GENERALIZATION FOR STUDENTS WITH SEVERE HANDICAPS

Strategies and Solutions

GENERALIZATION FOR STUDENTS WITH SEVERE HANDICAPS

Strategies and Solutions

Norris G. Haring, Editor

University of Washington Press
Seattle and London

Published by the **University of Washington Press** for the Washington Research Organization,
an Institute for Research in Education of the Severely Handicapped

Norris Haring, Principal Investigator
Kathleen Liberty, Project Coordinator

Michael Boer, Production Editor and Designer

The activity which is the subject of this report was supported in whole or in part by the U.S.
Department of Education (Contract No. 300–82–0364). However, the opinions expressed herein do
not necessarily reflect the position or policy of the U.S. Department of Education, and no official
endorsement by the Department should be inferred.

ISBN 0-295-96807-9

Printed in the United States of America

First printing, 1988

Acknowledgements

We have successfully met each of the overall goals for this project. This would not have been possible without the assistance provided by concerned educators.

The Washington State Office of the Superintendent of Public Instruction coordinated the contribution of IEP data by more than 150 school districts statewide, under the leadership of Dr. Judy Schrag, Assistant Superintendent, Division of Special Services and Professional Programs, and Dr. Greg Kirsch, Director of Special Education and Institutions.

Public school districts that facilitated teacher, staff, and student participation in the research included:

1. Bellevue School District #405, Dr. Sharon Hill, Director of Special Education;
2. Experimental Education Unit of the University of Washington's Child Development and Mental Retardation Center, Dr. Joseph Jenkins, Director, and Dr. Kevin Cole, Principal;
3. Highline School District #401, Dr. John Jewell, Director, Special Education;
4. Issaquah School District #411, Dr. Abby Adams, Director of Special Services;
5. Lake Washington School District #414, Dr. Ralph Bohannon, Director of Special Services;
6. Northshore School District #417, Mr. Fred Row, Director of Special Education; and
7. Tacoma School District #10, Mr. John Pearson, Acting Director, Special Education.

In addition, we would like to thank the following people: our work would have been impossible without their help:

Stephanie Abernathy, Joe Affronte, Angie Ahn, Jean Atcheson, Ralph Allen, Matt Anderson

Evelyn Baken, Steven Baum, Renee Beebe, Troy Bellerud, Bonnie Berenz, Ann Berman, Catherine Bilvue, Ruth Bingle, Nicole Blanton, Michael Boer, Lynn Bourcier, Lisa Brateng, James Brenchley, Beth Burnell

David Carter, Ernie Catlett, Rosemary Chamberlain, Danny Chapin, Jeanine Chriest, Rosemarie Cluck, Michael Colburn, Robert Connors, Eric Conway, Jim Cornwall, Keith Criss, Richard Crabb, Sheila Creighton

Felicia Davis, Nancy Davis, Christine Delorenzo, Laura Dickinson, Teri Doane, Mary Doyle, Carol Duncan-Smith, Lora Ebey, Dave Ehman

Robin Farman, Gaye Fedorchak, Tim Fergason, Phillip Fergason, Laura Fernandes, Sharon Field, Robin Figuracion, Cynthia Fischer, Cindy Flegenheimer, James Fleming, Genevieve Frankenberg

Angie Galipeau, Phyllis Gamas, Julie Gardner, Rachel Garner, Ali Gharib, Jim Gibson, Sally Gillard, Carl Gilles, David Glascock, Barbara Goodell, Chris Gray, Kevin Greer, Anthony Gridley, Leo Griffin, Sheri Griffith, Devon Gruver, Teresa Guthrie

Diane Hardee, Jenny Harris, Ruth Hayes, Mary Healy, Joan Herbert, Michael David Hill, Kerry Hogan, Kelli Holcomb, Cheryl Homiak, Steve Horton, Teddy Huffman, Shirley Inveen, Peg Jaskar, Betty Johnson

Table of Contents

PREFACE

This book was written as an outgrowth of our work with public school students in Washington. Although based on our experiences with learners with moderate, severe, and profound handicaps, we believe that the procedures may be useful with all students.

Two major purposes are served by this text. The primary objective is to provide educators with a means of systematically eliminating skill generalization problems. The strategies presented have been validated by public school teachers of students with moderate, severe, and profound handicaps. The second purpose of this text is to present information on the empirical basis for the strategies, to underscore both the importance and effectiveness of implementing the strategies.

The first section of this book provides an introduction to generalization, and describes the empirical basis for understanding the procedures. Following the initial five chapters, the second section is designed to guide practitioners in the implementation of the steps to be followed in a systematic approach to generalization:

- Carefully assess skills for generalization.
- Teach for acquisition and generalization.
- Probe for generalization during and after instruction.
- Use decision rules to identify generalization problems.
- Implement strategies as indicated to solve problems.
- Reprobe until generalization is achieved.

The second section includes descriptions of the specific types of problems students encounter when they generalize skills, and examples of how strategies can overcome these problems.

I. RESEARCH FOUNDATIONS FOR GENERALIZATION TECHNOLOGY

Ms. Cindy Burchart is pleased with her new job at the Seattle Hotel. She has loaded the industrial dishwasher for the first time: all of the plates on the bottom in neat rows and all of the glasses on the top. It was easy to figure out where they went. She closes the door with satisfaction. But where are the buttons to start the machine? They're not on the front of the machine, nor on the side. Behind the dishwasher, on the wall, Cindy sees a row of buttons, switches, dials, and lights. Some of the lights are dark, while others are glowing red or green. She stands bewildered before the display. The manager of the kitchen rushes over, glares at Cindy, and rapidly pushes some buttons, sets a dial, and flicks a switch. He barks, "Start on the next load," wondering why he ever agreed to give a retarded person a chance, anyway.

Mr. White gazes at the assessment data for Richard. He is depressed; this is the third year he has had Richard in his class, the third year he has conducted assessments, and the third year he must prepare instructional objectives for Richard's IEP. Last year he taught Richard to say, "My name is Richard Clark," when asked "What's your name?" or "Who are you?" This year, he only answers with, "Richard." "That really won't help if he gets lost," sighs Mr. White. He ruefully writes the objective for "says own name" for the second year in a row. He looks at some more assessment data, collected over the first six weeks of school. It is taking Richard even longer to learn to say his address than it did to say his name, and it looks like there is no guarantee that he will remember it next year. Mr. White considers just getting him an ID bracelet, but remembers what Richard's parents said. He writes an objective for "says own address" and shakes his head.

Jody is screaming so loudly that his face is eggplant purple. Mrs. Loomis stares helplessly at him. She goes over and picks up the tennis shoes from the corner where he threw them moments ago. She knows that Jody's teacher told her that Jody was able to put on these very same shoes without any help. The screaming is now broken by gasps, as Jody winds up to an even higher pitch. Mr. Loomis yells up the stairs, "Where are you? We're all in the car waiting!" Mrs. Loomis quickly picks up Jody, puts his shoes on him, and carries him downstairs. Jody quits screaming when they go out the door. "Thank goodness," she says to herself.

The problem for Cindy, Richard, and Jody is generalization, or the lack of it, to be more precise. The setting changes, time passes, and it is somehow as if they had never learned what to do in the first place. This is one of the most critical problems we have had to face in education, and it is one that must be solved if education is to effectively prepare students for life in society. In the first section of this book, we take a critical look at generalization, and at the research that has been conducted. We have paid special attention to the problems of skill generalization by students with severe handicaps, but we have found that their problems are not unique. All learners and teachers face them together.

Chapter 1

A TECHNOLOGY FOR GENERALIZATION

Norris G. Haring

Generalization is, perhaps, the most important phase of learning. We recognize that acquisition of a new skill or behavior is where learning begins, and that building the skill to a functional level of proficiency embodies the process of teaching. But ensuring that skills will be used requires that our teaching plans include generalization. While a technology can and does exist for all stages of learning, generalization has certainly come under the sharp focus of applied science in recent years.

When we refer to the technology of generalization, we are referring to the application of results from studies which show that tactics or strategies can facilitate the process of generalization. As our science has developed, we have established certain principles that can guide us in facilitating generalization. Most recently our research has built on and refined those principles to establish a procedure for making decisions about how best to match instructional strategies with behavior patterns to increase the probability that newly acquired skills will generalize across persons, materials, and settings. We are moving toward an explicit technology of generalization, though as any good scientist would say, we may never be exactly there.

It is only within the short span of the last two decades that teaching models for learners with severe handicaps have been successfully demonstrated. As a result of systematic instruction, students with severe handicaps have demonstrated that they have the ability to acquire and master self-help, social, vocational, and a wide variety of other critical skills.

Having attained some success, educators are facing another problem: Acquisition of skills rarely guarantees that the individual can apply those skills in natural settings. Skills which only appear in training situations are practically valueless—and certainly won't provide the necessary foundation for independence and integration. Instead, educators must apply strategies which facilitate the generalization of skills from training to natural settings. In order to generalize a skill, the student must recognize that the setting is appropriate for the skill, and identify and respond to antecedent stimuli with a specific skill appropriate to that situation. For the generalized skill to maintain, the consequence provided must reinforce the behavior. A problem at any one point in the chain will probably be sufficient for generalization to fail.

What is Meant by Generalization?

Definition of Generalization

Broadly speaking, skill generalization is appropriate responding in untrained situations. In the training situation, the student is taught to perform a skill under certain conditions. The elements of the training situation include the setting, the people around, the teacher, cues, directions, materials, praise, assistance—in short, everything within the situation, even if it is not directly associated with the instructional goal. In the generalization situation, the student must respond to different forms of those elements—forms which were not trained. For example, when a student learns a skill in the classroom and then uses it appropriately at home or elsewhere, we say that the skill has generalized.

The true purpose of teaching generalized responding is to provide individuals with the means of adapting to new situations, solving problems, and living in different settings. The generalized response must be both appropriate and functional. "Hi, my name is Charles," may be said perfectly in a new setting, but if it follows the stimulus, "Put on your jacket," it is entirely wrong. The student must also be able to modify, or physically adapt the response to the demands of the new setting. Many instances of generalization involve changes in the physical actions that constitute the response. For example, putting on a T–shirt with long sleeves requires slightly different physical movements than putting on a short-sleeved T–shirt. In other cases very different physical responses will be required to achieve the same effect as that achieved by performing the trained response. For example, training a student to put on a shoe achieves the effect of covering and protecting the feet. Putting on a pair of rubber boots achieves the same effect, but physically different responses are usually involved.

Dimensions of Generalization

Sometimes we specify the dimension across which generalization occurs. Such descriptors can allow us to determine the nature of the differences between the training situation and the target generalization situation. Some of the more common descriptors include:

Generalization across persons. Usually this means that the only difference between the training and the generalization situation is the people with whom the learner interacts in order to perform the skill.

Generalization across objects or materials (or verbal directions or other specific stimuli). Here, the difference is in the objects the learner manipulates or responds to in performing the skill.

Generalization to natural consequences. In this case, the consequences used during training—such as praise for appropriate responding and verbal feedback for errors—are not provided in the generalization situation, and the student responds appropriately to the consequences available— such as ignoring appropriate behavior and ridiculing errors.

Generalization across stimuli. Here, all of the antecedent events, or the constellation of antecedent events, differ, while consequences do not.

Generalization across settings. This more general term encompasses changes in most of the antecedent and consequent events which control responding.

Generalization across time. This refers to skill generalization during periods in which training contingencies are not in effect. For example, if "answering yes/no questions," which is trained in the classroom in the morning, also is observed in the classroom in the afternoon, it would probably be labeled as "generalization across time." In addition, skills that are maintained after training is discontinued may be described as generalizing over time.

The generalization phenomenon has been recognized and studied in research laboratories for many years, but the need for application of strategies to facilitate generalization has never been more critical than it is now. As we face the integration of persons with severe handicaps into all facets of society, we realize that the main stumbling block is the difficulty encountered with skill generalization. In fact, without the application of specific strategies we can honestly expect that only about 25% of the skills we teach will be useful in natural settings.

Review and Analysis of Generalization Studies

In 1977, Trevor Stokes and Don Baer published a major review and analysis of studies of generalization. They urged that efforts be directed at understanding generalization and at investigating strategies which facilitate it. They concluded that simply hoping that generalization would follow acquisition just wasn't enough—that specific strategies must be applied to actively program for generalization. Their article heralded the first major step in the development of a technology of generalization.

By the early 1980s, researchers had studied a variety of generalization strategies. We have identified 172 experimental studies of generalization conducted between 1977 and 1986; special strategies were employed in 89% of them (see Chapter 2). Educators also have recognized the critical importance of this phase of learning; textbooks and teacher preparation programs have incorporated ideas and strategies about generalization. However, we found that less than one out of every eight objectives written for the IEPs of students with severe handicaps included even the intent to produce generalized skills (Billingsley, Doyle, Radovich, & Thompson, 1985; Billingsley, Berman, & Opalski, 1983; Billingsley, Thompson, Matlock, & Work, 1984). Not surprisingly, we found a correspondingly low rate of skill generalization by students with severe handicaps attending local public school programs: 40%, 30%, and 8.3% in consecutive years (Billingsley, Berman, & Opalski, 1983; Billingsley, Doyle, Radovich, & Thompson, 1985; Billingsley, Thompson, Matlock, & Work, 1984).

The Washington Research Organization

In 1982, the Office of Special Education and Rehabilitation Services of the U.S. Department of Education contracted with the Washington Research Organization of the University of Washington to:

1. Identify and validate a set of intervention strategies for teaching specific skills to individuals with severe handicaps in a manner which would lead to the generalization and adaptation of those skills across environments.
2. Develop performance-based guidelines for matching and adjusting generalization-relevant intervention procedures to meet the specific needs of individual learners with severe handicaps.

We have concluded five years of research conducted to meet our goals. The research studies have involved four different but interrelated approaches to fundamental questions about generalization. "Ecological studies" were conducted to extend our understanding of factors in school settings which affect generalization. "Self-control studies" were conducted to extend our information about ways of teaching students with severe handicaps to manage their own behavior, a strategy that can produce generalized responding. "Performance pattern studies" provided information on the characteristic patterns of individual learners' responses to generalization situations and on the effectiveness of generalization strategies. "Strategy implementation studies" were conducted to determine the effects of strategies and decision rules for facilitating generalization when they are implemented in typical classroom settings.

Retrospective Analysis

As part of the performance pattern strand of research, we conducted a retrospective analysis of literature on generalization. We developed a coding system to analyze the relative success of a variety of strategies that have been used to facilitate generalization. We reviewed a total of 172 studies from 151 published articles, involving 623 subjects and 12 different generalization strategies. We found, for example, that general case programming had been effective with 100% of the subjects and programming indiscriminable contingencies was effective with 85.7% of the subjects with severe handicaps. On the other hand, training in the natural setting had produced good generalization in only 20% of the students with severe handicaps. Although the numbers of subjects for several of the strategies were quite low, this meta analysis gave us a good picture of what was available for training strategies.

Application of Strategies and Rules

More than 300 students with handicaps and nearly 200 direct service staff participated in our research. In addition, more than 150 school districts provided data for our studies into IEP objectives. With the cooperation of these individuals, our investigations have identified (a) specific factors associated with improved skill generalization, (b) strategies that educators can implement in schools to improve generalization, and (c) rules for making decisions about what strategy to use to promote generalization of a particular skill by a specific learner. In our research, we found that if we replace a "train first and then hope for generalization" approach with specific strategies, generalization can improve from about 25% of skills generalizing (Billingsley, Doyle, Radovich,

& Thompson, 1985; Billingsley, Berman, & Opalski, 1983; Billingsley, Thompson, Matlock, & Work, 1984) to anywhere from 30 to 100% (see Chapter 2). When practitioners apply specific strategies to improve generalization, 75% of the skills may generalize (see Chapter 4). This is a very good start on solving the problems caused by failure to generalize.

However, we can now go even further, and apply decision rules to help us decide which strategy will be most likely to solve generalization problems. When practitioners use decision rules to guide the selection of strategies, 78 to 88% of skills may generalize (see Chapters 4 and 5). We believe that educators who apply strategies selected through the decision rule process can significantly reduce the number of generalization failures by students with severe handicaps.

General Factors Affecting Generalization

Generalization can occur spontaneously during or after skill acquisition, but most often it does not. Instead of hoping for generalization, we must actively program for it. Thus, the first factor to recognize is our intention to aim for generalized skills. The first step toward achieving that goal is to closely examine the type of skill targeted for instruction.

1. Select Naturally Reinforced Skills.

Skills which the student will use in other situations are ones which will help him/her achieve some goal—that is, the student will be reinforced for performing the skill. If the skill is not reinforced, it will not be used by the student, since it serves no purpose from the student's point of view. A naturally reinforced skill is one which provides the student a means of gaining reinforcement. Skills which function to access available reinforcers are more likely to generalize than skills which do not.

For example, teaching a student to communicate "yes" and "no" might allow the student to access a whole new set of reinforcers, since this skill fosters natural interactions with others. If the student had no means of acceptable expressive language prior to learning to answer yes/no, generalization might be almost immediate and at a level which accesses sufficient reinforcement to ensure maintenance (Liberty, 1984a; 1984b).

Sometimes skills which are useful to others in the students' environment are considered "functional." For example, dressing skills are often labeled as functional. Such skills are practical, because they can reduce caretaking time, but they may not be naturally reinforcing skills for the student. Consider—if a student has no dressing skills, then s/he is dressed by others, an interaction which results in a considerable and sustained interpersonal interaction, involving verbal, gestural, and physical contact. The student who dresses her/himself may miss out on such interaction. If the child's "goal" or need is for sustained interactions involving lots of physical contact, then "not dressing oneself" is naturally reinforced and self-dressing skills are not. Functional skills may or may not access natural reinforcers. However, if the student acquires a functional skill, s/he may be more likely to be reinforced by parents and caretakers, but this additional reinforcement for independence can't be taken for granted. If it doesn't occur, the student may perform independently one or two times and then stop generalizing (see Chapter 8).

We can devise and implement strategies which will facilitate generalization of functional skills—for example by changing the nature and density of reinforcement used during acquisition for both self-dressing and for being dressed by others.

2. Select Skills That Are Useful in Many Situations and That Can Be Used Frequently.

Skills which are useful in more than one situation are also more likely to generalize. Thus, we would expect that specific communication skills, which are useful in virtually every situation, will generalize more readily than a floor-cleaning skill, which is likely to be limited in usefulness to work and house-cleaning situations.

Another important factor is the number of opportunities the student will have to use the skill. Usually, the greater the opportunities, the more likely that generalization will occur and maintain, because the student will have more chances to recognize appropriate antecedents cuing the skill, and more frequent reinforcement to maintain it. Functional skills, by their very nature, are more likely to be frequently requested.

We can devise strategies that will facilitate generalization of skills which are useful in only a few settings, and which are needed only occasionally. However, recognizing these cases prior to programming can allow us to improve instruction before any problem with generalization, by paying specific attention to the number of opportunities which can be provided in any setting, and by strengthening reinforcement available for infrequently used skills.

3. Write IEP Objectives for Generalization.

Once skills have been targeted for instruction, the objectives written for the students' Individual Education Plan (IEP) must specify that generalization is a criterion for passing the objective, by describing the nontraining situations in which performance will be tested. Our research into this factor was conducted by Dr. Felix Billingsley, who explains:

> One of the major functions of instructional objectives is that of guidance. By stating the desired educational outcome, objectives guide the teacher in his or her search for appropriate methods of instruction and pupil progress evaluation . . . It is perhaps obvious that the desired educational outcome for pupils with severe handicaps is not the acquisition of functional skills which will be demonstrated only in artificial training settings in the presence of one or two specific trainers. Rather, adaptation within natural environments requires a generalized outcome in order that skills may be performed in each appropriate setting, and in the presence of persons other than the original trainer(s) . . . Because generalization cannot be assumed to be a passive phenomenon . . . and because it possesses its own technology . . . pupils will be most effectively served when educators select instructional methods which are specifically designed to achieve generalized effects. The inclusion of generality as an outcome in objectives could increase the likelihood that educators will attend to the need for active generalization programming (Streifel & Cadez, 1983). In addition, it seems probable that statements of generalized outcome will act to promote the cross-situational measurement of instructional effects. Unless generalization is prescribed by objectives, educators may find themselves evaluating pupil progress toward stimulus-bound performance. This possibility was implicitly recognized in the recommendation by Brown, Nietupski, & Hamre-Nietupski (1976) that educators adopt a zero degree inference strategy in relation to skill generalization. In order to effectively serve their guidance function, then, objectives should include generalized performance as a desired outcome. Indeed, Streifel and Cadez (1983) have proposed that any evaluation of the quality of IEP content should include an assessment not only of the technological adequacy and functionality of objectives, but of performance generality as stated in objectives as well (see also Whitney & Streifel, 1981). (Billingsley, 1984, p. 186-187.)

Chapter 6 describes how to write objectives for generalized skills.

4. Select Skills for Acquisition Carefully and Probe for Generalization before Instructing.

We should recognize that before generalization can occur, the skill must be acquired. The first step is to identify whether a particular skill has been previously acquired. This is often not as obvious as it may first appear. In one of our studies, 21% of the skills selected for acquisition training by experienced teachers had already been acquired by the students, who were performing them in other settings as well (see Chapter 4). Parents have reported that as many as 56% of IEP objectives target skills the student already does at home (Billingsley, Thompson, Matlock, & Work, 1984). The problem obviously wasn't one of acquisition, it was one of compliance—of getting the student to perform previously acquired skills. And different tactics must be used.

Often teachers' autumn assessments show that skills were not maintained over the summer. However, if skills are not maintained over time, instruction should not be directed at acquisition, but at generalization. Perhaps as many as 30% of IEP objectives written for students with severe handicaps inappropriately target acquisition of previously mastered skills (Hilton & Liberty, 1986). Instructional time is our most valuable resource, and the most costly. We can help ensure that it is properly used by careful assessment in training (c.f., Browder, 1987; Snell, 1987) and in generalization situations (see Chapter 7) *before* we begin instruction.

5. Avoid Instructional Strategies That Can Cause Generalization Problems.

Once we have appropriately identified a skill as "not acquired," we must be careful that our instruction does not cause generalization problems. Problems may arise when specific antecedent and consequent events that occurred during training are not present in the generalization situation. For example, the consequences available during instruction, such as candy or hugs, may not occur as natural reinforcers in the generalization situation. If the student performs the skill, and the reinforcer which controlled responding during training (i.e., candy and hugs) does not occur, the skill may not be reinforced, and therefore the skill may not be performed again. Or if the student has learned that the verbal cue "take a bite" or "sign sandwich" precedes the opportunity to eat, s/he may sit quietly in a restaurant waiting for the cue to occur.

The nature of the differences between the training and the target situation must be identified prior to instruction in the skill, since problems caused by these differences can be ameliorated or even overcome by the instructional strategies we program, beginning with initial skill acquisition. These strategies are described in Chapter 2.

6. Use Decision Rules and Strategies to Solve Generalization Problems.

We must actually measure and observe to verify that generalization has occurred following instruction, and that the IEP objective has been met. If it hasn't, then the problem must be identified and solved. The data we collect during our probes of performance in the generalization situation are used to answer questions posed in the decision rule sequence. The questions guide the user in identifying the nature of the problem that is impeding generalization (see Chapter 9). Then, the rules assist in the identification of a strategy that is likely to be effective (see Chapter 8). After we have implemented the new strategy, we will again test for generalization. This process should be repeated until successful generalization is achieved.

Enough is known now to state with adequate confidence that, as a field of study, we do have the beginnings of an explicit technology of generalization. Using naturalistic tactics to teach skills in natural settings, selecting naturally reinforced skills, selecting skills that are useful in many situations and are used frequently, developing instructional objectives which include generalization, carefully selecting skills for acquisition, probing for generalization, applying strategies to facilitate generalization, and using decision rules and strategies to solve generalization problems— each of these principles can be used to increase the probability that individuals will generalize new skills across persons and materials, across stimuli and settings.

Although we need more research into effective strategies, and investigations to improve the decision rules, we have a technology of generalization that can help educators now. Educators must be able to demonstrate that they can teach skills which generalize to untrained, natural community settings before claiming success in preparing students with severe handicaps to live and work with their peers.

This book is about our development of decision rules for generalization, and the application of strategies to ensure that all skills which are taught will be useful outside of training. In the first section, we review the literature on generalization strategies, and describe two of the studies we conducted to develop and validate the decision rules. The second part describes how strategies may be implemented by practitioners.

References

Billingsley, F. F. (1984). Where are the generalized outcomes? (An examination of instructional objectives). *Journal of the Association for Persons with Severe Handicaps, 9*(3), 186-192.

Billingsley, F. F., Berman, A., & Opalski, C. (1983). Generalization and the educational ecology of severely handicapped learners: A descriptive study. In N. G. Haring (Principal

Investigator), *Institute for education of severely handicapped children: Washington Research Organization; Annual report FY 82-83*. (U.S. Department of Education, Contract No. 300-82-0364). Seattle: University of Washington, College of Education.

Billingsley, F. F., Doyle, M., Radovich, S., & Thompson, M. (1985). Generalization and the educational ecology of severely handicapped learners: A descriptive study—third project year. In N. G. Haring (Principal Investigator), *Institute for education of severely handicapped children: Washington Research Organization; Annual report FY 84-85*. (U.S. Department of Education, Contract No. 300-82-0364). Seattle: University of Washington, College of Education.

Billingsley, F. F., Thompson, M., Matlock, B., & Work, J. (1984). Generalization and the educational ecology of severely handicapped learners: A descriptive study—second project year. In N. G. Haring (Principal Investigator), *Institute for education of severely handicapped children: Washington Research Organization; Annual report FY 83-84*. (U.S. Department of Education, Contract No. 300-82-0364). Seattle: University of Washington, College of Education.

Browder, D. M. (1987). *Assessment of individuals with severe handicaps*. Baltimore: Paul H. Brooks.

Brown, L., Nietupski, J., & Hamre-Nietupski, S. (1976). Criterion of ultimate functioning. In M. A. Thomas (Ed.), *Hey, don't forget about me: Education's investment in the severely, profoundly and multiply handicapped* (pp. 2-15). Reston, VA: Council for Exceptional Children.

Haring, N. G. (Principal Investigator). (1984). *Investigating the problem of skill generalization: Literature review I*. (U.S. Department of Education, Contract No. 300-82-0364). Seattle: University of Washington, College of Education. (ERIC Document Reproduction Service No. ED 249 738)

Haring, N. G. (Principal Investigator). (1985). *Investigating the problem of skill generalization* (3rd edition, with literature reviews). (U.S. Department of Education, Contract No. 300-82-0364). Seattle: University of Washington, College of Education. (ERIC Document Reproduction Service No. ED 265 695)

Haring, N. G. (Principal Investigator). (1987). *Investigating the problem of skill generalization: Literature review III*. (U.S. Department of Education, Contract No. 300-82-0364). Seattle: University of Washington, College of Education. (ERIC Document Reproduction Service No. ED 287 270)

Hilton, A., & Liberty, K. (1986, November). *Analysis of progress of integrated secondary students with profound mental retardation*. Paper presented at the meeting of the Association for Persons with Severe Handicaps, San Francisco, CA.

Liberty, K.A. (1984a). Effects of a generalization package alone and with self-monitoring on generalized yes/no answers of profoundly handicapped subjects. In N. G. Haring (Principal Investigator), *Institute for education of severely handicapped children: Washington Research Organization; Annual report FY 83-84*. (U.S. Department of Education, Contract No. 300-82-0364). Seattle: University of Washington, College of Education.

Liberty, K.A. (1984b). Acquisition and generalization of self-monitoring and self-reinforcement and their effects on question answering. In N. G. Haring (Principal Investigator), *Institute for education of severely handicapped children: Washington Research Organization; Annual report FY 83-84*. (U.S. Department of Education, Contract No. 300-82-0364). Seattle: University of Washington, College of Education.

Snell, M. (Ed.) (1987). *Systematic instruction of persons with severe handicaps* (3rd edition). Columbus, OH: Charles E. Merrill.

Stokes, T. F., & Baer, D. B. (1977). An implicit technology of generalization. *Journal of Applied Behavior Analysis, 10*(2), 349-367.

Streifel, S., & Cadez, M. J. (1983). *Serving children and adolescents with developmental disabilities in the special education classroom: Proven methods*. Baltimore: Paul H. Brookes.

Whitney, R., & Streifel, S. (1981). Functionality and generalization in training the severely and profoundly handicapped. *Journal of Special Education Technology, 4*(3), 33-39.

Strategies that were successful in teaching new skills to students with severe handicaps were identified by the early 1970s, although research into more efficient methods continues. Unfortunately, acquisition and even skill mastery are often not sufficient to ensure that the student will apply her newly learned skills in other situations. Investigators began examining this problem. In 1977, Trevor Stokes, of the University of Manitoba, and Don Baer, of the University of Kansas, published a review of the "embryonic technology" of generalization. They reported that 77% of the literature related to skill generalization had been published since 1970, and identified 120 studies which were central in identifying strategies for meeting the problems related to the failure to generalize.

In this chapter, we review studies from the period 1977-1986, and identify the growth of the technology. We also examine the overall effectiveness of the new technology in promoting skill generalization.

Chapter 2

REVIEW AND ANALYSIS OF STRATEGIES FOR GENERALIZATION

Owen R. White, Kathleen A. Liberty,
Norris G. Haring, Felix F. Billingsley,
Michael Boer, Ann Burrage, Robert Connors,
Robin Farman, Gaye Fedorchak,
B. Douglas Leber, Sara Liberty–Laylin,
Sarah Miller, Cheryl Opalski, Claire Phifer, and
Ike Sessoms

Until recently, many people expected generalization to occur after training and thus a passive approach to instructing for generalization has been common. In 1977, Trevor Stokes, of the University of Manitoba, and Don Baer, of the University of Kansas, published a major analysis and summary of research in generalization. They argued that it is better to view generalization as an active process and to try to develop instructional methods that ensure that generalization does occur. Their article, and the discussion it provoked, had a major impact on shaping subsequent research in generalization.

In the ten years since Stokes' and Baer's analysis was published, data on the effectiveness of various generalization strategies have appeared in hundreds of articles. The result has been a deepening of our understanding of generalization and the problems that may impede it, and a better understanding of strategies that can be used effectively to promote it. This literature review summarizes studies of different strategies and discusses the theoretical and empirical basis for specific strategies.

Method

A systematic review of the applied literature was undertaken to identify studies concerning generalization. Articles were included in the review only if they allowed the meaningful analysis of generalization at an individual subject level, since research which summarizes effects only at a group level can misrepresent the effectiveness of strategies with individual learners (Sidman, 1960; White, 1984). The majority of studies concerned the performance of individuals with severe handicaps, but a sampling of studies involving less handicapped or nonhandicapped subjects were also included in the review for comparative purposes.

Articles were coded to identify the number of subjects, the most severe handicaps, subject ages, the functionality of the behaviors studied, the types of generalization strategies employed, and the number of subjects who generalized well.[1] Each experiment reported in an article was coded separately; in this paper, each experiment is referred to as a "study." Studies were categorized in this review as including at least one student displaying one or more of the following characteristics: severe mental retardation, profound mental retardation, moderate mental retardation with severe physical disabilities, multiple handicaps, severe behavioral disturbance/autism, or deaf-blind.

Generalization Strategies

Each study was coded to indicate the type(s) of generalization strategies employed during training. The original list of strategies was drawn from those suggested by Stokes and Baer (1977), but was expanded to include additional strategies developed since the conduct of their review. The final list of strategies included: train and hope, sequential modification, introduction to natural maintaining contingencies, training sufficient exemplars, training loosely, using indiscriminable contingencies, programming common stimuli, mediating generalization, training to generalize, the use of multiple exemplars, and general case programming. Each of those strategies will be defined and discussed later in this chapter in the results and discussion section, and they are summarized in Table 2–1.

Several problems were encountered in coding the generalization strategies employed in some studies. First, many articles failed to provide sufficiently detailed information concerning the procedures they employed. That was especially important when making discriminations among various strategies which entail special pretraining preparation in materials or procedures. For example, the critical distinction between "multiple exemplars" and "general case programming" is the degree to which training stimuli adequately represent all relevant dimensions of stimulus variation likely to be encountered in generalization settings. When authors failed to provide adequate information concerning the manner in which potential stimulus variation was evaluated and eventual training stimuli selected, the code "multiple exemplars" was used, perhaps erroneously.

Second, coders were occasionally misled by direct statements made by authors concerning the strategies they employed. In one study, for example, authors stated that all the behaviors they trained could be "viewed as those that are likely to be maintained by the natural consequences in a classroom" (Reese & Filipczak, 1980, p. 221). That statement led the coder to select "introduce to the natural maintaining contingencies" as one of the strategies employed in the study. The authors went on to say, however, that "no systematic analysis of [nontraining classrooms] was conducted" (ibid.). In fact, no evidence was provided in the study to suggest that those natural consequences ever actually occurred or, if they did, that they were reinforcing to the subject.

Third, many studies employed several different generalization strategies, either in succession or simultaneously. The use of multiple strategies expanded the difficulty in identifying component strategies per se, and often made it impossible to attribute generalization outcomes to any single strategy. The results presented later in this chapter will focus on only those studies were effects could be meaningfully attributed to a single generalization strategy.

Generalization Outcomes

Coders inspected the individual subject data for each study and recorded the number of subjects generalizing "well." In order to classify a subject as generalizing "well," two conditions had to be met. First, the subject must have generalized a functionally meaningful level of performance. For example, a subject who generalized enough steps in a bus-riding sequence to independently ride a bus on an untrained route would be considered to have acquired a meaningful level of performance (e.g., Neef, Iwata, & Page, 1978). A subject who generalized all the steps for

---

[1] A copy of the recording form, the coding manual, and/or computer listings of actual codes may be obtained from the authors for cost of reproduction and mailing.

Table 2-1

Strategies for Facilitating Generalization

Strategy	Definition	Example
Train & Hope	Providing simple instruction and then "hoping" that generalization will occur. Actually the *absence* of any special strategy.	Three preschool boys who were blind and severely or profoundly retarded were taught to reach for noise-making toys always presented at the midline. None of the boys generalized to objects presented on the right or left (Correa, Poulson, & Salzberg, 1984).
Setting *Train in the Natural Setting*	Training is conducted directly in at least one type of setting in which the skill will be used. Generalization is then probed in other nontraining settings.	The social interaction skills of several individuals with severe handicaps were trained in the classroom and courtyard during class breaks (Gaylord-Ross & Holvoet, 1985).
Sequential Modification	Training is provided in one setting, and generalization is probed in other settings. If necessary, training is conducted sequentially in more and more settings until generalization to all desired settings is observed.[2]	One girl with moderate handicaps needed articulation training in 3 settings before generalizing to all remaining situations of interest; a second girl only required training in two situations before generalizing (Murdock, Garcia, & Hardman, 1977).
Consequences *Introduce to Natural Maintaining Contingencies*	Ensuring that the learner experiences the natural consequences of a behavior by: (1) teaching a functional skill which is likely to be reinforced outside instruction; (2) training to a level of proficiency that makes the skill truly useful; (3) making sure the learner actually does experience the natural consequence; and/or (4) teaching the learner to solicit or recruit reinforcement outside instruction.	Three teens who were multiply handicapped and severely retarded were taught to use symbols and pictures to request objects. Generalization was encouraged by using objects which would be regularly encountered outside instruction, making sure the boys always carried their communication boards, and that someone would always be present to provide any requested items (Hurlbut, Iwata, & Green, 1982).
Use Indiscriminable Contingencies	If natural consequences cannot be expected to encourage and maintain generalization, artificial consequences or schedules of natural consequences might be used. However, it is best if the learner cannot determine precisely when those consequences will be available, and so must behave as if they always are.	Two behavior disordered and five normal preschool children always generalized their interaction and study skills better when verbal praise by the teacher was provided after progressively greater delays, rather than immediately following each behavior (Fowler & Baer, 1981).
Train to Generalize	The learner is only reinforced for performing some generalized instance of the target skill. Performing a previously reinforced version of the response is no longer reinforced.	Four youths with severe retardation were taught to name specific items. Contingencies were then altered so they were only reinforced if they named *untrained* items. After 3 sessions, all youths generalized well to untrained items (Warren, Baxter, Anderson, Marshall, & Baer, 1981).

---

[2]   Stokes & Baer (1977) described this strategy as training in one situation and, if that fails to produce generalization, training in all remaining situations of interest. The more literally "sequential" nature of the procedure as described above seems better suited for describing current application of the strategy.

Table 2-1 (continued)

Strategy	Definition	Example
Antecedents *Program Common Stimuli*	Selecting a salient, but not necessarily task-related, stimulus from the situation to which generalization is desired, and including that stimulus in the training program.	Stokes & Baer (1977) report a case in which an individual with severe retardation was taught exercise skills to facilitate integration in a physical education class. Music was played during the PE class, so music was also introduced into the individual's training sessions to make the two situations more similar.
Sufficient Exemplars	A strategy similar to Sequential Modification, involving sequential addition of stimuli to the training program until generalization to all related stimuli occurs.[3]	An adolescent with severe handicaps was taught to name objects, and probed with other objects from the same class. Some objects required only a single exemplar to produce generalized naming, while other objects required 5 exemplars before generalization occurred (Anderson & Spradlin, 1980).
Multiple Exemplars	Several examples of the stimulus class to which generalization is desired are trained at the same time.	Three adults with profound mental retardation were trained in three types of exercise. Generalization occurred to a group exercise program and to two untrained exercises (Stainback, Stainback, Wehman, & Spangiers, 1983).
General Case Programming	The universe to which generalization is desired is analyzed and representative examples of positive stimuli (stimuli in the presence of which the skill should be used), negative stimuli (stimuli in the presence of which the skill should not be used), and irrelevant stimuli (stimuli which should not effect skill use, but might inappropriately do so) are selected for training.	Six young men with moderate or severe retardation were trained on three vending machines which reflected the range of machine-types found in the community. Good generalization was obtained to 10 untrained machines in the community (Sprague & Horner, 1984).
Other *Train Loosely*	Settings, cues, prompts, materials, response definition, and other features of the training situation are purposely varied to avoid a ritual, highly structured, invariate program which might inhibit generalization.	Mothers were taught to vary the type of stimuli and reinforcers they used in working with their children's motor skills. All children learned their skills quickly and generalized well to another setting (Filler & Kasari, 1981).
Mediate Generalization	Teaching a secondary behavior or strategy which will help an individual remember or figure out how and when to generalize, or which will dispel the differences between the training and generalization situations.	Five adolescents with moderate or severe mental retardation were taught to self-instruct task completion using a picture sequence. They then used the self-instruction skill to generalize task completion of a new task with a new picture sequence (Wacker & Berg, 1983).

---

[3] Stokes & Baer used this label to describe the successive introduction of new stimuli or settings, but separating the two variations seemed more advisable for the current study (see note 2, above).

boarding a bus, but failed to generalize critical skills for determining when and how to get off the bus, would not be considered to have generalized well. Second, the behavior in the generalization setting was not trained in that setting. For example, a subject who required special prompts in a novel setting before beginning to engage in the target behavior would not be considered to have generalized well, even if only a few prompts were needed to produce independent performance at criterion level (e.g., Hill, Wehman, & Horst, 1982).

Review and Discussion

Twelve journals were examined covering the years 1977-1986.[4] A total of 151 articles including 172 studies were identified which provided information on the generalization of individual subjects. In all, 623 subjects participated in those studies, and generalization data were provided for 616 subjects; the other 7 subjects were not available at the time generalization data were collected. A complete list of articles which were coded is provided at the end of this chapter.

In this review, each of the major strategies is discussed individually, with examples drawn from the literature, and a summary of the strategy's impact.

No Strategy: Train and Hope

The first of Stokes and Baer's (1977) categories is "train and hope," which is not really a method of programming for generalization at all. Generally, this category involves probing for skill generalization following training which did not include specific generalization-facilitating strategies—one simply "trains" and then "hopes" that generalization occurs.[5]

Generalization *can* occur even when instructional procedures are not overtly directed at generalization. For example, six adult employees of a sheltered workshop, described as mildly or moderately retarded, with deficits in interpersonal skills, received individualized social skills training using instructions, modeling, rehearsal, feedback, and social reinforcement (Bornstein, Bach, McFall, Friman, & Lyons, 1980). Training was conducted in a room adjacent to the workshop. Skills and problems addressed included number of words spoken, speech latency, hand-to-face gestures, sitting posture, enunciation, speech content, loudness, intonation, eye contact, and speech rate. Each subject was trained on four behaviors/skills. Generalization was probed in role-playing situations similar to those used in training and in different situations. Training was successful in improving 23 of the 24 behaviors. Improvement in one skill did not generalize to improvement in the other three skills of each student. However, generalization of 23 of the 24 behaviors to untrained similar role-play and to 13 of 24 behaviors in dissimilar situations did occur. These levels generally were maintained one month following training.

Unfortunately, we can't often rely on training to produce generalization. For example, Correa, Poulson, and Solzberg (1984) reported that three preschool blind boys, described as severely or profoundly retarded, were individually instructed to reach and grasp a noisemaking toy. The trainer provided successive prompts following consecutive 10 second allowable latency periods (graduated prompts included verbal, physically assisted demonstration, physically molded). During training, toys were presented at the child's midline. Training increased independent reach/grasp from 0% to 77%, 100%, and 22% of the trials for subjects 1 through 3, respectively. However, this phase of training did not produce a single instance of generalized responding to toys presented to the left or right of midline.

Overall, 14 articles (16 studies) that included at least 1 subject with severe handicaps ("Severe

---

[4] Articles from 12 journals were included in the retrospective analysis. Circa 49% of all articles were published in the *Journal of Applied Behavior Analysis*, 18% in the *Journal of the Association for Persons with Severe Handicaps*, 15% in *Behavior Modification*, and 6% in *Education and Training of the Mentally Retarded*. The remaining 22% of the articles were distributed among the *American Journal of Mental Deficiency*, *Behavior Research and Therapy*, *Behavior Research of Severe Developmental Disabilities*, *Behavior Therapy*, *Education and Treatment of Children*, *Journal of Applied Research in Mental Retardation*, *Journal of Experimental Child Psychology*, and *Mental Retardation*.

[5] In many studies, "train and hope" was coded for one phase, usually as a baseline for another method. Such studies are classified according to the alternate method, unless separate experiments were presented.

Studies") were identified as train and hope and 9 articles (9 studies) reported train and hope with 40 other persons.

Train and Hope Alone

	Studies	Subjects	Subjects Generalizing Well
Severe Studies	9	30	73.3% (22/30)
Other Studies	3	11	81.8% (9/11)
Total	12	41	75.6% (31/41)

A simple train and hope approach appears to produce generalization about three quarters of the time, but several cautions are in order. First, it is possible that research in which generalization failed to occur might be published less frequently; few studies showing failure of any kind are published. Second, as other strategies were developed, the use of train and hope alone decreased. The most recent study which we could locate which used train and hope as the sole strategy was published in 1984. However, train and hope is often the first condition or baseline in studies of other strategies.

In establishing a research design, experimenters often predict that generalization will *not* occur during a train and hope baseline so that the effects of special generalization strategies can be tested in subsequent phases. This practice permits a different approach to estimating the effectiveness of train and hope. Of the 172 studies we examined, 48 studies involved train and hope as a baseline condition preceding use of a special strategy. In these studies, train and hope did not produce generalization. If we were to combine the two groups, our table would include all subjects with whom a train and hope approach was attempted.

Train and Hope Total

	Studies	Subjects	Subjects Generalizing Well
Severe Studies	38	136	16.2% (22/136)
Other Studies	22	79	11.4% (9/79)
Total	60	215	14.4% (31/215)

This procedure produces a significantly lower estimate of the effectiveness of train and hope (i.e., 75.6% vs 14.4%). An intermediate figure of 25% was produced in a compilation of data from longitudinal studies, in which it was assumed that train and hope was used alone (Billingsley, Berman, & Opalski, 1983; Billingsley, F. F., Doyle, M., Radovich, S., & Thompson, M., 1985; Billingsley, F. F., Thompson, M., Matlock, B., & Work, J., 1984). In the two studies reported in chapters 4 and 5 of this book, train and hope as a "baseline" strategy produced generalization in 8.3% and 17.3% of the skills respectively; (subjects were measured on more than one skill).

The range of figures associated with train and hope indicates how imprecise this definition is; it is likely that differences in the instructional procedures used during initial training effect generalization. In fact, almost all of the special strategies which have been investigated rely on *altering* typical training procedures. These strategies may be incorporated into the initial instructional plan or, if generalization fails to occur following initial skill acquisition, they may be applied in subsequent instructional phases.

Strategies Affecting Settings

The first set of strategies affects the location of instruction. Of course, when the setting of instruction changes, antecedents and consequences might also change; however, these changes are subordinate to the changes in setting. Two strategies which involve setting changes are "train in the natural setting" and "sequential modification."

1. Train in the Natural Setting.

One strategy not included by Stokes and Baer (1977), but which has been increasingly advocated, especially for students with severe handicaps, is to train directly in the environments in which the behavior is desired (e.g., Falvey, 1986) or in which the behavior is expected to occur naturally (Neel et al., 1983). Some skills, like mobility and communication, would naturally occur in almost all settings, so it is difficult to determine precisely how this strategy might be applied to some skills. Some skills, such as assembling semiconducters, would be most useful only in a single setting; training conducted in the desired setting would bypass any generalization problems. Sometimes training in the natural setting can not be arranged to occur frequently or conveniently, and simulated natural settings might be used. Gaylord-Ross and Holvoet (1985) describe natural environments this way:

> Some skills, such as getting out materials, locomotion, communication, eating, using the toilet, and grooming, can be taught easily in the natural school context. Other skills, such as cooking, making a bed, dressing, eating family style, doing laundry, and setting the table, may not occur in the natural school context, but a realistic context can be created or simulated within the school setting. Still other skills, such as shopping, using public transportation, bowling, and eating at restaurants, require a community context . . . (p.96)

This strategy is based on the theory that training in the natural setting ensures that naturally occurring stimuli will come to control responding. Examples of natural and artificial settings and behaviors for the studies included in this discussion are shown in Table 2-2. It should be empha-sized that it is the training setting which is coded here, since the generalization settings are natural by definition.

Training in the natural setting as the single strategy used to facilitate generalization was identified in 13 articles (13 studies). An analysis of the overall impact of those studies indicates that merely shifting the location of instruction without incorporating other strategies to facilitate generalization will not be effective for many students. In studies with severe subjects, training in the natural setting is only as effective as train and hope.

Natural Setting

	Studies	Subjects	Subjects Generalizing Well
Severe Studies	7	25	20.5% (5/25)
Other Studies	6	29	37.5% (11/29)
Total	13	54	29.6% (16/54)

2. Sequential Modification

Sequential modification is a technique for the introduction or sequencing of changes in settings. Basically, a skill is trained in one situation and then generalization is probed in one or more nontraining situations. If generalization across situations is not evident, training is pro-grammed for an additional setting. This process is continued until training has been completed in all target situations or generalization to all remaining target situations is observed. Sequential modification may not be a very practical solution to most generalization problems, since it may require training to occur each time the individual encounters a new situation; however, it may be practical if only a few settings are required.

Stokes and Baer (1977) originally defined sequential modification as the use of train and hope procedures applied sequentially "in every nongeneralized condition, *i.e.*, across responses, subjects, settings, or experimenters" (p. 352). The difference between "sequential modification" and "sufficient exemplars" is unclear in the Stokes and Baer article, since sequential introduction to different settings is also cited as sufficient exemplars. One difference might be whether every setting is included in the training or not. However, even the examples cited are confusing, since not all settings where the behavior should occur are included. This distinction made coding difficult.

To facilitate coding, the following conventions were decided upon: the term "sufficient exemplars" would apply to the sequential introduction of new examples of the class of target stimuli (e.g., objects, cues) into training *within a single general setting* (i.e., place or time); and the

Table 2-2

Examples of Settings

Study	Behaviors	Setting of Instruction	Natural ?
Ackerman & Shapiro, 1984	packaging	sheltered workshop	Yes
Bornstein, et al., 1980	variety of social skills	small room adjacent to workshop (only trainer was present)	No
Burney, Russel, & Shores, 1977	verbal & nonverbal interaction skills	students' classroom	Yes
Correa, Poulson, & Salzberg, 1984	reach & grasp toy	small therapy room close to classroom	No
Dowrick & Dove, 1980	swimming	small room in pool building	No
Gaylord-Ross et al., 1985	social interaction skills	classroom & courtyard used for "break"	Yes
Hurlbut, Iwata, & Green, 1982	nonverbal communication skills	students' classroom	Yes
Kissel & Whitman, 1977	toy play	structured, free, and isolate play situations in a classroom	Yes
Mithaug & Wolfe, 1976	verbal interaction skills	small room with one person	No
Murdock, Garcia, & Hardman, 1977	verbal articulation of words	small therapy room close to classroom	No
VanBiervliet, Spangler, & Marshall, 1981	verbal and physical social interaction skills	mealtimes in the cafeteria	Yes

term "sequential modification" would be applied to cases in which training was sequentially introduced *across general settings*. In either case, training would be provided for new instances (stimuli or settings) until generalization to untrained instances occurred, or responding to all instances had been directly trained. These definitions are at some variance with those originally suggested by Stokes and Baer (1977), but they seemed somewhat more useful for purposes of the present investigation.

As an example of sequential modification, the way we have defined it, Murdock, Garcia, and Hardman (1977) used social consequences for correctly articulated words and immediate modeling of correct response for errors to improve the articulation of two girls with moderate handicaps. Articulation of one subject was probed in five settings: small therapy room, corner of regular classroom, learning center, at a desk in the hallway, and classroom lunch period. The five settings for the second girl included: small therapy room, corner of regular classroom, another corner, third corner, and classroom lunch period. Four different trainers (assigned to specific settings) worked with subject 1 and three with subject 2. The number of classmates present also varied, except in the therapy room setting. For subject 1, training was introduced sequentially in settings 1, 2, and 3. Although training in setting 1 produced some generalized effects in all other settings, good generalization in all 5 settings was not achieved until training had produced criterion performance levels in 3 settings. For subject 2, good generalization occurred once training was initiated in the second setting. It is likely that this occurred because settings 2-5 were in the classroom. In this study, generalization to a nontrainer in the untrained settings also occurred. The authors point out that increases in training time associated with the introduction into other settings may have produced the generalization.

As an example of a situation in which sequential modification needed to be applied to all target settings, reinforcement and prompting, including physical guidance, were implemented to train toy play to a 14-year-old teenager characterized as profoundly retarded (Kissel & Whitman, 1977). A hand over correction procedure was also implemented to reduce hand-to-mouth, head-back, and rocking behaviors. Training was first implemented in a structured play situation (i.e., teacher next to student, frequent cues). Improved frequency of play and deceleration in the frequency of mouthing did not generalize to free play (teacher more distant, fewer cues) or to isolate play (teacher still more distant, only one cue). Training was then introduced in the free play situation, but effects did not generalize to isolate play. Finally, training was introduced in the third situation, isolate play. The authors report that changes also failed to generalize to the teen's residential ward, and that training was subsequently introduced there as well.

Sequential modification was never coded as the only technique in instruction to promote generalization. Twenty studies reported using sequential modification in conjunction with one or more other strategies. It was most frequently paired with "introduce to natural contingencies" and "use sufficient exemplars" (e.g., Charlop & Walsh, 1986; Odom, Hogson, Jamieson, & Strain, 1985; Shafer, Egel, & Neef,1984).

Strategies Affecting Consequences

The second set of strategies affects both the scheduling and selection of consequences which follow the target response. Stokes and Baer (1977) distinguished the following strategies: introduce to natural maintaining contingencies, use indiscriminable contingencies, and train to generalize.

1. Introduce to Natural Maintaining Contingencies

This method is designed to ensure that the response comes under the control of consequences which naturally occur in nontraining environments. Achievement of that goal can be facilitated by: (a) teaching functional skills which should be reinforced in nontraining situations; (b) training the skill to a level of proficiency that allows the student to access natural reinforcers in an efficient manner; (c) making sure the learner actually does experience the natural consequence; and/or (d) training the student to specifically recruit reinforcement from others in the environment.

Teach functional skills. Recent curricula for the moderately, severely, and profoundly handicapped emphasize the importance of teaching functional skills which *should* provide access to naturally occurring consequences (Bates, Morrow, Pancsofar, & Sedlak, 1984; Brown, Branston, Hamre-Nietupski, Certo, & Gruenwald, 1979; Brown, Branston-McClean, Baumgart, Vincent, Falvey, & Schroeder, 1979; Falvey, 1986; Neel, Billingsley, & Lambert, 1983).

Of the 172 studies reviewed, 154 taught skills rated as immediately functional in other settings. A functional skill which generalized well was taught to 51.8% of the subjects, while only 43% of subjects were taught a nonfunctional skill which generalized well. However, most studies included other strategies as well, so this result cannot be interpreted as the "effect" of teaching functional skills.

Training behaviors which *should* be reinforced may not be sufficient, however. One must also provide assurances that the behavior actually *does* occur in nontraining situations (so it can be reinforced), that the consequences for that behavior are in fact *reinforcing* to the student, and that the consequences actually follow the behavior with sufficient *frequency* to bring the behavior under their control. It might be necessary, therefore, to deliberately program certain of those "natural conditions" before one can confidently assert that the student has been adequately "introduced" to them.

Provide opportunities. It may not be sufficient to simply teach a functional skill if occasions for the use of the skill are limited. For example, Thompson, Braam, and Fuqua (1982) taught three students with moderate handicaps to use a washer and dryer to do their laundry. At a follow-up check for maintenance 10 months later, two of the men did very poorly. Questioning revealed that the staff in the group home had failed to provide many opportunities for the men to use the laundry facilities. A follow-up study of skills trained to 17 young men and women reported similar problems when students did not have the chance to apply functional skills (Horner, Williams, & Knobbe, 1985).

The situation might also be arranged so that the response is required, and thus the natural consequence can occur and eventually maintain the behavior. Mithaug and Wolfe (1976) arranged a task where one moderately handicapped and three mildly handicapped 10 to 12 year-old boys were given candy for putting a puzzle together and where either one other or three other boys had the pieces required by one boy. The target behavior, requesting a piece, was followed by the natural consequence, receiving the piece. In an ABAB design, the task required 2-person (A) then 4-person (B) exchanges. The students were always seated in groups of four and were required to verbally request puzzle pieces from each other. Rate and direction of requests generally increased during the 4-person interdependence conditions. Experimenters measured other verbalizations to determine if the increased number of verbal requests would generalize to other verbalizations, and whether verbalizations would be directed at each member of the group. Three students did increase verbalizations, while one student decreased verbalizations during the four conditions, and ceased verbalizing to one person by the fourth phase. In this study, the students were "forced" to interact by the requirements of the task, and they were therefore introduced to the natural contingencies, which in turn not only reinforced requests, but produced generalized increases in other communication as well.

Develop Proficiency. Natural contingencies may exist, but the student may lack the proficiency in the use of the skill required to actually evoke those contingencies. One way to improve generalization is to ensure that the behavior can be performed at a level which will be reinforced. Burney, Russel, and Shores (1977) measured the generalization of vocalizing, smiling, and sharing of two boys described as profoundly mentally retarded in a toy play situation with a young woman, also described as profoundly mentally retarded. The two boys' vocalizations occurred at 1 in 3 minutes and 1 in 6 minutes initially during baseline, while the woman's fell from almost 3 per minute to zero. The woman's social interactions did not reappear until the boys' skills training began to generalize to their interactions with her, and their rate of verbalizations rose. The authors hypothesize that the boys' initial failure to respond extinguished her behaviors in that situation. In addition, her reinforcement of their verbalizations was available to them only after their skills increased in proficiency.

Ensure reinforcement. In other cases, the situation in which the behavior is to occur may need to be altered in order to establish the conditions under which the behavior, if it occurs, will be reinforced. For example, VanBiervliet, Spangler, and Marshall (1981) arranged a relatively simple change in the way food was served to make the natural community of reinforcers for language available to five young men classified as either moderately or severely mentally retarded living in a residential center. In a multiple baseline design, family style serving (i.e., bowls, platters, and pitchers of food placed on tables) replaced institutional serving (i.e., individuals picked up food on trays at a serving counter and carried them to tables) at dinner, breakfast, and lunch. This encouraged verbal requests for food, and set the stage for other interactions, such as passing the food. It also introduced the student to the natural contingencies (e.g., conversation, receiving food) which were available to reinforce interactive behavior. Three of the students showed increased and maintained frequencies of interaction in all three situations. A fourth student showed an increase from 0 or 1 verbalization in 9 minutes to 1 or 2; however, he had a very minimal social and verbal skill repertoire at the time of the study. The fifth man's rate varied across situations over time, and he appeared to have high language frequency with traditional institutional-style serving.

Problems might be encountered when the response occurs, but is not reinforced in the target generalization situations. For example, a student may be taught to sign, but if signing is ignored by parents and/or teachers, the response is likely to extinguish. In order to avoid this situation, experimenters have often arranged events to provide better assurances that appropriate responses will be reinforced in the generalization situation.

For example, three teens with multiple handicaps/severe mental retardation were taught to point to Bliss symbols for 10 objects they encountered at least twice per day in school (Hurlbut, Iwata, & Green, 1982). They were also taught to point to drawings for 10 other objects. Two steps were taken to ensure that spontaneous usage of symbols/pictures was reinforced outside of training: the students' communication boards remained with them all day and an experimenter remained in the classroom all day to ensure that language was reinforced. Four types of generalization were probed. First, students were asked to respond to an item trained in the morning during afternoon sessions to test maintenance. Each student maintained the learned pictures much more often (range 75%-100%) than the trained Bliss symbols (range 29%-92%). Second, the student was shown an object differing in irrelevant stimulus characteristics from the specific object used to train the symbol/picture (e.g., a sock of a different color) and asked to identify it by symbol/picture. Two students were much more likely to use pictures to name untrained objects than symbols. For one student, variability obscured any meaningful difference. Third, the student was provided a picture and a symbol for 10 untrained objects. Each student used pictures much more often than symbols, and each used untrained pictures to name untrained objects. Fourth, spontaneous usage of symbols/pictures in the classroom outside of the training sessions was assessed. All students generalized both symbols and pictures, although pictures generalized first and occurred at greater frequencies.

Teach to recruit reinforcement. People may also be taught to actively recruit reinforcement. Stokes, Fowler, and Baer (1978) taught eight preschool children, including four classified as "deviant," to self-evaluate their own work and then to cue their teachers to deliver praise for good work by asking questions such as "How is this work?" and "Have I been working carefully?" Probes were conducted with other trainers, but generalization required that the "new" trainer ask the students to work carefully, evaluate their work, and ask about their work before full generalization was achieved.

Summary. Five articles (6 studies) involving at least 1 subject with severe handicaps ("Severe Studies") implemented natural contingencies and 4 articles (5 studies) reported the use of natural contingencies with 27 other persons. Natural contingencies were used in combination with other strategies in 47 articles (53 studies).

Natural Contingencies

	Studies	Subjects	Subjects Generalizing Well
Severe Studies	6	18	52.9% (9/17)
Other Studies	5	14	85.7% (12/14)
Total	11	32	67.7% (21/31)

4. Use Indiscriminable Contingencies

It has also been hypothesized that generalized responding might not occur or maintain because the consequences available in natural settings either are not reinforcing to the individual or do not occur with sufficient frequency. Under such conditions the behavior might extinguish.

The use of indiscriminable contingencies involves the gradual replacement of training consequences and schedules with the contingencies which will be found in natural settings. In this manner, naturally available consequences acquire reinforcing powers through pairing with programmed consequences, before training consequences are discontinued. Similarly, the schedule of one consequence for each response commonly used during training is gradually replaced with a schedule of intermittent consequences, so that the student is unable to discriminate when a response is likely to be reinforced. This method is designed to ensure that generalized responding will occur and endure when only infrequent natural consequences are available outside of training settings. Reinforcement might also be programmed to occur after progressively longer delays, and/or artificial consequences might be continued, but only under conditions which make it impossible for the student to discriminate *when* they might occur.

For example, Fowler and Baer (1981) compared feedback and reinforcement schedules for interactive and study behavior of two behavior disordered and five normal preschool children during morning training settings and afternoon generalization settings. Delaying reinforcement for appropriate behavior in the morning until the end of the school day produced much better generalization than delivering it at the end of the morning session. Coders identified that six of the seven subjects (85.7%) generalized well.

With the exception of Fowler and Baer (1981), indiscriminable contingencies were always applied in conjunction with other strategies. For example, Russo and Koegel (1977) identified a 5-year-old autistic boy who was at risk for being expelled from kindergarten because of inappropriate social behaviors, verbal responses, and stereotypic behavior. Following baseline, a therapist provided prompting and tokens for appropriate social and verbal behavior, and used restraint, a verbal reprimand, and token loss for stereotyped behavior. As the student's behavior improved, the schedule of tokens was reduced from 1:1 to variable interval schedules. Social reinforcement and tokens were provided for periods of "appropriate behavior." Also, the student and therapist moved from a separate section of the classroom to the "front" of the room with the other students. Then the therapist gradually moved his/her chair further and further away behind the student. In addition, the therapist taught the teacher to deliver tokens, to praise, and to remove tokens for stereotyped behavior. The teacher gradually assumed these responsibilities. In the final phase, the teacher delivered tokens only twice a day and social reinforcement was intermittent. The therapist was not present. The child's behavior had improved to acceptable levels and he completed kindergarten without reassignment.

After the summer vacation, the student returned to previous problem levels of behavior. Identical procedures were implemented and similar changes produced. The behavior then maintained at acceptable levels for the rest of first grade. There were no problems in either second or third grades. Fading control by the therapist, establishing control by the teacher, learning the reinforcement schedule, developing an intermittent and variable interval schedule for the delivery of tokens, and implementing procedures in a second setting all served to produce indiscriminable contingencies.

This study also incorporated several other strategies, including sequential modification (i.e., intervention in kindergarten and first grade were sufficient to produce generalization to second and third grade), introduction to natural maintaining contingencies (i.e., training functional behaviors, training teachers to ensure that reinforcement occurred), training loosely (i.e., contingencies for reinforcement were shifted from specific social and verbal behaviors to "appropriate behavior"), and multiple exemplars (i.e., at least three different trainers were involved).

In another study, five sheltered workshop employees were praised and prompted to increase their productivity (Ackerman & Shapiro, 1984). When effects did not generalize to other work periods for the same task, clients were taught to actuate a counter for each package completed and to circle a numeral representing the total completed at the end of the work period. Training independent self-monitoring was achieved in 35 minutes. Once the clients were trained, the praise and prompting for good production was dropped. Self-monitoring alone was sufficient to maintain the increases, indicating that the counter activation and charting reinforced production rate. The counter and production chart were not available at other times, and the increased productivity did not generalize. When identical materials became available (i.e., self-monitoring counters were present at all times), the differences in available contingencies between trained and untrained situations became indiscriminable and productivity immediately increased.

5. Train to Generalize

With this technique the learner is not reinforced for performing a previously reinforced response, but only for a new form of the response, or for appropriately responding in the presence of untrained stimuli. The technique seems to be at odds with most established instructional methods directed at acquisition, since consequation occurs only for generalized responding. However, Stokes and Baer (1977) also describe the possibility of "instructed generalization," in which the student is informed of the "possibility of generalization and then ask[ed] for it" (p. 363). For example, Warren, Baxter, Anderson, Marshall, and Baer (1981) studied four severely retarded youths who had failed to maintain generalized asking "What is that?" questions 2 1/2 years after training ended, and whose skill did not return even after observing a peer model the behavior. Training was introduced which included new items (generalization stimuli) and trained items. Asking a "what" question when first shown a novel object resulted in a token reinforcement, later exchanged for toy or edible, but no tokens were provided for naming familiar items. After 3 sessions with 10 novel objects included in each, all 4 youths demonstrated generalization in probe sessions.

Endo and Sloane (1982) taught four elementary grade children to make poetic statements which personified inanimate objects (e.g., "The shirt hated to get starched," "The roses smiled when the sun came up"). During training, a model made a personified statement and received a token; the child was reinforced with a token only for stating a different personification for the same picture. The children did well in training, but when new items were shown to the children, they were unable to state personifications ("poor generalization"). In a follow-up study reported in the same article (Endo & Sloane, 1982), three elementary grade boys were similarly taught—except that the model demonstrated five consecutive statements for five different elements in a single set, instead of the one exemplar for one set used in Experiment I. Then the child had a chance to make five statements regarding items drawn from a second set. In this study, the children responded to about 80% of untrained items in the first generalization probe. The lack of any reinforcement or feedback during the probes may have affected the level and amount of generalization recorded, and may explain why the performances of two of the children dropped during the second probe. In both studies, the model demonstrated and the student was reinforced for nonpersonified statements in a subsequent phase (e.g., "The shirt is yellow and green;" "The roses bloom during the springtime"). Experimental control over generalized responding was demonstrated in the second study when the children failed to make personified statements during the generalization probe after the nonpersonified statement reinforcement phase.

A total of four studies in three articles included "train to generalize" as one of the components of instruction, but no studies were identified which used this strategy in isolation. Two articles involving subjects with severe disabilities and two other articles were coded as applying this strategy in addition to other strategies, and only 2 of the 20 study participants in those studies (10%) were identified as generalizing well.

Strategies Affecting Antecedents

Two strategies for the manipulation of stimuli were described by Stokes and Baer (1977): "programming common stimuli" and "training sufficient exemplars." Since then, other methods have been identified which also manipulate stimuli.

These methods focus on the discrimination of events which occur before or concurrent with the response. In discrimination training, the centerpiece of most research in instruction and learning, specific stimuli come to evoke specific responses through differential reinforcement. If the response fails to generalize, it is hypothesized that discrimination training was so successful that differences between stimuli in "training" and "generalization" situations inhibited generalization. The methods that follow suggest techniques for selecting stimuli that minimize the differences between training stimuli and stimuli in the generalization situation.

6. Program Common Stimuli

As the label implies, this technique involves providing instruction which includes stimuli which occur most frequently in the target generalization settings (Stokes and Baer, 1977).

For example, Jones, Van Hasselt, and Sisson (1984) attributed the low levels of generalization of fire drill skills to two primary factors:

> [a] lack of specific programming for transfer of training, and [b] specific instructions frequently provided to subjects by night staff to assist their roommates during drills. Behaviors emitted in assisting roommates (e.g., holding their hands, walking quickly out of room) were frequently incompatible with trained responses. (p. 269)

Therefore, in a second study, the authors' aim was to "expand the breadth of stimuli that exert control over these responses" (p. 269). They trained three blind teens at night, in their bedrooms, to assist in the evacuation of their roommates during fire drills and they trained the roommates to follow the target teen from the bedroom. The roommates, the sound of the alarm, the location, and the time of day were the stimuli common to both training and generalization situations. Following training, two of the target teens and their three roommates participated correctly in the school nighttime fire drill. One young man, however, jumped out of bed and ran to the door, in violation to the trained safety procedures. His roommate stopped him and made him start again, whereupon he completed the sequence correctly (Jones, Sisson, & Van Hasselt, 1984).

In cases where it is not possible or practical to employ stimuli which will actually occur in natural settings, it might be possible to effectively *simulate* those stimuli. For example, Page, Iwata, and Neef (1976) constructed a cardboard model of four city blocks, including streets, houses, cars, trees, people, and pedestrian and traffic control lights. Five moderately retarded young men then were trained to manipulate a doll and verbalize the doll's actions in getting to a designated location in the simulated environment. The men were tested on street crossing under actual city traffic conditions and successful generalization occurred. In this study, the experimenters simulated the stimuli common to both situations, since duplication within the classroom would have been impossible.

Overall, only 5 studies (5 articles) were identified as employing "common stimuli" as the single method to facilitate generalization. However, this technique was used in combination with other strategies in 64 studies (58 articles).

Common Stimuli

	Studies	Subjects	Subjects Generalizing Well
Severe Studies	4	21	66.7% (14/21)
Other Studies	1	3	100.0% (3/3)
Total	5	24	70.8% (17/24)

7. Train Sufficient Exemplars

Stokes and Baer (1977) differentiated sequential modification from "train sufficient exemplars" primarily on the basis of the number of situations to which generalization is desired. If the response is desired in only a few situations, then "sequential modification" may suffice. However, if the response is applicable in many situations, "sufficient exemplars" would involve "teaching another exemplar of the same generalization lesson, and then another, and then another, and so on until the induction is formed (i.e., until generalization occurs sufficiently to satisfy the problem posed)" (p. 355). As noted earlier, for purposes of this study we further defined "sufficient exemplars" as the sequential introduction of new target *stimuli within settings,* and used the term "sequential modification" to reference the introduction of training *across* settings.

The strategy, as we define it, requires the introduction of many different instances of the class of target antecedents into the training situation. By training sufficient exemplars, the student is thought to learn a general category of stimuli to which to respond. If training on one does not produce generalization, training is directed to another exemplar, and so on, until generalization to other exemplars is noted. For example, instead of teaching "putting on a sweater" with just long-sleeved crew-necked sweaters, V-necked sweaters, short-sleeved sweaters, and so on are trained. With more varied instructional antecedents, generalization to untrained sweaters (e.g., turtlenecks) may occur.

As an example, an adolescent with severe handicaps was taught to match objects to an exemplar to demonstrate "match to sample" skills for six classes of objects (i.e., car, bowl, hat, doll, shoe, and book) (Anderson & Spradlin, 1980). In generalization probes, untrained objects of different colors, shapes, sizes, and materials were presented. The subject generalized matching for each class at or above 87% of the untrained exemplars presented after 3 training sessions. The matching skill was the first step. In the second step, the youth was asked to name the class to which the exemplar belonged. Following baseline assessment of 36 objects (6 per class), one bowl and one car exemplar were selected for training. When the student correctly labeled the training exemplar in 80% of the trials, untrained objects were probed. If generalization occurred to less than 80% of the exemplars for the trained class, a second exemplar was trained to criterion. This process was repeated until sufficient exemplars had been trained to produce 80% generalization to untrained members of the class. Then, the entire procedure was repeated with another class of objects. The first exemplar for the car and bowl classes required 2060 trials, but subsequent exemplars required a maximum of 850 trials, and the first exemplar in shoe and book required only 250 trials. Car and bowl required only 1 exemplar to produce within class generalization, book required 3 exemplars, hat required 4 exemplars, and doll required 5 exemplars.

In another study, stimulus classes included peers and objects to be used in social interaction. Gaylord-Ross, Haring, Breen, and Pitts-Conway (1984) trained an adolescent to respond to interactions initiated by an autistic youth. The trainer prompted and reinforced interactions with a nonhandicapped teen in both the classroom and the school courtyard. During training, the subject was first taught to use a video game, then a portable radio, and then chewing gum, as content for the interactions. Generalization to peers who had not participated in training was probed in a trained setting (the courtyard), during a school break.

The number of initiations by the autistic teen and the duration of the exchanges increased as each object was trained, and initiations when the student did not have the object increased as well. Training in one object did not generalize to offering to share untrained objects during breaks. Thus, generalization occurred across one stimulus dimension (peers) but did not occur across another (untrained objects). This is certainly understandable, since the student did not know how to use any of the objects prior to training. In addition, the authors were most interested in generalization across nonhandicapped peers. Therefore, the sequential introduction of the objects seems like an instructional convenience rather than an attempt to obtain generalization across objects. However, in this case, one must conclude that one peer was a "sufficient exemplar" while three objects were insufficient exemplars.

Anderson and Spradlin (1980) identified a number of pertinent questions regarding the application of "sufficient exemplars."

1. "What is the most efficient method of training sufficient examples? . . . a more efficient technique may be training several examples concurrently, instead of serially" (p. 155).
2. Since the "number of examples sufficient to produce generalization may vary, . . . it is reasonable to suppose that the diversity of properties reflected by the examples chosen for training may affect the extent of generalization," [and] ". . . further analysis is needed to determine the proper balance" in the selection of examples (pp. 155-156).

Until these questions have been adequately answered, "train sufficient exemplars" may be difficult to define precisely and to implement exactly.

A total of five articles (with five studies) were identified that employed sufficient exemplars as the sole strategy for facilitating generalization.

Sufficient Exemplars

	Studies	Subjects	Subjects Generalizing Well
Severe Studies	3	9	55.6% (5/9)
Other Studies	2	9	66.7% (6/9)
Total	5	18	61.1% (11/18)

8. Multiple Exemplars

Within this strategy, representatives of the stimuli which are included in the targeted class are concurrently trained. However, a systematic method is apparently not applied to select the stimuli. We were unable to identify an article with multiple exemplars as the sole strategy, but it was reported in combination with other strategies in six articles. For example, Lagomarcino, Reid, Ivancic, and Faw (1984) sequentially trained three types of dance movements (sufficient exemplars) concurrently in three settings and partnered their five dancers labeled as severely or profoundly retarded with three to six other persons (multiple partner exemplars). However, the authors did not describe the criteria for selecting the number of type of exemplars trained. Two students showed improvements in dancing at community dances, although one later decelerated in appropriate dancing. For two others, however, it was necessary to introduce training in the community setting (sequential modification) to produce generalization.

Stainback, Stainback, Wehman, and Spangiers (1983) provided individual training in three physical fitness exercises to three adults with profound mental retardation. All three adults generalized performing the trained exercises to a group exercise setting, and also showed increasing skills in performing two untrained exercises. Since common stimuli and indiscriminable contingencies were also programmed, however, it is difficult to determine the effects of the multiple exercise exemplars. In another study, Sprague and Horner (1984) used multiple exemplars of vending machines, but they were carefully selected to be non-representative, since their use preceded training in machines selected with a general case method (see below). The careful selection of similar exemplars seems to preclude using this as an example of multiple exemplars.

Anderson and Spradlin's (1980) second concern has also been addressed in the literature. Becker, Engelmann, and Thomas (1975), and Engelmann and Carnine (1982) have described a procedure for selecting examples that represent the range of stimuli and associated response variation. This approach has been labeled the "general case" method (Horner, Sprague, & Wilcox, 1982).

9. General Case Exemplars

Exemplars chosen for training are systematically selected to represent the range of stimuli included in the category to which responding is desired. For example, to select vending machines to use in training, Sprague and Horner (1984) analyzed a number of machines and chose three which represented the range of stimuli and associated response variations likely to be encountered by the subjects in terms of the location and action of the coin insertion and return slots and mechanism for item selection and delivery. Six young men with moderate or severe handicaps showed little generalization to untrained machines following training on a single machine or following training on three similar machines. However, following instruction involving the three "general case" machines, good generalization to untrained machines was obtained.

In a second experiment to teach social skills to two young men with autism, Gaylord-Ross, Haring, Breen, and Pitts-Conway (1984) sequentially trained the use of objects. In addition, however, they selected peers without handicaps to sample the range of peer types in senior high school. The attributes sampled included grade, sex, and whether the peer was known or unknown to the trainee. During generalization probes, the youths initiated responses with 28 and 33 peers respectively, an enormous increase from the 0 recorded prior to training.

Eight studies (8 articles) applied general case strategies, but six of those studies included other strategies for comparative purposes. Coding was not difficult, since all clearly identified and referenced the strategy. When used as a sole strategy, all subjects generalized well.

General Case

	Studies	Subjects	Subjects Generalizing Well
Severe Studies	1	3	100.0% (3/3)
Other Studies	1	5	100.0% (5/5)
Total	2	8	100.0% (8/8)

Other Strategies

Two other strategies defined by Stokes and Baer, "Train Loosely" and "Mediate Generalization," are not easily classified within the categories we have used above, so we will discuss them separately below.

10. Train Loosely

Tight stimulus control which may inhibit generalization may also be avoided by relaxing the stimulus events which precede responding and by reinforcing response variants which produce similar critical effects. Stokes and Baer (1977) called this "loose training."

For example, Campbell and Stremel-Campbell (1982) instructed two boys with moderate handicaps to ask what/where/why questions using "is/are" (e.g., "What are you doing?"). Next, they were taught to ask questions requiring a yes or no answer (e.g., "Is this mine?"). One boy was also taught to make statements (e.g., "This is mine.") in response to questions. Although teachers prompted the responses at first, events and objects which occurred naturally constituted the stimulus events. Since specific training stimuli were not defined and the responses which were reinforced also varied (i.e., over 400 different syntactic structures were emitted by each boy), the authors classified their procedure as "training loosely." Spontaneous use of the language forms was assessed during peer and adult interactions which occurred during a free play period (generalization probes). For both boys, what/where/why questions increased from 1 or fewer in 150 minutes to about 1 every 5 minutes. "Yes/no" questions increased from 1 or fewer in 150 minutes to about 1 every 6 minutes. For both boys, incorrect usage also increased somewhat.

As a second example, Filler and Kasari (1981) taught mothers to work with their severely involved infants to turn their heads to follow visual stimuli and track sounds with one infant; and to reach for objects, and to bear weight in two different positions with a second infant. The mothers varied the stimuli, and reinforced variations of the responses—training "loosely." All skills were quickly acquired and generalized very well to their twice weekly center-based program.

"Train loosely" was coded as an isolated strategy for three articles (three studies) involving at least one person with severe handicaps and one other study, with the generalization results shown in the following table.

Train Loosely

	Studies	Subjects	Subjects Generalizing Well
Severe Studies	3	8	37.5% (3/8)
Other Studies	1	6	100.0% (6/6)
Total	4	14	64.3% (9/14)

11. Mediate Generalization

The final strategy considered in this discussion is designed to "bridge the gap" between training and generalization settings. The "gap" can be bridged by teaching the individual behaver to control the stimuli and reinforcers which affect his own generalization. For example, if the target behavior is insufficiently reinforced in the generalization situation, the individual can be taught self-reinforcement. The behavior of self-reinforcement must be trained. Then, the self-reinforcement act provides the additional reinforcers necessary to mediate the differences between the training situation and the target situation. In a similar way, self-instruction, or self-control of stimuli which occur before the response, can be used to mediate differences in the controlling stimuli.

For example, Wacker and Greenbaum (1984) found that training seven moderately or severely mentally retarded adolescents to verbally label a shape prior to sorting it (self-instruction) improved generalization to novel shapes and dimensions much more than training which did not involve training verbal labeling. Wacker and Berg (1983) taught five moderately and severely mentally retarded adolescents to self-instruct steps in complex assembly tasks using a picture sequence. They were then able to use a new set of pictures to complete novel tasks.

Teaching students to self-monitor can result in self-reinforcement in the generalization situation. Apparently the act of counting a behavior serves to positively reinforce it (Liberty, 1984; 1985). Self-monitoring was also used to mediate differences in four studies (Ackerman & Shapiro, 1984; Heins, Lloyd, & Hallahan, 1986; Matson & Andrasik, 1982).

In some studies, students were taught both self-instruction and self-monitoring. For example, Sowers, Verdi, Bourbeau, and Sheehan (1985) used a self-control package which included pictures for self-instruction and self-monitoring to teach four severely to moderately retarded teens, who maintained performance on 13 complex tasks after training ceased. In addition, two students were given novel tasks and were able to acquire them very rapidly.

An alternative approach to self-control procedures which can be used to mediate differences involves teaching "general" skills or "strategies"—skills that are useful in a variety of situations. For educational situations, skills which are useful in a variety of settings include: attending, completing work on time, and "good behavior." Many studies have attempted to modify discrete student behaviors. However, in this new approach, students are taught the general rules or expectations as a strategy for achieving success in other situations. For example, the strategy of "staying on task" is taught to a high school student in a resource room and then generalization to the regular classrooms (e.g., History, English, etc.) is evaluated. Only three studies were identified in which students were taught general skills which were useful in a variety of situations. For example, Reese and Filipczak (1980) taught students in a resource room classroom behavior, attendance, and other skills which generalized to other settings, although similar strategies were not effective with other individuals in a study conducted by Kirschenbaum, Dillman, and Karoly (1982).

Mediate Generalization

	Studies	Subjects	Subjects Generalizing Well
Severe Studies	1	4	75.0% (3/4)
Other Studies	1	2	0.0% (0/2)
Total	2	6	50.0% (3/6)

Mediating generalization was identified as the sole strategy in two articles involving six learners, and only three of them generalized well. In a separate analysis of published and unpublished data, Liberty (1987) found that of 20 subjects trained in self-control techniques, 16 (80%) either generalized or showed improved generalization as a result of the self-control training. Of the 20 subjects, 14 were severely handicapped, and 91% showed improved generalization.

Results and Discussion

A total of 151 articles involving 172 studies provided information for the evaluation of generalization with 616 subjects. Of those studies, 106 included persons with severe handicaps and involved 373 subjects. The remaining 66 studies involving 243 subjects did not include persons with severe handicaps. No statistically reliable differences between the two sets of studies were found, so they were combined in the analyses of strategy effectiveness presented below.

Reliability

Coding reliabilities were estimated with 10 independent raters forming 25 comparisons in the coding of 19 studies (approximately 11% of all studies coded). Overall agreement across items averaged 91%. The specific item reliabilities are reported in Table 2-3. Reliabilities involving binomial coding (e.g., "yes/no" indications that a particular strategy was employed) were evaluated via the formula: (number of agreements)/(number of agreements + number of disagreements). Reliabilities involving values other than 0 or 1 (e.g., the number of subjects generalizing "well") were evaluated using the formula: (lowest number coded)/(highest number coded).

Table 2-3

Coding Reliabilities

Characteristic Coded	Mean Reliability
Number of Subjects	100%
Most Severe Handicapping Condition of a Single Subject	92%
Age Range of Subjects	99%
Functionality of Behavior	94%
Generalization Strategy/Strategies	86%
Number of Subjects Generalizing Well	77%

Train and Hope Expectancies

A surprisingly high proportion (76%) of the subjects in published studies of simple train and hope approaches generalized well to nontraining situations. However, one must bear in mind that such studies would not ordinarily have been published unless they were successful. If one also considers all the studies of special strategies that used train and hope as a comparative baseline, estimates of effectiveness in that condition drop to 14.4%. Of course, those studies might severely *underestimate* the overall effectiveness of such training, since it is unlikely they would have been published if subjects had generalized well under baseline conditions. In the face of such divergent estimates, data were collected to reflect more accurately the success which teachers might be expected to enjoy in public schools.

Observational data collected for our baseline studies in classrooms serving pupils with severe handicaps revealed that only 8 out of 32 skills (25%) generalized well when instruction did not include any special strategies to facilitate generalization (Billingsley, Berman, & Opalski, 1983; Billingsley, F. F., Doyle, M., Radovich, S., & Thompson, M., 1985; Billingsley, F. F., Thompson, M., Matlock, B., & Work, J., 1984). Another UWRO study of public school instruction (see Chapter 4) showed that of 24 skills found to generalize, only one (4.2%) had been taught with a simple train and hope approach. The 25% figure seemed a conservative compromise among the various alternatives, and so was used in all the comparative analyses presented below.

Single Strategies vs. Train and Hope

The effectiveness of individual strategies used in isolation could be ascertained in 43 studies involving a total of 162 subjects. Three strategies—training to generalize, sequential modification, and programming multiple exemplars—were not studied in isolation in any of the articles reviewed. The effectiveness of the remaining strategies when used in isolation is presented in Table 2-4 and Figure 2-1.

All eight of the special strategies studied in isolation produced higher proportions of subjects generalizing well than a simple train and hope approach. However, those differences proved to be statistically reliable in only six cases, using chi-square analysis (see Table 2-5). Mediating generalization appeared to produce substantial increases in the proportion of subjects generalizing well, but too few subjects were included in the analysis to deem those improvements statistically reliable. The other strategy failing to reach significance, training in the natural environment, was evaluated with a good number of subjects (n=54), but produced outcomes that were not reliably better than those produced by a simple train and hope approach. Providing training in natural environments does, of course, result in the acquisition of a skill which can be effectively employed within at least one meaningful context. However, it would appear that training in one natural environment does not necessarily improve generalization to other natural environments.

Relative Single Strategy Effectiveness

Single strategy effectiveness ranged from a low of 29.6% (i.e., training in the natural setting) to a high of 100% (i.e., general case programming), with the bulk of strategies falling within the range of 50% to 65%. Despite that rather large range, no between-strategy differences proved to be statistically reliable except for differences between training in the natural environment and the use of other special strategies. The failure to show differences among other strategies is most likely due to small sample sizes.

As shown in Table 2-6, other strategies proved to be reliably superior to training in the natural environment in all but one case. The remaining strategy—mediating generalization—was not studied with enough subjects for meaningful comparison. Those outcomes support the notion that simply training in the natural environment, without the use of other special strategies, might not be very effective in facilitating generalization across a range of target situations.

Strategy Class Effectiveness

More powerful analyses can be conducted to determine if any general approach to facilitating generalization appears superior by forming classes of strategies. Most special strategies can be placed in one of three classes describing the major focus concern: setting or situational strategies; antecedent or stimulus event strategies; and consequence or reinforcement strategies.

General setting strategies. Two of the strategies studied—training in the natural environment and sequential modification—concern themselves with the location and general context of training. The types of stimuli and consequences available for responding might be changed but not necessarily in any particular manner, so this is considered a separate class from the other two. A total of 14 studies, involving 57 subjects, were found where training in the natural environment and/or sequential modification were the only special strategies employed.

As a class, general setting strategies produced a slightly higher proportion of subjects generalizing well than train and hope, but the increase did not prove to be statistically reliable ($x^2=0.170$, $p(x^2) = 0.6803$). The class was significantly less effective than the other two classes.

General antecedent strategies. Four of the strategies studied involve the systematic manipulation of stimulus events antecedent to the response—the use of common stimuli, sufficient exemplars, multiple exemplars, and general case programming. None of those strategies necessarily involve the manipulation of specific settings or locations, nor any particular strategy for the consequation of correct or incorrect responding. A total of 45 studies involving 158 subjects were found where one or more of the antecedent strategies were the only special strategies employed.

As a group, the class of antecedent strategies proved significantly more effective than either a simple train and hope approach ($x^2 = 11.384$, $p(x^2) = 0.0007$) or the class of general setting strategies ($x^2 = 11.985$, $p(x^2) = 0.0005$). The class of antecedent strategies also performed somewhat better than the class of consequence-related strategies, but that advantage was not statistically meaningful ($x^2 = 0.146$, $p(x^2) = 0.7025$).

General consequent strategies. Three strategies involve the manipulation of consequences or the contingencies for delivering consequences—introduction to natural contingencies, the use of indiscriminable contingencies, and training to generalize. Eighteen studies with 56 subjects were identified in which natural contingencies and/or indiscriminable contingencies were employed as the only special strategies. No studies were found which used training to generalize as a strategy in isolation, or in combination only with other consequence-related strategies.

As a group, consequence-related strategies were significantly more effective than a simple train and hope approach ($x^2 = 6.424$, $p(x^2) = 0.0113$) or the use of general setting strategies ($x^2=5.5471$, $p(x^2) = 0.0183$).

Effectiveness of Cross-Class Combinations

Only 43 of the 172 coded studies focused on the evaluation of a single strategy. The remaining 129 (75%) of the studies, involving 454 (73.7%) of the subjects, evaluated various combinations of strategies, usually in ways which made the effects of individual strategies impossible to determine. Moreover, the variation in strategy combination was very large, making the meaningful evaluation of each type of combination impossible with the number of subjects available for analysis.

The proportions of subjects generalizing well for each strategy used in combination are reported in Table 2–4 and Figure 2–1, but caution should be used in interpreting those results. While all cases reported under a given strategy involved the use of that strategy, each study also used some combination of one to four other strategies. To attribute outcomes primarily to the labeled strategy would be ill advised. Also, while the analyses of strategies used in isolation could carefully partition articles and subjects into separate, nonoverlapping cells, that is not the case in the study of strategy combinations. If a study used three different strategies, that study and its subjects would be tallied under each of those strategies in the summary table. Such subject overlap obviates the direct comparison of effects among strategy categories. However, since studies classified as an "isolated study" are separate from those classified as a "combined study," it is possible to statistically evaluate any change in outcome produced by combining a given strategy with one or more other strategies.

Of the eight strategies studied in isolation, six produced poorer results when used in combination with other strategies, although only two—natural contingencies and indiscriminable contingencies proved to have a statistically reliable decrement in outcome (see Table 2–7). Training in the natural environment showed a statistically reliable increase in effectiveness when used in combination with other strategies, and general case programming was 100% effective in both conditions.

That training in the natural setting improved in effectiveness when combined with other strategies only serves to underscore the observations made earlier—training in one natural setting does not necessarily ensure stimulus or consequence variation representative of all the settings to which generalization might be desired. Adding the strategies of, for example, multiple exemplars

Table 2-4

Percent of Subjects Generalizing Well with the Use of
Strategies Alone and in Combination

	Strategy Used Alone			Strategy Used with Other Strategies		
	# Studies	# Subjects	% Gen Well	# Studies	# Subjects	% Gen Well
Setting Strategies						
Train in Natural Setting	13	54	29.6%	59	201	53.2%
Sequential Modification	0	0	-	20	69	46.4%
Any Combination of Setting Strategies	16	57	31.6%	63	221	50.2%
Consequent Strategies						
Natural Contingenices	11	31	67.7%	53	207	45.4%
Indiscriminable Contingencies	1	7	85.7%	8	22	22.7
Train to Generalize	0	0	-	4	20	10.%
Any Combination of Consequation Strategies	18	56	55.4%	56	221	42.1%
Antecedent Strategies						
Common Stimuli	5	24	70.8%	64	220	51.4%
Sufficient Exemplars	5	18	61.1%	66	239	37.7%
Multiple Exemplars	0	0	-	6	22	90.9%
General Case Programming	2	8	100.0%	6	18	100.0%
Any Combination of Antecedent Strategies	45	158	59.5%	63	221	43.9%
Other Strategies						
Train Loosely	4	14	64.3%	7	33	57.6%
Mediate Generalization	2	6	50.0%	18	63	34.9%

Figure 2-1

Effect of Strategies Used in Isolation and Combination

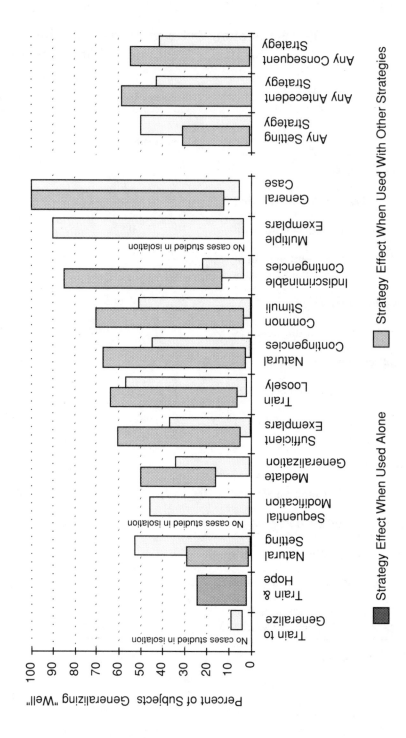

Table 2-5

Comparisons of Strategy Effectiveness
Relative to Train & Hope

Strategy	Chi square[6]	Significantly Better Than Train & Hope?	P(x2)
Setting Strategies			
Train in a Natural Setting	0.046	No	
Sequential Modification		Comparison not made[7]	
Any Combination of Setting Strategies	0.170	No	
Consequent Strategies			
Natural Contingencies	9.923	Yes	0.0016
Indiscriminable Contingencies	6.752	Yes	0.0094
Train to Generalize		Comparison not made[7]	
Any Combination of Consequent Strategies	6.424	Yes	0.0113
Antecedent Strategies			
Common Stimuli	9.877	Yes	0.0017
Sufficient Exemplars	4.936	Yes	0.0263
Multiple Exemplars		Comparison not made[7]	
General Case Programming	12.038	Yes	0.0005
Any Combination of Antecedent Strategies	11.384	Yes	0.0007
Other Strategies			
Train Loosely	4.875	Yes	0.0272
Mediate Generalization	0.560	No	

[6] All chi square values have been corrected for discontinuity to account for small cell sizes.
[7] Comparison was not made because no studies in which this strategy was used in isolation were identified.

Table 2-6

Comparisons of Strategy Effectiveness Relative to Train in the Natural Setting

Strategy	Chi square[8]	Significantly Better Than Train in Natural Setting?	P(x2)
Consequent Strategies			
Natural Contingencies	10.139	Yes	0.0015
Indiscriminable Contingencies	6.196	Yes	0.0128
Train to Generalize		Comparison not made[9]	
Any Combination of Consequent Strategies[10]	5.571	Yes	0.0183
Antecedent Strategies			
Common Stimuli	9.931	Yes	0.0016
Sufficient Exemplars	4.444	Yes	0.0350
Multiple Exemplars		Comparison not made[9]	
General Case Programming	11.728	Yes	0.0006
Any Combination of Antecedent Strategies[10]	11.985	Yes	0.0005
Other Strategies			
Train Loosely	4.350	Yes	0.0370
Mediate Generalization	0.308	No	

or sequential modification across a series of natural settings could improve the prospects of generalization considerably.

The constant effectiveness of general case programing, used either alone or in combination with other strategies, is impressive. Since general case programming represents the most extensive and systematic approach for facilitating generalization of all those studied, the results are not entirely unexpected. However, some caution should be taken in positing the invincibility of general case programing. Only two studies with a total of eight subjects using that approach in isolation, and only an additional 7 studies with 21 subjects evaluating that approach in combination with other strategies, were included in the review. Until additional studies are completed, general case programming must be considered a very promising, but not extensively tested, approach for facilitating generalization.

[8] All chi square values have been corrected for discontinuity to account for small cell sizes.
[9] Comparison was not made because no studies in which this strategy was used in isolation were identified.
[10] Includes Train in the Natural Setting alone and in combination with Sequential Modification (Combined Setting Strategies).

Table 2-7

Comparisons of Strategy Effectiveness Used Alone
Relative to Combined with Other Strategies

Strategy	Chi square[11]	Significantly Better Used . . .	P(x2)
Setting Strategies			
Train in a Natural Setting	8.576	With other strategies	0.0034
Sequential Modification		Comparison not made[12]	
Consequent Strategies			
Natural Contingencies	4.527	Alone	0.0334
Indiscriminable Contingencies	6.473	Alone	0.0110
Train to Generalize		Comparison not made[12]	
Antecedent Strategies			
Common Stimuli	2.560	No reliable difference	
Sufficient Exemplars	2.940	No reliable difference	
Multiple Exemplars		Comparison not made[12]	
General Case Programming		No difference[13]	
Other Strategies			
Train Loosely	0.011	No reliable difference	
Mediate Generalization	0.084	No reliable difference	

Strategy Selection

It would appear, on the basis of admittedly limited evidence, that general case programming is the strategy of choice for facilitating generalization from instructional to applied situations. Unfortunately, while general case programming is not necessarily a difficult process to employ, it can be very time-consuming and laborious. The "universe" of positive, negative, and irrelevant stimuli must be defined, identified, and carefully sampled to provide a good representation of the situations to which generalization is desired. That sampling must then be tested carefully and adjusted in accord with observed trainee error patterns before confidence in the program can be

---

[11] All chi square values have been corrected for discontinuity to account for small cell sizes.
[12] Comparison was not made because no studies in which this strategy was used in isolation were identified.
[13] All subjects generalized, whether used alone or in combination with other strategies.

achieved. Quite simply, it is not likely that classroom teachers and other applied practitioners will be able to mount such an effort very often. Good "prepackaged" general case programs have been and are being developed to meet a variety of needs for persons with severe handicaps (c.f., Sprague & Horner, 1984), but those programs cannot meet all the needs of individuals with severe handicaps. There will be times when the teacher must turn to one or more of the other strategies for facilitating generalization.

At first it might seem logical to simply select the alternative strategy with the next highest probability of facilitating generalization. If that fails to work, the next strategy on the list could be tried, and so on until generalization is achieved. As noted earlier, however, there were no statistically reliable differences among most strategies. Almost any strategy might do as well as any other, but could still fail to facilitate good generalization with between 15% and 50% of the learners. It is not at all clear, therefore, where one should start; and simply trying all strategies in succession could be inefficient and time consuming.

To provide multiple assurances of success, one might be tempted to use several strategies, each designed to address different aspects of the conditions which should promote generalization. One might, for example, combine the use of multiple exemplars with an introduction to natural contingencies and sequential modification across natural settings. Counter-intuitively, however, the evidence presented earlier would suggest that the indiscriminate combination of multiple strategies might actually reduce the effectiveness of instruction. Some combinations might be quite effective, but the sample sizes available for analyses in the current study simply do not allow all the various combinations to be meaningfully evaluated.

If it is inadvisable to combine strategies indiscriminately, then one is left with the original problem—which strategy or strategies should be employed? All strategies, including a simple train and hope approach, did produce good generalization with at least some subjects. The problem, then, would seem to be one of identifying the circumstances under which each strategy is most likely to succeed. A decision rule approach to guide selection offers an alternative to guesswork. The development and validation of decision rules are very needed steps in the realization of Stokes' and Baer's vision of a technology of generalization.

References

Ackerman, A. M., & Shapiro, E. S. (1984). Self-monitoring and work productivity with mentally retarded adults. *Journal of Applied Behavior Analysis, 17*(3), 403-407.

Anderson, S. R., & Spradlin, J. E. (1980). The generalized effects of productive labeling training involving common object classes. *Journal of the Association for the Severely Handicapped, 5*(2), 143-157.

Bates, P., Morrow, S., Pancsofar, E., & Sedlak, R. (1984). The effect of functional vs. non-functional activities on attitudes/expectations of non-handicapped college students: What they see is what we get. *Journal of the Association for Persons with Severe Handicaps, 9*(2), 73-78.

Becker, W., Engelmann, S., & Thomas, D. (1975). *Teaching 2: Cognitive learning and instruction* (pp. 57-92). Chicago: Science Research Associate.

Billingsley, F. F., Berman, A., & Opalski, C. (1983). Generalization and the educational ecology of severely handicapped learners: A descriptive study. In N. G. Haring (Principal Investigator), *Institute for education of severely handicapped children: Washington Research Organization; Annual report FY 82-83.* (U.S. Department of Education, Contract No. 300-82-0364). Seattle: University of Washington, College of Education.

Billingsley, F. F., Doyle, M., Radovich, S., & Thompson, M. (1985). Generalization and the educational ecology of severely handicapped workers: A descriptive study—third project year. In N. G. Haring (Principal Investigator), *Institute for education of severely handicapped children: Washington Research Organization; Annual report FY 82-83.* (U.S. Department of Education, Contract No. 300-82-0364). Seattle: University of Washington, College of Education.

Billingsley, F. F., Thompson, M., Matlock, B., & Work, J. (1984). Generalization and the educational ecology of severely handicapped workers: A descriptive study—second project year. In N. G. Haring (Principal Investigator), *Institute for education of severely handicapped children: Washington Research Organization; Annual report FY 82-83.* (U.S. Department of Education, Contract No. 300-82-0364). Seattle: University of Washington, College of Education.

Bornstein, P. H., Bach, P. J., McFall, M. E., Friman, P. C., & Lyons, P. D. (1980). Application of a social skills training program in the modification of interpersonal deficits among retarded adults: A clinical replication. *Journal of Applied Behavior Analysis, 13*(1) 171-176.

Brown, L., Branston, M., Hamre-Nietupski, S., Pumpian, I., Certo, N., & Gruenewald, L. (1979). A strategy for developing chronological-age-appropriate and functional curricular content for severely handicapped adolescents and young adults. *Journal of Special Education, 13*(1), 81-90.

Brown, L., Branston-McClean, M. B., Baumgart, D., Vincent, L., Falvey, M., & Schroeder, J. (1979). Using the characteristics of current and subsequent least restrictive environments in the development of curricular content for severely handicapped students. *American Association for the Education of the Severely/Profoundly Handicapped Review, 4*(4), 407-424.

Burney, J. D., Russel, B., & Shores, R. E. (1977). Developing social responses in two profoundly retarded children. *American Association for the Education of the Severely/Profoundly Handicapped Review, 2*(2), 53-60.

Campbell, C. R., & Stremel-Campbell, K. (1982). Programming "loose training" as a strategy to facilitate language generalization. *Journal of Applied Behavior Analysis, 15*(2), 295-302.

Correa, V. I., Poulson, C. L., & Salzberg, C. L. (1984). Training and generalization of reach-grasp behavior in blind, severely/profoundly mentally retarded young children. *Journal of Applied Behavior Analysis, 17*(1), 57-69.

Dowrick, P. W., & Dove, C. (1980). The use of self-modeling to improve the swimming performance of spina bifida children. *Journal of Applied Behavior Analysis, 13*(1), 51-56.

Endo, G. T., & Sloane, H. J., Jr. (1982). Generalization of a semantic-syntactic structure. *Behavior Modification, 6*(3), 389-406.

Engelmann, S., & Carnine, D. (1982). *Theory of instruction: Principles and applications* (pp. 1-54). New York: Irvington.

Falvey, M. (1986). *Community-based curriculum: Instructional strategies for students with severe handicaps.* Baltimore: Paul H. Brookes.

Filler, J., & Kasari, C. (1981). Acquisition, maintenance and generalization of parent-taught skills with two severely handicapped infants. *Journal of the Association for the Severely Handicapped, 6*(1), 30-38.

Fowler, S. A., & Baer, D. M. (1981). "Do I have to be good all day?" The timing of delayed reinforcement as a factor in generalization. *Journal of Applied Behavior Analysis, 14*(1), 13-24.

Gaylord-Ross, R. J., Haring, T. G., Breen, C., & Pitts-Conway, V. (1984). The training and generalization of social interaction skills with autistic youth. *Journal of Applied Behavior Analysis, 17*(2), 229-247.

Gaylord-Ross, R. J., & Holvoet, J. F. (1985). *Strategies for educating students with severe handicaps.* Boston: Little, Brown.

Hawkins, R. P., & Dotson, V. A. (1975). Reliability scores that delude: An Alice in Wonderland trip through the misleading characteristics of interobserver agreement scores in interval recording. In E. Ramp & G. Semb (Eds.), *Behavior Analysis: Areas of research and application*, Englewood Cliffs, NJ: Prentice-Hall.

Heins, E. D., Lloyd, J. W., & Hallahan, D. P. (1986). Cued and noncued self-recording of attention to task. *Behavior Modification, 10*(2), 235-254.

Hill, J. W., Wehman, P., & Horst, G. (1982). Toward generalization of appropriate leisure and social behavior in severely handicapped youth: Pinball machine use. *Journal of the Association for Persons with Severe Handicaps, 6*, 38-44.

Horner, R. H., Sprague, J., & Wilcox, B. (1982). Constructing general case programs for community activities. In B. Wilcox & T. Bellamy (Eds.), *Design of high school for severely handicapped students* (pp. 61-98). Baltimore: Paul H. Brookes.

Horner, R. H., Williams, J. A., & Knobbe, C. A. (1985). The effect of "opportunity to perform" on the maintenance of skills learned by high school students with severe handicaps. *Journal of the Association for Persons with Severe Handicaps*, *10*(3), 172-175.

Hurlbut, B. I., Iwata, B. A., & Green, J. D. (1982). Nonvocal language acquisition in adolescents with severe physical disabilities: Blissymbol versus iconic stimulus formats. *Journal of Applied Behavior Analysis*, *15*(2), 241-258.

Jones, R. T., Sisson, L. A., & Van Hasselt, V. B. (1984). Emergency fire-safety skills for blind children and adolescents: Group training and generalization. *Behavior Modification*, *8*(2), 267-286.

Jones, R. T., Van Hasselt, V. B., & Sisson, L. A. (1984). Emergency fire-safety skills: A study with blind adolescents. *Behavior Modification*, *8*(1), 59-78.

Kirschenbaum, D. S., Dillman, J. S., & Karoly, P. (1982). Efficacy of behavioral contracting: Target behaviors, performance criteria, and settings. *Behavior Modification*, *6*(4), 499-518.

Kissel, R. C., & Whitman, T. L. (1977). An examination of the direct and generalized effects of a play-training and overcorrection procedure upon the self-stimulatory behavior of a profoundly retarded boy. *American Association for the Severely and Profoundly Handicapped Review*, *2*(3), 131-146.

Lagomarcino, A., Reid, D. H., Ivancic, M. T., & Faw, G. D. (1984). Leisure-dance instruction for severely and profoundly retarded persons: Teaching an intermediate community-living skill. *Journal of Applied Behavior Analysis*, *17*(1), 71-84.

Lancioni, G. E. (1982). Normal children as tutors to teach social responses to withdrawn mentally retarded schoolmates: Training, maintenance and generalization. *Journal of Applied Behavior Analysis*, *15*(1), 17-40.

Liberty, K. A. (1987). Self-monitoring and skill generalization: A review of current research. In N. G. Haring (Principal Investigator), *Investigating the problem of skill generalization: Literature review III*. (U.S. Department of Education, Contract No. 300-82-0364). Seattle: University of Washington, College of Education. (ERIC Document Reproduction Service No. 287 270)

Liberty, K. A. (1987). Behaver control of stimulus events to facilitate generalization. In N. G. Haring (Principal Investigator), *Investigating the problem of skill generalization: Literature review III*. (U.S. Department of Education, Contract No. 300-82-0364). Seattle: University of Washington, College of Education.

Liberty, K. A., & Michael, L. J. (1985). Teaching retarded students to reinforce their own behavior: A review of process and operation in the current literature. In N. G. Haring (Principal Investigator), *Investigating the problem of skill generalization* (3rd edition, with literature reviews). (U.S. Department of Education, Contract No. 300-82-0364). Seattle: University of Washington, College of Education. (ERIC Document Reproduction Service No. ED 265 695)

Mithaug, D. E., & Wolfe, M. S. (1976). Employing task arrangements and verbal contingencies to promote verbalizations between retarded children. *Journal of Applied Behavior Analysis*, *9*(3), 301-314.

Murdock, J. Y., Garcia, E. E., & Hardman, M. L. (1977). Generalizing articulation training with trainable mentally retarded subjects. *Journal of Applied Behavior Analysis*, *10*(4), 717-733.

Neef, N. A., Iwata, B. A., & Page, T. J. (1978). Public transportation training: In vivo versus classroom instruction. *Journal of Applied Behavior Analysis*, *11*(3), 331-344.

Neel, R. S., Billingsley, F. F., & Lambert, C. (1983). IMPACT: A functional curriculum for educating autistic youth in natural environments. In R. B. Rutherford, Jr. (Ed.), *Monograph in behavior disorders: Severe behavior disorders of children and youth* (Series No. 6, pp. 40-50). Reston, VA: Council for Children with Behavioral Disorders.

Neel, R. S., Billingsley, F. F., McCarty, F., Symonds, D., Lambert, C., Lewis-Smith, N., & Hanashiro, R. (1983). *Teaching autistic children: A functional curriculum approach*. Seattle: Experimental Education Unit, University of Washington.

Page, T. J., Iwata, B., & Neef, N. A. (1976). Teaching pedestrian skills to retarded persons: Generalization from the classroom to the natural environment. *Journal of Applied Behavior*

Analysis, 9(4), 433-444.

Reese, S. C., & Filipczak, J. (1980). Assessment of skill generalization: Measurement across setting, behavior, and time in an educational setting. *Behavior Modification, 4*(2), 209-223.

Russo, D., & Koegel, R. L. (1977). A method for integrating an autistic child into a normal public school classroom. *Journal of Applied Behavior Analysis, 10*(4), 579-590.

Sailor, W., & Guess, D. (1983). *Severely handicapped students: An instructional design.* Boston: Houghton-Mifflin Co.

Sisson, L. A., Van Hasselt, V. B., Hersen, M., & Strain, P. S. (1985). Peer interventions: Increasing social behaviors in multihandicapped children. *Behavior Modification, 9*(3), 293-321.

Sowers, J., Verdi, M., Bourbeau, P., & Sheehan, M. (1985). Teaching job independence and flexibility to mentally retarded students through the use of a self-control package. *Journal of Applied Behavior Analysis, 18*(1), 81-85.

Sprague, J. R., & Horner, R. H. (1984). The effects of single instance, multiple instance, and general case training on generalized vending machine use by moderately and severely handicapped students. *Journal of Applied Behavior Analysis, 17*(2), 273-278.

Stainback, S., Stainback, W., Wehman, P., & Spangiers, L. (1983). Acquisition and generalization of physical fitness exercises in three profoundly retarded adults. *Journal of the Association for the Severely Handicapped, 20*(4), 260-267.

Stokes, T. F., & Baer, D. B. (1977). An implicit technology of generalization. *Journal of Applied Behavior Analysis, 10,* 349-367.

Stokes, T., Fowler, S., & Baer, D. (1978). Training preschool children to recruit natural communities of reinforcement. *Journal of Applied Behavior Analysis, 11*(2), 285-303.

Thompson, T. J., Braam, S. J., & Fuqua, R. W. (1982). Training and generalization of laundry skills: A multiple probe evaluation with handicapped persons. *Journal of Applied Behavior Analysis, 15*(1), 177-182.

VanBiervliet, A., Spangler, P. F., & Marshall, A. M. (1981). An ecobehavioral examination of a simple strategy for increasing mealtime language in residential facilities. *Journal of Applied Behavior Analysis, 14*(3), 295-305.

Wacker, D. P., & Berg, W. L. (1983). The effects of picture prompts on the acquisition of complex vocational tasks by mentally retarded adolescents. *Journal of Applied Behavior Analysis, 16*(4), 417-433.

Wacker, D. P., & Greenbaum, F. T. (1984). Efficacy of a verbal training sequence on the sorting performance of moderately and severely retarded adolescents. *American Journal of Mental Deficiency, 88*(6), 653-660.

Warren, S. F., Baxter, D. K., Anderson, S. R., Marshall, A., & Baer, D. M. (1981). Generalization of question-asking by severely retarded individuals. *Journal of the Association for the Severely Handicapped, 6*(3), 15-22.

White, O. R. (1984). Selected issues in program evaluation: Arguments for the individual. In B. K. Keogh (Ed.), *Advances in special education, Vol. 4.* Greenwich, CT: JAI Press Inc.

Bibliography of Coded Articles

Ackerman, A. M., & Shapiro, E. S. (1984). Self-monitoring and work productivity with mentally retarded adults. *Journal of Applied Behavior Analysis, 17*(3), 403-407.

Adkins, J., & Matson, J. L. (1980). Teaching institutionalized mentally retarded adults socially appropriate leisure skills. *Mental Retardation, 18*(5), 249-252.

Anderson, S. R., & Spradlin, J. E. (1980). The generalized effects of productive labeling training involving common object classes. *Journal of the Association for the Severely Handicapped, 5*(2), 143-157.

Baer, R.A., Williams, J. A., Osnes, P. G., & Stokes, T. F.(1984). Delayed reinforcement as an indiscriminable contingency in verbal/nonverbal correspondence training. *Journal of Applied Behavior Analysis, 17*(4), 429-440.

Bornstein, P. H., Bach, P. J., McFall, M. E., Friman, P. C., & Lyons, P. D. (1980). Application of a social skills training program in the modification of interpersonal deficits among retarded adults: A clinical replication. *Journal of Applied Behavior Analysis, 13*(1), 171-176.

Bornstein, M. R., Bellack, A. S., & Hersen, M. (1977). Social-skills training for unassertive children: A multiple-baseline analysis. *Journal of Applied Behavior Analysis, 10*(2), 183-195.

Bourbeau, P. E., Sowers, J., & Close, D. W. (1986). An experimental analysis of generalization of banking skills from classroom to bank settings in the community. *Education and Training of the Mentally Retarded, 21*(2), 98-107.

Brady, M. P., Shores, R. E., Gunter, P., McEvoy, M. A., Fox, J. L., & White, C. (1984). Generalization of an adolescent's social interaction behavior via multiple peers in a classroom setting. *Journal of the Association for Persons with Severe Handicaps, 9*(4), 278-286.

Breen, C., Haring, T., Pitts-Conway, V., & Gaylord-Ross, R. (1985). The training and generalization of social interaction during breaktime at two job sites in the natural environment. *Journal of the Association for Persons with Severe Handicaps, 10*(1), 41-50.

Browder, D. M., Moris, W. W., & Snell, M. E. (1981). Using time delay to teach manual signs to a severely mentally retarded student. *Education and Training of the Mentally Retarded, 16*(4), 252-258.

Bryant, L. E., & Budd, K. S. (1982). Self-instructional training to increase independent work performance in preschoolers. *Journal of Applied Behavior Analysis, 15*(2), 259-271.

Burgio, L. D., Whitman, T. L., & Johnson, M. R. (1980). A self-instructional package for increasing attending behavior in educable mentally retarded children *Journal of Applied Behavior Analysis, 13*(3), 443-460.

Burney, J. D., Russel, B., & Shores, R. E. (1977). Developing social responses in two profoundly retarded children. *American Association for the Education of the Severely/Profoundly Handicapped Review, 2*(2), 53-60.

Campbell, C. R., & Stremel-Campbell, K. (1982). Programming "loose training" as a strategy to facilitate language generalization. *Journal of Applied Behavior Analysis, 15*(2), 295-302.

Charlop, M. H., Schriebman, L., & Thibodeau, M. G. (1985). Increasing spontaneous verbal responding in autistic children using a time delay procedure. *Journal of Applied Behavior Analysis, 18*(2), 155-166.

Charlop, M. H., & Walsh, M. E. (1986). Increasing autistic children's spontaneous verbalizations of affection: An assessment of time delay and peer modeling procedures. *Journal of Applied Behavior Analysis, 19*(3), 307-314.

Combs, M. L., & Lahey, B. B. (1981). A cognitive social skills training program. *Behavior Modification, 5*(1), 39-59.

Cooke, T. P., & Apolloni, T. (1976). Developing positive social-emotional behaviors: A study of training and generalization effects. *Journal of Applied Behavior Analysis, 9*(1), 65-78.

Coon, M. E., Vogelsberg, R. T., & Williams, W. (1981). Effects of classroom public transportation instruction on generalization to the natural environment. *Journal of the Association for the Severely Handicapped, 6*(2), 46-53.

Correa, V. I., Poulson, C. L., & Salzberg, C. L. (1984). Training and generalization of reach-grasp behavior in blind, severely/profoundly mentally retarded young children. *Journal of Applied Behavior Analysis, 17*(1), 57-69

Cuvo, A. J., Leaf, R. B., & Borakove, L. S. (1978). Teaching janitorial skills to the mentally retarded: Acquisition, generalization and maintenance. *Journal of Applied Behavior Analysis, 11*(3), 345-355.

Dineen, J. P., Clark, H. B., & Risely, T. R. (1977). Peer tutoring among elementary students: Educational benefits to the tutor. *Journal of Applied Behavior Analysis, 10*(2), 231-238.

Dowrick, P. W., & Dove, C. (1980). The use of self-modeling to improve the swimming performance of spina bifida children. *Journal of Applied Behavior Analysis, 13*(1), 51-56.

Duker, P. C., & Michielsen, H. M. (1983). Cross-setting generalization of manual signs to verbal instructions with severely retarded children. *Journal of Applied Research in Mental Retardation, 4*(1), 29-40.

Duker, P. C., & Morsink, H. (1984). Acquisition and cross-setting generalization of manual signs with severely retarded individuals. *Journal of Applied Behavior Analysis, 17*(1), 93-103.

Dunlap, G., Koegel, R. L., & Koegel, L. K. (1984). Continuity of treatment: Toilet training in multiple community settings. *Journal of the Association for Persons with Severe Handicaps, 9*(2), 134-141.

Endo, G. T., & Sloane, H. N., Jr. (1982). Generalization of a semantic-syntactic structure. *Behavior Modification, 6*(3), 389-406.

Farb, J., & Thorne, J. M. (1978). Improving the generalized mnemonic performance of a Down's syndrome child. *Journal of Applied Behavior Analysis, 11*(3), 413-419.

Filler, J., & Kasari, C. (1981). Acquisition, maintenance and generalization of parent-taught skills with two severely handicapped infants. *Journal of the Association for the Severely Handicapped, 6*(1), 30-38.

Fowler, S. A., & Baer, D. M. (1981). "Do I have to be good all day?" The timing of delayed reinforcement as a factor in generalization. *Journal of Applied Behavior Analysis, 14*(1), 13-24.

Foxx, R. M., McMorrow, M. J., Bittle, R. G., & Ness, J. (1986). An analysis of social skills generalization in two natural settings. *Journal of Applied Behavior Analysis, 19*(3), 299-305.

Foxx, R. M., McMorrow, M. J., & Mennemeier, M. (1984). Teaching social/vocational skills to retarded adults with a modified table game: An analysis of generalization. *Journal of Applied Behavior Analysis, 17*(3), 343-352.

Frank, A. R., Wacker, D. P., Berg, W. K., & McMahon, C. M. (1985). Teaching selected microcomputer skills to retarded students via picture prompts. *Journal of Applied Behavior Analysis, 18*(2), 179-185.

Garcia, E. E. (1976). The development and generalization of delayed imitation. *Journal of Applied Behavior Analysis, 9*(4), 499. (National Auxiliary Publications Service No. 02835)

Gaylord-Ross, R. J., Haring, T. G., Breen, C., & Pitts-Conway, V. (1984). The training and generalization of social interaction skills with autistic youth. *Journal of Applied Behavior Analysis, 17*(2), 229-247.

Giangreco, M. F. (1983). Teaching basic photography skills to a severely handicapped young adult using simulated materials. *Journal of the Association for the Severely Handicapped, 8*(1), 43-49.

Guevremont, D. C., Osnes, P. G., & Stokes, T. F. (1986a). Preparation for effective self-regulation: The development of generalized verbal control. *Journal of Applied Behavior Analysis, 19*(1), 99-104.

Guevremont, D. C., Osnes, P. G., & Stokes, T. F. (1986b). Programming maintenance after correspondence training interventions with children. *Journal of Applied Behavior Analysis, 19*(2), 215-219.

Haavik, S. F., Spradlin, J. E., & Altman, K. I. (1984). Generalization and maintenance of language responses: A study across trainers, schools, and home settings. *Behavior Modification, 8*(3), 331-359.

Hall, C., Sheldon-Wildgen, J., & Sherman, J. A. (1980). Teaching job interview skills to retarded clients. *Journal of Applied Behavior Analysis, 13*(3), 433-442.

Halle, J. W., Marshall, A. M., & Spradlin, J. E. (1979). Time delay: A technique to increase language use and facilitate generalization in retarded children. *Journal of Applied Behavior Analysis, 12*(3), 431-439.

Handleman, J. S. (1979). Generalization by autistic-type children of verbal responses across settings. *Journal of Applied Behavior Analysis, 12*(2), 273-282.

Handleman, J. S., Powers, M. D., & Harris, S. L. (1984). Teaching of labels: An analysis of concrete and pictorial representations. *American Journal of Mental Deficiency, 88*(6), 625.

Haring, T. (1985). Teaching between-class generalization of toy play behavior to handicapped children. *Journal of Applied Behavior Analysis, 18*(2), 127-139.

Haring, T. G., Roger, B., Lee, M., Breen, C., & Gaylord-Ross, R. (1986). Teaching social language to moderately handicapped students. *Journal of Applied Behavior Analysis, 19*(2), 159-171.

Hart, B. & Risley, T. R. (1980). In vivo language intervention. *Journal of Applied Behavior Analysis, 13*(3), 407-432.

Heins, E. D., Lloyd, J. W., & Hallahan, D. P. (1986). Cued and noncued self-recording of attention to task. *Behavior Modification, 10*(2), 235-254.

Hendrickson, J. M., Strain, P. S., Tremblay, A., & Shores, R. E. (1982). Interactions of behaviorally handicapped children: Functional effects of peer social initiations. *Behavior Modification, 6*(3), 323-353.

Hester, P., & Hendrickson, J. (1977). Training functionally expressive language. *Journal of Applied Behavior Analysis, 10*(2), 316.

Hill, J. W., Wehman, P., & Horst, G. (1982). Toward generalization of appropriate leisure and social behavior in severely handicapped youth: Pinball machine use. *Journal of the Association for the Severely Handicapped, 6*, 38-44.

Hill, J. W., Wehman, P., & Pentecost, J. (1980). Developing job interview skills in mentally retarded adults. *Education and Training of the Mentally Retarded, 15*(3), 179-186.

Hodges, P. M., & Deich, R. F. (1978). Teaching an artificial language to non-verbal retardates. *Behavior Modification, 2*(4), 489-509.

Horner, R. H., & Budd, C. M. (1985). Acquisition of manual sign use: Collateral reduction of maladaptive behavior, and factors limiting generalization. *Education and Training of the Mentally Retarded, 20*(1), 39-47.

Horner, R. H., Jones, D. N., & Williams, J. A. (1985). A functional approach to teaching generalized street crossing. *Journal of the Association for Persons with Severe Handicaps, 10*(2), 71-78.

Horner, R. H., & McDonald, R. S. (1982). Comparison of single instance and general case instruction in teaching a generalized vocational skill. *Journal of the Association for Persons with Severe Handicaps, 7*(3), 7-20.

Hunt, P., Goetz, L., Alwell, M., & Sailor, W. (1986). Using an interrupted behavior chain strategy to teach generalized communication responses. *Journal of the Association for Persons with Severe Handicaps, 11*(3), 196-204

Hurlbut, B. I., Iwata, B. A., & Green, J. D. (1982). Nonvocal language acquisition in adolescents with severe physical disabilities: Blissymbol versus iconic stimulus formats. *Journal of Applied Behavior Analysis, 15*(2), 241-258.

Jackson, G. M. (1979). The use of visual orientation feedback to facilitate attention and task performance. *Mental Retardation, 17*(6), 281-284.

James, S. D., & Egel, A. L. (1986). A direct prompting strategy for increasing reciprocal interactions between handicapped and nonhandicapped siblings. *Journal of Applied Behavior Analysis, 19*(2), 173-186.

Jeffree, D. M., & Cheseldine, S. E. (1984). Programmed leisure intervention and the interaction patterns of severely mentally retarded adolescents: A pilot study. *American Journal of Mental Deficiency, 88*(6), 619.

Johnson, B. F., & Cuvo, A. J. (1981). Training mentally retarded adults to cook. *Behavior Modification, 5*, 187-202.

Jones, R. T., Sisson, L. A., & Van Hasselt, V. B. (1984). Emergency fire-safety skills for blind children and adolescents: Group training and generalization. *Behavior Modification, 8*(2), 267-286.

Jones, R. T., Van Hasselt, V. B., & Sisson, L. A. (1984). Emergency fire-safety skills: A study with blind adolescents. *Behavior Modification, 8*(1), 59-78.

Kayser, J. E., Billingsley, F. F., & Neel, R. S. (1986). A comparison of in-context and traditional instructional approaches: Total task, single trial versus backward chaining, multiple trials. *Journal of the Association for Persons with Severe Handicaps, 11*(1), 28-38.

Kirby, K. C., & Holborn, S. W. (1986). Trained, generalized, and collateral behavior changes of preschool children receiving gross-motor skills training. *Journal of Applied Behavior Analysis, 19*(3), 283-288.

Kirschenbaum, D. S., Dillman, J. S., & Karoly, P. (1982). Efficacy of behavioral contracting: Target behaviors, performance criteria, and settings. *Behavior Modification, 6*(4), 499-518.

Kissel, R. C., Johnson, M. R., & Whitman, T. L. (1980). Training a retarded client's mother and teacher through sequenced instructions to establish self-feeding. *Journal of the Association for the Severely Handicapped, 5*(4), 382-394.

Kissel, R. C., & Whitman, T. L. (1977). An examination of the direct and generalized effects of a play-training and overcorrection procedure upon the self-stimulatory behavior of a profoundly retarded boy. *American Association for the Severely and Profoundly Handicapped Review, 2*(3), 131-146.

Koegel, R. L., Egel, A. L., & Williams, J. A. (1980). Behavioral contrast and generalization across settings in the treatment of autistic children. *Journal of Experimental Child Psychology, 30*(3), 422-437.

Kohl, F. L., Karlan, G. R., & Heal, L. W. (1979). Effects of pairing manual signs with verbal cues upon the acquisition of instruction following behaviors and the generalization to expressive laguage with severely handicapped students. *American Association for the Severely and Profoundly Handicapped Review, 4*(3), 291-300.

Kohl, F. L., Wilcox, B. L., & Karlan, G. R. (1978). Effects of training conditions on the generalization of manual signs with moderately handicapped students. *Education and Training of the Mentally Retarded, 13*(3), 327.

Lagomarcino, A., Reid, D. H., Ivancic, M. T., & Faw, G. D. (1984). Leisure-dance instruction for severely and profoundly retarded persons: Teaching an intermediate community living skill. *Journal of Applied Behavior Analysis, 17*(1), 71-84.

Lahey, B. B., Busmeyer, M. K., O'Hara, C., & Beggs, V. E. (1977). Treatment of severe perceptual-motor disorders in children diagnosed as learning disabled. *Behavior Modification, 1*(1), 123-140.

Lancioni, G. E. (1982). Employment of normal third and fourth graders for training retarded children to solve problems dealing with quantity. *Education and Training of the Mentally Retarded, 17*(2), 93-102.

Lancioni, G. E. (1982). Normal chilldren as tutors to teach social responses to withdrawn mentally retarded schoolmates: Training, maintenance and generalization. *Journal of Applied Behavior Analysis, 15*(1), 17-40.

Lancioni, G. E., & Ceccarani, P. S. (1981). Teaching independent toileting within the normal daily program: Two studies with profoundly retarded children. *Behavior Research of Severe Developmental Disabilities, 2*, 79-96.

Lemanek, K. L., Williamson, D. A., Gresham, F. M., & Jensen, B. J. (1986). Social skills training with hearing-impaired children and adolescents. *Behavior Modification, 10*(1), 55-71.

Livi, J., & Ford, A. (1985). Skill transfer from a domestic training site to the actual homes of the moderately handicapped students. *Education and Training of the Mentally Retarded, 20*(1), 69-82.

MacKenzie, M. L., & Budd, K. S. (1981). A peer tutoring package to increase mathematics performance: Examination of generalized changes in classroom behavior. *Education and Treatment of Children, 4*(1), 1-15.

Marholin, D., O'Toole, K., Touchette, P. E., Berger, P. J., & Doyle, D. (1979). "I'll have a Big Mac, large fries, large coke, and apple pie . . . " or teaching adaptive community skills. *Behavior Therapy, 10*(2), 236-248.

Marholin, D., II, & Steinman, W. M. (1977). Stimulus control in the classroom as a function of the behavior reinforced. *Journal of Applied Behavior Analysis, 10*(3), 465.

Matson, J. L., & Adkins, J. (1980). A self-instructional social skills training program for mentally retarded persons. *Mental Retardation, 18*(5), 245-248.

Matson, J. L., & Andrasik, F. (1982). Training leisure time social-interaction skills to mentally retarded adults. *American Journal of Mental Deficiency, 86*(5), 533-542.

Matson, J. L. (1981). Assessment and treatment of clinical fears in mentally retarded children. *Journal of Applied Behavior Analysis, 14*(3), 287-294.

McDonnell, J. J., Horner, R. H., & Williams, J. A. (1984). Comparison of three strategies for teaching generalized grocery purchasing to high school students with severe handicaps. *Journal of the Association for Persons with Severe Handicaps, 9*(2), 123-133.

McGee, G. G., Krantz, P. J., & McClannahan, L. E. (1985). The facilitative effects of incidental teaching on preposition use by autistic children. *Journal of Applied Behavior Analysis, 18*(1), 17-31.

McMorrow, M. J., & Foxx, R. M. (1986). Some direct and generalized effects of replacing an autistic man's echolalia with correct responses to questions. *Journal of Applied Behavior Analysis, 19*(3), 299-305.

Miller, S. M. & Sloane, H. N. (1976). The generalization effects of parent training across stimulus settings. *Journal of Applied Behavior Analysis, 9*(3), 355-370.

Mithaug, D. E. (1978). Case study in training generalized instruction-following responses to preposition-noun combinations in a severely retarded yound adult. *American Association for the Severely and Profoundly Handicapped Review, 4*(3), 230-245.

Mithaug, D. E. & Wolfe, M. S. (1976). Employing task arrangements and verbal contingencies to promote verbalizations between retarded children. *Journal of Applied Behavior Analysis, 9*(3), 301-314.

Mosk, M. D., & Bucher, B. (1984). Prompting and stimulus-shaping procedures for teaching visual-motor skills to retarded children. *Journal of Applied Behavior Analysis, 17*(1), 23.

Murdock, G. Y., Garcia, E. E., & Hardman, M. L. (1977). Generalizing articulation training with trainable mentally retarded subjects. *Journal of Applied Behavior Analysis, 10*(4), 717-733.

Neef, N. A., Iwata, B. A., & Page, T. J. (1978). Public transportation training: In vivo versus classroom instruction. *Journal of Applied Behavior Analysis, 11*(3), 331-344.

Neef, N. A., Walters, J., & Egel, A. L. (1984). Establishing generative yes/no responses in developmentally disabled children. *Journal of Applied Behavior Analysis, 17*(4), 453-460.

Nietupski, J., Clancy, P., & Christiansen, C. (1984). Acquisition, maintenance, and generalization of vending machine purchasing skills by moderately handicapped students. *Education and Training of the Mentally Retarded, 19*(2), 91-96.

Nietupski, J., Welch, J., & Wacker, D. (1983). Acquisition, maintenance, and transfer of grocery item purchasing skills by moderately and severely handicapped students. *Education and Training of the Mentally Retarded, 18*(4), 279-286.

Nutter, D., & Reid, D. H. (1978). Teaching retarded women a clothing selection skill using community norms. *Journal of Applied Behavior Analysis, 11*(4), 475-487.

Odom, S. L., Hogson, M., Jamieson, B., & Strain, P. S. (1985). Increasing handicapped preschoolers' peer social interactions: Cross-setting and component analysis. *Journal of Applied Behavior Analysis, 18*(1), 3-16.

Oliver, C. B., & Halle, J. W. (1982). Language training in the everyday environment: Teaching functional sign use to a retarded child. *Journal of the Association for the Severely Handicapped, 7*(3), 50-62.

Page, T. J., Iwata, B., & Neef, N. A. (1976). Teaching pedestrian skills to retarded persons: Generalization from the classroom to the natural environment. *Journal of Applied Behavior Analysis, 9*(4), 433-444.

Paine, S. C., Hops, H., Walker, H. M., Greenwood, C. R., Fleischman, D. H., & Guild, J. J. (1982). Repeated treatment effects: A study of maintaining behavior change in socially withdrawn children. *Behavior Modification, 6*(2), 171-199.

Pancsofar, E. L., & Bates, P. (1985). The impact of the acquisition of successive training exemplars on generalization. *Journal of the Association for Persons with Severe Handicaps, 10*(2), 95-104.

Parsonson, B. S., & Baer, D. M. (1978). Training generalized improvisation of tools by preschool children. *Journal of Applied Behavior Analysis, 11*(3), 363-380.

Reese, S. C. & Filipczak, J. (1980). Assessment of skill generalization: Measurement across setting, behavior, and time in an educational setting. *Behavior Modification, 4*(2), 209-223.

Reichle, J., & Brown, L. (1986). Teaching the use of a multipage direct selection communication board to an adult with autism. *Journal of the Association for Persons with Severe Handicaps, 11*(1), 68-73.

Reichle, J., Rogers, N., & Barrett, C. (1984). Establishing pragmatic discriminations among the communicative functions of requesting, rejecting, and commenting in an adolescent. *Journal of the Association for Persons with Severe Handicaps, 9*(1), 31-36.

Reid, D. H., & Hurlbut, B. (1977). Teaching nonvocal communication skills to multihandicapped retarded adults. *Journal of Applied Behavior Analysis, 10*(4), 591-603.

Richman, G. S., Reiss, M. L., Bauman, K. E., & Baily, J. S. (1984). Teaching menstrual care to mentally retarded women: Acquisition, generalization, and maintenance. *Journal of Applied Behavior Analysis, 17*(4), 441-451.

Richman, J. S., Sonderby, T., & Kahn, J. V. (1980). Prerequisite vs. in vivo acquisition of self-feeding skill. *Behavior Research and Therapy, 18*, 327-332.

Riordan, M. M., Iwata, B. A., Finney, J. W., Wohl, M. K., & Stanley, A. E. (1984). Behavioral assessment and treatment of chronic food refusal in handicapped children. *Journal of Applied Behavior Analysis, 17*(3), 327-341.

Risley, R., & Cuvo, A. J. (1980). Training mentally retarded adults to make emergency telephone calls. *Behavior Modification, 4*(4), 513-526.

Rogers-Warren, A., & Warren, S. F. (1980). Mands for verbalization: Facilitating the display of newly trained language in children. *Behavior Modification, 4*(3), 361-382.

Russo, D., & Koegel, R. L. (1977). A method for integrating an autistic child into a normal public school classroom. *Journal of Applied Behavior Analysis, 10*(4), 579-590.

Rychtarick, R. G. & Bornstein, P. H. (1979). Training conversational skills in mentally retarded adults: A multiple baseline analysis. *Mental Retardation, 17*(6), 289-293.

Salmon, D. J., Pear, J. J., & Kuhn, B. A. (1986). Generaliation of object naming after training with picture cards and with objects. *Journal of Applied Behavior Analysis, 19*(1), 53-58.

Sarber, R. E., & Cuvo, A. J. (1983). Teaching nutritional meal planning to developmentally disabled clients. *Behavior Modification, 7*(4), 503-530.

Schleien, S. J., Ash, T., Kiernan, J., & Wehman, P. (1981). Developing independent cooking skills in a profoundly retarded woman. *Journal of the Association for the Severely Handicapped, 6*(2), 23-29.

Schriebman, L., & Carr, E. G. (1978). Elimination of echolalic responding to questions through the training of a generalized verbal response. *Journal of Applied Behavior Analysis, 11*(4), 453-463.

Shafer, M. S., Egel, A. L., & Neef, N. A. (1984). Training mildly handicapped peers to facilitate changes in the social interaction skills of autistic children. *Journal of Applied Behavior Analysis, 17*(4), 461-476.

Simic, J., & Bucher, B. (1980). Development of spontaneous manding in language deficient children. *Journal of Applied Behavior Analysis, 13*(3), 523-528.

Sisson, L. A., & Dixon, M. J. (1986). Improving mealtime behaviors through token reinforcement: A study with mentally retarded behaviorally disordered children. *Behavior Modification, 10*(3), 333-354.

Sisson, L. A., Van Hasselt, V. B., Hersen, M., & Strain, P. S. (1985). Peer interventions: Increasing social behaviors in multihandicapped children. *Behavior Modification, 9*(3), 293-321.

Smeege, M. E., Page, T. J., Iwata, B. A., & Ivancic, M. J. (1980). Teaching measurement skills to mentally retarded students: Training, generalization and followup. *Education and Training of the Mentally Retarded, 15*(3), 224-230.

Sowers, J., Verdi, M., Bourbeau, P., & Sheehan, M. (1985). Teaching job independence and flexibility to mentally retarded students through the use of a self-control package. *Journal of Applied Behavior Analysis, 18*(1), 81-85.

Sprague, J. R., & Horner, R. H. (1984). The effects of single instance, multiple instance, and general case training on generalized vending machine use by moderately and severely handicapped students. *Journal of Applied Behavior Analysis, 17*(2), 273-278.

Stainback, S., Stainback, W., Wehman, P., & Spangiers, L. (1983). Acquisition and generalization of physical fitness exercises in three profoundly retarded adults. *Journal of the Association for the Severely Handicapped, 8*(2), 47-55.

Sternberg, L., McNerney, C. D., & Pegnatore, L. (1985). Developing co-active imitative behaviors with profoundly mentally handicapped students. *Education and Training of the Mentally Retarded, 20*(4), 260-267.

Sternberg, L., Pegnatore, L., & Hill, C. (1983). Establishing interactive communication behaviors with profoundly handicapped students. *Journal of the Association for the Severely Handicapped, 8*(2), 39-46.

Stokes, T., Fowler, S., & Baer, D. (1978). Training preschool children to recruit natural communities of reinforcement. *Journal of Applied Behavior Analysis, 11*(2), 285-303.

Storey, K., Bates, P., & Hanson, H. B. (1984). Acquisition and generalization of coffee purchase skills by adults with severe disabilities. *Journal of the Association for Persons with Severe Handicaps, 9*(3), 178-185.

Strain, P. S., Shores, R. E., & Timm, M. A. (1977). Effects of peer social initiations on the behavior of withdrawn preschool children. *Journal of Applied Behavior Analysis, 10*(2), 289-298.

Thompson, T. J., Braam, S. J., & Fuqua, R. W. (1982). Training and generalization of laundry skills: A multiple probe evaluation with handicapped persons. *Journal of Applied Behavior Analysis, 15*(1), 1, 177-182.

Tofte-Tipps, S., Mendonca, P., & Peach, R. V. (1982). Training and generalization of social skills: A study with two developmentally handicapped, socially isolated children. *Behavior Modification, 6*(1), 45-71.

Touchette, P. E., & Howard, J. S. (1984). Errorless learning: Reinforcement contingencies and stimulus control transfer in delayed prompting. *Journal of Applied Behavior Analysis, 17*(2), 175.

Trace, M. W., Cuvo, A. K., & Criswell, J. L. (1977). Teaching coin equivalence to the mentally retarded. *Journal of Applied Behavior Analysis, 10*(1), 85-92.

Trap, J. J., Milner-Davis, P., Joseph, S., & Cooper, J. O. (1978). The effects of feedback and consequences on transitional cursive letter formation. *Journal of Applied Behavior Analysis, 11*(3), 381-394.

Tucker, D. J., & Berry, G. W. (1980). Teaching severely multihandicapped students to put on their own hearing aids. *Journal of Applied Behavior Analysis, 13*(1), 65-75.

van den Pol, R. A., Iwata, B., Ivanic, M. T., Page, T. J., Neef, N. A., & Whitley, P. F. (1981). Teaching the handicapped to eat in public places: Acquisition, generalization and maintenance of restaurant skills. *Journal of Applied Behavior Analysis, 14*(1), 61-69.

VanBiervliet, A., Spangler, P. F., & Marshall, A. M. (1981). An ecobehavioral examination of a simple strategy for increasing mealtime language in residential facilities. *Journal of Applied Behavior Analysis, 14*(3), 295-305.

Vogelsburg, R. T., & Rusch, F. R. (1979). Training severely handicapped students to cross partially controlled intersections. *Journal of the Association for the Severely Handicapped, 4*(3), 264-273.

Wacker, D. P., & Berg, W. L. (1983). The effects of picture prompts on the acquisition of complex vocational tasks by mentally retarded adolescents. *Journal of Applied Behavior Analysis, 16*(4), 417-433.

Wacker, D. P., Berg, W. K., Berrie, P., & Swatta, P. (1985). Generalization and maintenance of complex skills by severely handicapped adolescents following picture prompt training. *Journal of Applied Behavior Analysis, 18*(4), 329-336.

Wacker, D. P., & Greenbaum, F. T. (1984). Efficacy of a verbal training sequence on the sorting performance of moderately and severely retarded adolescents. *American Journal of Mental Deficiency, 88*(6), 653-660.

Warren, S. F., Baxter, D. K., Anderson, S. R., Marshall, A., & Baer, D. M. (1981).

Generalization of question-asking by severely retarded individuals. *Journal of the Association for the Severely Handicapped, 6*(3), 15-22.

Warren, S. F., & Rogers-Warren, A. K. (1983). A longitudinal analysis of language generalization among adolescents with severe handicapping conditions. *Journal of the Association for Persons with Severe Handicaps, 8*(4), 18-31.

Wehman, P., Renzaglia, A., Berry, G., Schultz, R., & Karan, O. (1978). Developing a leisure skill repertoire in severely and profoundly handicapped persons. *American Association for the Education of the Severely/Profoundly Handicapped Review, 3*(3), 162-172.

Welch, S. J., & Pear J. J. (1980). Generalization of naming responses to objects in the natural environment as a function of training stimulus modality with retarded children. *Journal of Applied Behavior Analysis, 13*(4), 629-643.

The strategies identified by Stokes and Baer, and newer strategies, like general case programming, illustrate that special strategies can raise skill generalization from about 25% to about 55 or 60%—even higher in some cases. This is great news for teachers.

The next question is how this information can be put to practical use. What educators need is a way to determine which strategy will work best with each student and with each skill. The decision rule approach offers a way of organizing information to help determine solutions to problems. In this chapter, the characteristics and foundations of decision rules are discussed.

Chapter 3

CHARACTERISTICS AND FOUNDATIONS OF DECISION RULES

Kathleen A. Liberty

Individualized instruction is the hallmark of special education: no other type of education attempts to tailor the curriculum and instructional techniques to the needs of each learner. In order to meet the goals of individualized instruction, educators and parents must decide what skills should be taught, the sequence of skill steps, and what instructional methods to use, then, to modify decisions based on the evaluation of success of these choices. A systematic approach to this process has been described by Corrigan (1969):

1. It begins with specifying in exact, measurable "knowing and doing" performance terms what the student is to be able to do and to know at the completion of instruction, defines acceptable proficiency levels, and states how this will be tested.
2. It requires a careful preselection of only relevant material and skills that represent the final learning objectives.
3. It provides for the design of instructional steps best suited to the progressive and successful understanding by each learner, based on his existing knowledge and background.
4. It provides for continuous, active response by each student at each learning step in the instructional sequence.
5. It provides for the pacing of instruction based solely on the measured student understanding.
6. It provides for predictable student learning achievements which are controllable and measurable.
7. It provides for empirical evaluation of whether objectives have been achieved as the basis for revision of parts of the whole, for the purpose of upgrading performance. (Corrigan, 1969, p. 26)

A key to success in meeting the objectives of individualized instruction is the effective use of information in the feedback loop from initial selection of content of education (curriculum) to the effect of the process of education (instructional methods) in conveying the content. Information produced during the process of instruction is used to revise the initial decisions. Changes can be made in the instructional techniques used to teach the curricular objective or in the nature of the curriculum itself. The collection of data and its systematic and frequent analysis are required in order to maintain an effective individualized program. "Decision rules" are procedures which guide the evaluation of information to determine if changes in methods and/or content are needed.

The purpose of this paper is to examine the characteristics and foundations of decision rules, as illustrated by a review of 23 decision rule systems identified in the literature, and to present a case for the empirical validation of such systems.

Systems which were identified by their authors as decision rules or decision systems or which were identified by others as decision rules (cf. Reichle & Karlan, 1985) were included. Decision rules were often difficult to locate, since systems were often presented in the context of research or as part of a training package, and were not usually individually referenced. The decision rule systems discussed in this paper are not necessarily representative of existing systems, but do provide a basis for discussion.

Characteristics

Rule systems may be characterized by the nature of the decision to be made and the empirical and theoretical bases for the decision rules. Usually these characteristics are organized into a set of questions which are to be answered either "yes" or "no" based on information produced by the systematic implementation of individualized education programs. The questions are arranged in a sequence, and the sequence may branch from specific responses to a separate set of questions. When one arrives at the termination of the sequence, the strategy or objective to be selected as the decision is evident. Examples are shown in the figures.

Nature of Decision

The majority (15 of 23) of the identified rule systems are intended to guide decisions about instruction (Table 3-1). For example, Bailey and Wolery's (1984) question sequence guides choices between seven alternative programming methods (Figure 3-1). In this system, information on student performance, interfering behaviors, and current instructional methods determines new strategies ranging from "implement procedures for decreasing the rate of interfering behaviors" to "implement detailed but minimal instructions" to "implement errorless learning procedures" (Bailey & Wolery, p. 76).

Three rule systems (13%) guide intervention decisions for behavior which is identified as a problem by the decision maker (Table 3-1). For example, Evans and Meyer's (1985) sequence guides choices between behavioral change treatments such as "differential reinforcement of other behaviors" and direct instruction in a skill/behavior which replaces the function of the problem behavior in the learner's behavioral repertoire (Figure 3-2). Evans and Meyer's system depends on observation and analysis of the learner's behavior in the context of interactions with others to provide the information needed to progress through the sequence.

Most systems for selecting instructional procedures and systems for intervening with problem behavior include curricular changes or choices as one of the potential decisions. Examples of these types of decisions include: (a) reducing the difficulty of the skill being taught (e.g., Fredericks et al., 1979), (b) increasing the difficulty of the skill being taught (e.g., Haring, Liberty, & White, 1981), and (c) teaching a different skill (e.g., Evans & Meyers, 1985). However, systems may not identify the actual skill to be taught. Five of the identified rule systems were developed specifically to guide curricular choices (Table 3-1) in areas ranging from the mode of expressive communication to teach (e.g., Sailor et al., 1980, see Figure 3-3) to which functional skills to teach (e.g., Falvey, 1986).

Basis for Rules

Whether the specific outcome of the rule system is an instructional procedure, intervention, or curricular objective, the decision is reached by answering questions in a specific order using certain types of information. Questions, sequence, information used—these three fundamentals distinguish decision systems. Systems with identical questions arranged in identical sequences could lead to different outcomes, depending on the information used to answer questions. For example, one system could use information derived from analyzing a learners' attitude to learning, or graphed data collected on student performance, or sub-test scores from achievement tests.

Even when two systems pose similar questions, use similar information and in which similar decisions could be selected, the sequence in which questions are posed will affect which decision

Table 3-1

Nature and Foundations of Decision Rule Systems

System Reference	Nature of Decision	Foundation
Bailey & Wolery, (1984), p. 76	modify instructional procedures	hierarchy of "intensiveness & complexity" of instruction; Etzel & LeBlanc, 1979
Browder, Liberty, Heller, & D'Huyvetters, (1986)	modify instructional procedures	adapted from Haring, Liberty, & White, 1980
Deno & Mirkin, (1977), p. 25–26, 152–55	when to modify instructional procedures	adapted from Liberty, 1972; Bohannon, 1975
Evans & Meyer, (1985), p. 54–56	treatment of behavior problems	hierarchy of acceptable interventions based on function of behavior & impact on environment
Falvey, (1986), p. 16-18	determining what skill to teach	characteristics of functional curricula
Fredericks et al., (1979), p. 105	modify instructional procedures	analysis of children's learning patterns
Gaylord-Ross, (1980), pp. 138, 139, 141, 146, 147, 151	treatment of aberrant behavior	treatment hierarchy, ethical considerations, level of intrusiveness of intervention
Haring, Liberty, & White, (1978), p. 72; (1980), p. 163	modify instructional procedures	analysis of student performance in 341 instructional decisions
Haring, Liberty, & White (1981), p. 8-10	modify instructional procedures	empirical analysis of student performance in 1241 change decisions; Haring, Liberty, & White, 1978, 1979a; Liberty, 1972
Hasselbring & Hamlett (1983)	modify instructional procedures	Haring, Liberty, & White, 1981
Lent & McLean (1976), p. 226	instructional procedures	hierarchy from least to most assistance required to get response
Liberty (1972)	when to change instruction/ behavior program	analyses of student performance in 361 programs

Table 3-1 (continued)

System Reference	Nature of Decision	Foundation
Liberty (1985), p. 64	modify instructional procedures for maintenance, generalization and adaptation	analysis of student performance errors
McGreevy (1983), pp. VI 1–4	modify instructional procedures	adapted from White & Haring, 1980
Neel, Billingsley, & Lambert (1983)	modify instructional procedures	adaptation of earlier version of rules, supported by data on 15 students and 78 programs
Nietupski & Hamre–Nietupski (1979), p. 113	selecting communication systems	characteristics of communication system and child
Renzaglia & Aveno (1986a): Domestic skills, pp. 20–21; Leisure skills, pp. 10–11; Community skills, pp. 10–11.	what to teach	characteristics of student/current and future environments/ functional curriculum
Sailor, Guess, Goetz, Schuler, Utley, & Baldwin (1980), pp. 94, 98	input/output response modes for language	characteristics of communication mode and characteristics of child; research on instruction
Seay, Suppa, Schoen, & Roberts (1984), p. 41	treatment of behavior problems	hierarchy of positive to punishing interventions (least to most intrusive)
Sternberg, Ritchey, Pegnatore, Wills, & Hill (1986), pp. 59–61	move ahead in curriculum, modify instructional procedures	prompt hierarchy
Tawney, Knapp, O'Reilly, & Pratt (1979), pp. 491–527	when and how to modify instructional procedures	analysis of characteristics of children's learning patterns
White & Haring (1976), p. 239; (1980), p. 243	when and how to modify instructional procedures	analysis of student performance in 468 instructional programs; Liberty, 1972
York, Nietupski, Hamre–Nietupski (1985), p. 215	when to teach use of micro-switch (adaptation of response) and how to modify instruction to do so	characteristics of functional curriculum, as applied to micro-switches

Figure 3–1. Example of decision rules for instructional strategies. From *Teaching infants and preschoolers with handicaps* (p. 76) by D. B. Bailey, Jr. & M. Wolery, 1984, Columbus, OH: Charles E. Merrill Pub. Co. Used by permission of the original copyright-holder, Plenum Publishing Corp.

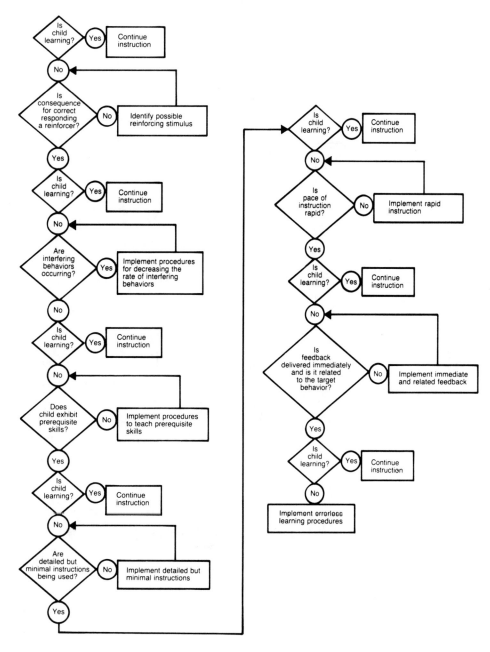

Flow chart describing procedures for enhancing instructional control when using direct instruction

Source: Etzel and LeBlanc (1979)

Figure 3-2. Example of decision rules to determine behavior interventions. From *An educative approach to behavior problems* (pp. 54-56) by Ian M. Evans & Luanna H. Meyer, 1985, Baltimore: Paul H. Brookes Pub. Co. Copyright 1985 by Paul H. Brookes Pub. Co. Used by permission of Paul H. Brookes Pub. Co.

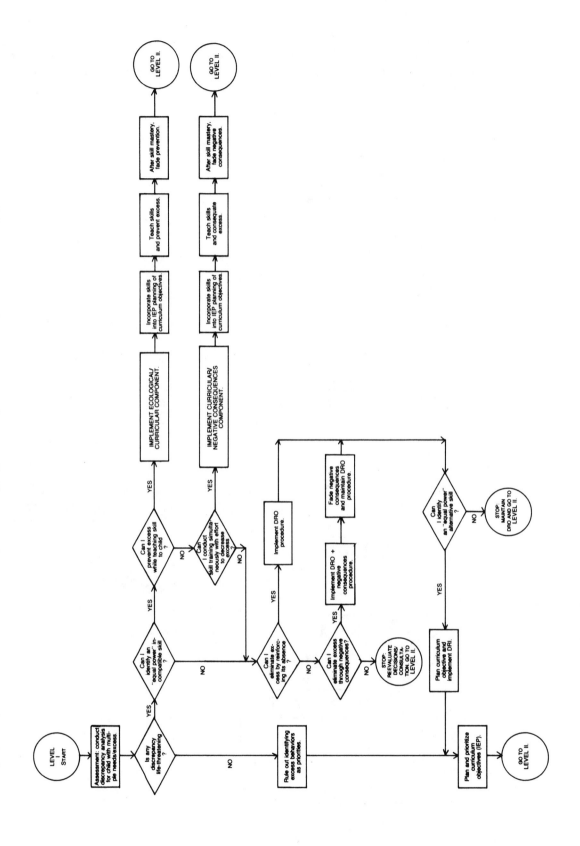

Figure 3–2 (continued)

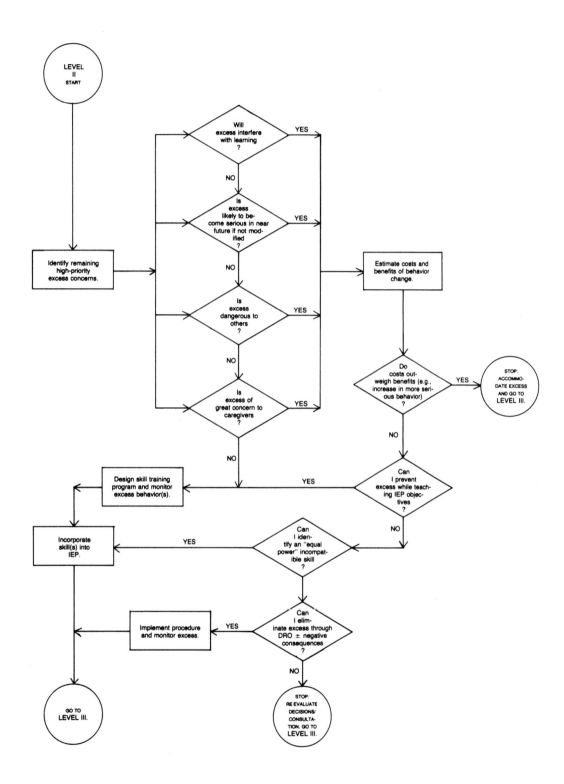

Figure 3–2 (continued)

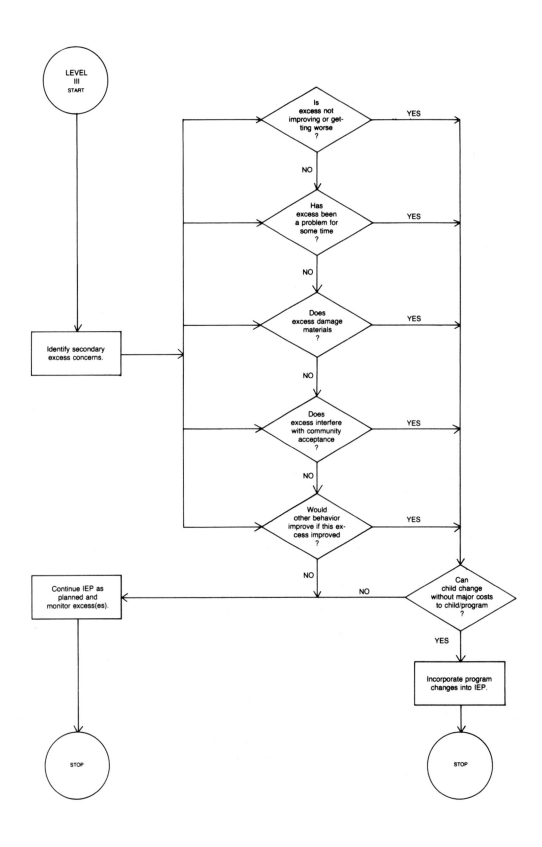

Figure 3-3. Example of decision rules to determine what skill to teach. From "Language and severely handicapped persons: Deciding what to teach to whom," by W. Sailor et al. in *Methods of instruction for severely handicapped students* (p.94) edited by W. Sailor, B. Wilcox, & L. Brown, 1980, Baltimore: Paul H. Brookes Pub. Co. Copyright 1980 by Paul H. Brookes Pub. Co. Used by permission of Paul H. Brookes Pub. Co.

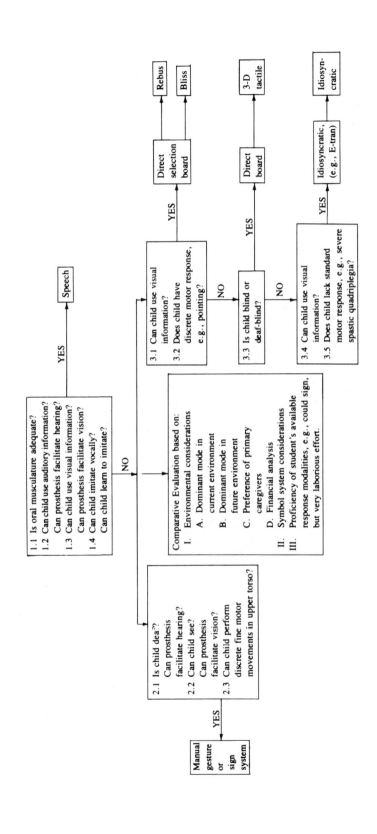

Figure 3-4. Example of decision rules for instructional strategies, Haring, Liberty, & White (1981). Reprinted by permission.

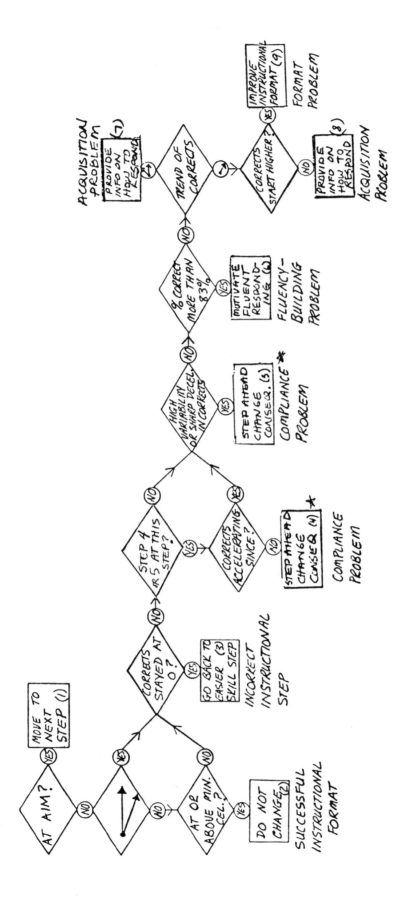

EXPERIMENTAL RULES FOR USE WITH MINIMUM CELERATION
ACCELERATE RATE OF RESPONDING

MARCH 1980

is reached. For example, while the rule systems shown in Figures 3-1 and 3-4 both include decision-choices relating to reinforcement[1] and to reducing skill difficulty[2], and each uses student progress to determine which method is selected, the decision to select one of these methods instead of the other is reached by two very different sequences. Bailey and Wolery's (1985) system identifies reinforcer change as the second ranked decision, following a decision to continue instruction without changes. Reducing skill difficulty is the fourth-ranked change procedure (see Figure 3-1). In contrast, Haring, Liberty, and White (1981) suggest changes in reinforcement and skill difficulty in reverse order, as decisions in the third and fourth positions, following decisions to increase skill difficulty and to continue instruction without changes (see Figure 3-4). Similar contrasts may be identified in any two systems which guide similar decisions. Such differences arise from the systems' foundations, either theoretical or empirical.

Theoretical bases. Systems with theoretical foundations are based on the authors' conviction of the fidelity of a particular logic system. Most often, such systems reflect a specific treatment hierarchy. Authors of such systems may cite research supporting the inclusion of specific strategies, but the nature, sequence, and information involved in the questions are selected and arranged so that the decisions reached reflect the treatment hierarchy supported by the author. Six of the systems surveyed are based on a hierarchy of treatment (Table 3-1).

For example, Evans and Meyer's (1985, see Figure 3-2) sequence guides the eventual decision according to the degree to which the target behavior is a problem for the student (e.g., self-abusive behavior) and/or a problem for family, friends, peers, eventual employers, etc. (e.g., stereotypic behavior). Within each level of severity, the treatment hierarchy begins with teaching positive behavior to replace the function of the problem behavior, then proceeds to reinforcement procedures and finally to procedures involving negative consequences. The authors provide a substantial logical argument for their formation of the treatment hierarchy for problem behavior (Evans & Meyer, 1985).

The Gaylord-Ross (1980) rules for problem behavior also are based on a hierarchy of treatment consisting of reinforcement, ecological, curricular, and finally punishment procedures. This system "is justified on empirical and ethical grounds" (p. 137). Movement through the sequence is based on conditions of the environment, child characteristics, and type of problem behavior.

Seay, Suppa, Schoen, and Roberts (1984) present a "least intrusive to most intrusive" treatment hierarchy for noncompliant behavior, including differential positive reinforcement, social reprimands, response cost, time-out, physical guidance, overcorrection, and physical restraint.

A similar hierarchy is the basis of Bailey and Wolery's (1984) system, which the authors based on Etzel and LeBlanc's (1979) discussion of instruction. Etzel and LeBlanc propose that instructional interventions proceed from the simplest teaching procedure (i.e., present task and consequence) to a more complex level of control (i.e., consistent instructional format and systematic analysis) and finally to the most complicated level, involving errorless learning, stimulus shaping, prompting, and so forth. Etzel and LeBlanc's article also points out factors which will be involved in the determination of the intrusiveness of educational control (i.e., incompatible responses, motivation, prerequisite skills, and effectiveness of instructions, feedback, and stimuli). Bailey and Wolery (1984) have translated and adapted Etzel and LeBlanc's text into a rule system in the format shown in Figure 3-1.

In Lent and McLean's (1976) system, interventions are based on a hierarchy of teaching prompts from least to most intrusive (i.e., independent without prompts; verbal cues; verbal cues with demonstration; verbal cues, demonstration, and physical cues). Snell and Smith (1978) reprint Lent and McLean's system as "increasing levels of assistance." Steinberg, Ritchey, Pegnatore, Wills, and Hill (1986) also incorporate "least to most" intrusive prompting in their decision rules for instructional change.

Sailor et al. (1980) developed a decision sequence to determine the modes of "input" (i.e., teacher's expressive language) and "output" (i.e., student's expressive language) for language

---

[1] "Identify possible reinforcing stimulus" (Bailey & Wolery, 1984) and "change consequences" (Haring, Liberty, & White, 1981).

[2] "Implement procedures to teach prerequisite skills" (Bailey & Wolery, 1984) and "go back to easier skill step" (Haring, Liberty, & White, 1981).

instruction. The authors argue that research and other literature on language instruction, acquisition, and assessment support the application of a hierarchy,

> with speech at the top as the preferred mode of expression . . . Following a decision not
> to instruct in speech, a decision to teach manual signs is made unless this system, too, is
> ruled out . . . If speech and manual communication (including "total communication"
> and gestural expression) have been ruled out, then the decision to instruct in a communi-
> cation board or physical, adaptive-aid system is necessitated. (p. 95)

The hierarchy of skills ranges from communication modes most commonly used by nonhandicapped students to those most unlike others'. The "input" hierarchy is similarly structured. Nietupski and Hamre-Nietupski's (1979) system also depends on a hierarchy from most-like-normal to least-like-normal to determine an "auxiliary" communication system to provide functional communication if students do not "verbalize or produce intelligible utterances by 5 to 8 years of age, and have not made adequate progress in verbal communication training programs" (ibid., p. 110).

Two other systems apply the authors' interpretation of theories of curriculum development rather than incorporating treatment hierarchies. York, Nietupski, and Hamre-Nietupski (1985) applied concepts of a functional curriculum to decisions about integrating the use of microswitches into the curriculum for learners with severe handicaps. Renzaglia and Aveno's (1986) system was developed to provide a tool for educators to accomplish a "functional, ecological assessment of each student's needs" (ibid., p. 3) in the domestic, leisure, and community domains. Their decision system involves a method of weighting such factors as degree of future skill independence, health and safety, current performance, and applicability and opportunity in multiple environments.

Empirical bases. Rule systems proceed from research in learning and are based on analysis of student performance. Rather than establish research to test a construct, such as levels of assistance, in which the theory precedes the research, these systems are derived from analysis of the performance records of students. The systems which are based on student performance data include: Liberty, 1972 (adapted by Deno & Mirkin, 1977); Fredericks et al. (1979); Tawney, Knapp, O'Reilly, & Pratt (1979); White & Haring (1976, 1980); and the rules developed by Haring, Liberty, & White (1975, 1976, 1977, 1978, 1979a, 1979b, 1980, 1981; and adapted by McGreevy, 1983, and by Browder, Liberty, Heller, & D'Huyvetters, 1986). Liberty's (1972) rules specify when a behavior or instructional program should be modified. All of the other systems provide rules for determining both when a change should be made and how instructional proce-dures should be modified.

Analytic procedures were similar across rule systems, and the following steps were generally used:

1. Student performance on each learning trial was recorded with a description of the instructional procedures in effect at the time of the response. If and when instructional procedures were changed, the effect on student performance was analyzed (e.g., did performance improve or worsen as a result of the change in instructional strategies?).
2. Identical or similar pre-change performances were matched on important variables (e.g., accuracy, sequence of correct and error responses, rate) and frequently occurring combinations of variables were labeled as patterns of performance. For example, Fredericks et al. (1979) identified a pattern labeled "intermittent success," characterized by a mixture of correct and incorrect responses, without 3 consecutive correct responses in 10 trials (an example of this pattern is shown in Figure 3-5). One of the patterns identified by Haring, Liberty, and White (1978, 1980) was labeled a "fluency-building problem." This pattern is characterized by a correct performance of less than 10 responses and which is either not improving or worsening in conjunction with error responses of greater than 2, which are worsening, decreasing, or maintaining (Figure 3–5).
3. The effects of post-change instructional procedures on identical pre-change performance patterns were analyzed (e.g., changes which improved performance for that performance pattern were compared with changes which did not).

4. The authors developed a performance pattern-instructional strategy match. Rules were formulated according to the procedure: when the student's performance matches this pattern, this type of change in instructional procedures is most likely to improve performance.

Individual rules are then sequenced, so that the decision maker compares an individual student's performance with the rules' specification by answering a series of questions. The sequence leads to the match of the student's performance with a particular performance pattern. The question sequence may be based on the frequency with which certain patterns appeared (e.g., questions used to identify high-frequency performance patterns occur first in the question sequence) or on the quickest method to discriminate performance patterns. Once the decision maker has answered the questions in sequence, the recommended instructional technique is identified.

Empirical analysis has produced decision rules with similar pattern-strategy rules. For example, for the patterns shown in Figure 3-5, Fredericks et al.'s rules (1979) specify a change in reinforcement, and Haring, Liberty, and White's rules (1978, 1980) direct that consequences be changed.

Effectiveness of Decision Rules

There are several different methods for evaluating system effectiveness. Two fundamental methods are to (a) measure impact variables before the system is introduced and while the system is in use, and/or (b) introduce the system to one group and compare results to a second group working without the system. Of course there are a number of other methods of evaluation which could be used (cf. Voeltz & Evans, 1983; White, 1984; 1985). The evaluation design should allow for system implementation over a suitable period of time, since users' familiarity with the system is likely to affect system use, adoption, and implementation of strategies, and since impact on students may not be immediately apparent. Second, the evaluation should assess the impact of the system on the progress of individual students, since systems are designed to aid decision-making for individuals.

Effective systems should result in decisions which are more beneficial than decisions which are not guided by such systems. Systems which guide decisions about instructional procedures should produce better learning than if no such rules are used. Curriculum systems should result in the identification of more appropriate and individualized education plans and perhaps increased numbers of mastered objectives than when rules are not applied.

An example can be seen in the procedures used to develop, evaluate, and revise the Decision Rules for Instruction (Haring, Liberty, & White, 1976, 1977, 1978, 1979, 1980, 1981; Figure 3-4). First, data were collected on student progress and the nature of teacher decisions. Then, teachers were trained to use the rules. Next, the researchers evaluated the nature of teacher decisions and student progress by (a) comparing progress to pre-training progress, and (b) comparing progress in programs in which rule-governed strategies were implemented and those in which teachers selected other strategies. The effectiveness was measured first by the frequency of students meeting their objectives and moving to the next skill step and second by the impact of the teacher's decisions on learning problems (Table 3-2). More than 55 educators and 365 students participated in the studies, conducted over five years. The rules resulted in an increase of 35% in decisions to advance in the curriculum and a 45% increase in successful remediations. Overall, a teacher who applied the final version of the decision rules would find that about 60% of his decisions would be to move to the next curricular step, and, of the remaining 40% of the decisions, 85% would be effective in correcting learning problems, a significant improvement over the decisions made by teachers who were without rules or who chose not to follow them.

In addition to empirically determining the impact of a system, the collection of effectiveness data could identify any "holes" or problems in the system, and thus guide revisions to improve effectiveness. An effectiveness field-test would also permit evaluation of whether practitioners can accurately and efficiently use the system, their attitude toward it, and its impact on planning time. For example, Haring, White, and Liberty (1981) found that about 72% of teachers trained in the rules decided to apply them, but the decision to adopt the system was not related to evaluations of the practitioners' guide or the training. For those who did adopt the system, planning time for

Figure 3–5. Two examples of performance patterns: (a) pattern indicating a change in reinforcer for correct responses is needed; (b) pattern indicating a change in consequences for either/both correct and error responses is needed. Part (a) from *A data-based classroom for the moderately and severely handicapped*, 3rd ed. (p. 113) by H. Fredericks et al., 1979, Monmouth, OR: Instructional Development Corporation. Copyright 1979 by Instructional Development Corporation. Adapted and used by permission. Part (b) from "Rules for data-based strategy decisions in instructional programs: Current research and instructional implications" by N. Haring, K. Liberty, & O. White in *Methods of instruction for severely handicapped students* (p. 163) edited by W. Sailor, B. Wilcox, & L. Brown, 1980, Baltimore: Paul H. Brookes Pub. Co. Copyright 1980 by Paul H. Brookes Pub. Co. Used by permission of Paul H. Brookes Pub. Co.

(a)

Teaching Research Infant and Child Center Raw Data Sheet

Name: _____ Program: _____

X = Correct
0 = Incorrect

Reinforcer	Phase	Step	1	2	3	4	5	6	7	8	9	10	Comments	Date
Social	II	2	X	0	X	X	0	X	0	0	X	0		2/4
Music Box/ Social	II	2	0	0	X	X	0	0	X	0	X	X		2/5

(b)

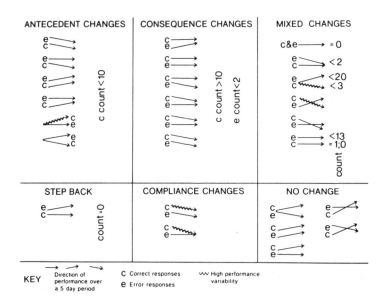

Table 3-2

Effectiveness of Decision Rules for Instructional Decisions[3]

	Curricular Advances[4]	Successful Remediations[5]
Decisions made without rules (baseline)	27.0%	40.4%
Decisions made with rules (version 1)	24.7%	64.6%
Decisions made with rules (version 2)	43.7%	79.6%
Decisions made with rules (version 3)	62.0%	85.9%

instruction was reduced from an average of a little over 4 hours per week to about 2.2 hours per week.

Conclusion

Decision rule systems offer the possibility of improving individualized education for persons with handicaps by shaping how educators use information to determine curriculum, instruction, and behavior interventions. Most systems reviewed are based on application of current trends and ideas regarding education and student learning. Although research in support of the system's foundation, strategies, or techniques often exists, data supporting the use of the system itself are often lacking. As demands on teachers increase, and as the heterogeniety of students within a classroom increases, the appeal and value of decision rules will increase. The next step is to determine if they can actually live up to their promise of improving our decisions.

References

Bailey, D. B., Jr., Wolery, M. (1984). *Teaching infants and preschoolers with handicaps*, Columbus, OH: Charles E. Merrill.

Billingsley, F., White, O., & Munson, R. (1980). Procedural reliability: A rationale and an example. *Behavioral Assessment, 2*, 229-241.

Bohannon, R. (1975). Direct and daily measurement procedures in the identification and treatment of reading behaviors of children in special education. *Dissertation Abstracts International, 37*(2), 914A. (University Microfilms No. 76-17,409)

Browder, D., Liberty, K., Heller, M., & D'Huyvetters, K. (1986). Self-management by teachers: Improving instructional decision making. *Professional School Psychology, 1*(3), 165-175.

---

[3]   From Haring, Liberty, & White (1976; 1977; 1978; 1979; 1981).

[4]   Percent of instructional decisions which advanced student in curriculum.

[5]   Percent of instructional decisions to remediate learning problems which accelerated learning performance when the rules-governed intervention was implemented.

Brown, L., Nietupski, J., & Hamre-Nietupski, S. (1976). The criterion of ultimate functioning. In M. A. Thomas (Ed.), *Hey, don't forget about me!* Reston, VA: CEC Information Center.

Carr, E. (1986). [Review of *An educative approach to behavior problems: A practical model for interventions with severely handicapped learners*]. *Child and Family Behavior Therapy, 7*(3), 63-68.

Corrigan, R. E. (1969). *A system approach for education.* Anaheim, CA: R. E. Corrigan Associates.

Deno, S. L., & Mirkin, P. K. (1977). *Data-based program modification: A manual.* Reston, VA: Council for Exceptional Children.

Donnellan, A., & Mirenda, P. L. (1983). A model for analyzing instructional components to facilitate generalization for severely handicapped students. *Journal of Special Education, 17*(3), 317-331.

Etzel, B. C., & LeBlanc, J. M. (1979). The simplest treatment alternative: The law of parsimony applied to choosing appropriate instructional control and errorless-learning procedures for the difficult-to-teach child. *Journal of Autism and Developmental Disorders, 9*(4), 361-382.

Evans, I. M., & Meyer, L. H. (1985). *An educative approach to behavior problems: A practical decision model for interventions with severely handicapped learners.* Baltimore: Paul H. Brookes.

Falvey, M. A. (1986). *Community-based curriculum: Instructional strategies for students with severe handicaps.* Baltimore: Paul H. Brookes.

Fredericks, H., Baldwin, V., Moore, W., Templeman, V., Grove, D., Moore, M., Gage, M., Blair, L., Alrick, G., Wadlow, M., Fruin, C., Bunse, C., Samples, L., Samples, B., Moses, C., Rogers, G., & Toews, J. (1979). *A data-based classroom for the moderately and severely handicapped* (3rd ed.). Monmouth, OR: Instructional Development Corporation.

Gaylord-Ross, R. (1980). A decision model for the treatment of aberrant behavior in applied settings. In W. Sailor, B. Wilcox, & L. Brown (Eds.), Methods of instruction for severely handicapped students (pp. 135-158). Baltimore: Paul H. Brookes.

Haring, N., Liberty, K., & White, O. (1975). *Field initiated research studies of phases of learning and facilitating instructional events for the severely/profoundly handicapped* (technical proposal). (U.S. Department of Education, Contract No. G007500593.) Seattle: University of Washington, College of Education.

Haring, N., Liberty, K., & White, O. (1976). *First annual report: Field initiated research studies of phases of learning and facilitating instructional events for the severely/profoundly handicapped* (U.S. Department of Education, Contract No. G007500593.) Seattle: University of Washington, College of Education.

Haring, N., Liberty, K., & White, O. (1977). *Second annual report: Field initiated research studies of phases of learning and facilitating instructional events for the severely/profoundly handicapped.* (U.S. Department of Education, Contract No. G007500593.) Seattle: University of Washington, College of Education.

Haring, N., Liberty, K., & White, O. (1978). *Third annual report: Field initiated research studies of phases of learning and facilitating instructional events for the severely/profoundly handicapped.* (U.S. Department of Education, Contract No. G007500593.) Seattle: University of Washington, College of Education.

Haring, N., Liberty, K., & White, O. (1979a). *Fourth annual report: Field initiated research studies of phases of learning and facilitating instructional events for the severely/profoundly handicapped.* (U.S. Department of Education, Contract No. G007500593.) Seattle: University of Washington, College of Education.

Haring, N., Liberty, K., & White, O. (1979b). *Handbook of experimental procedures.* (U.S. Department of Education, Contract No. G007500593.) Seattle: University of Washington, College of Education.

Haring, N., Liberty, K., & White, O. (1980). Rules for data-based strategy decisions in instructional programs:Current research and instructional implications. In W. Sailor, B. Wilcox, & L. Brown (Eds.), *Methods of instruction for severely handicapped students* (pp. 159-192). Baltimore: Paul H. Brookes.

Haring, N., Liberty, K., & White, O. (1981). *Final report: Field initiated research studies of phases of learning and facilitating instructional events for the severely/profoundly handicapped.* (U.S. Department of Education, Contract No. G007500593.) Seattle: University of Washington, College of Education.

Hasselbring, T., & Hamlett, C. (1983). *Aimstar: A computer software program* [Computer program]. Portland, OR: ASIEP Education Co.

Horner, R., Bellamy, G. T., & Colvin, G. T. (1984). Responding in the presence of nontrained stimuli: Implications of generalization error patterns. *Journal of the Association for the Severely Handicapped, 9*(4), 287-295.

Lent, J. R., & McLean, B. M. (1976). The trainable retarded: The technology of teaching. In N. Haring & R. Schiefelbusch (Eds.), *Teaching special children.* New York: McGraw-Hill.

Liberty, K. (1972). *Decide for progress: Dynamic aims and data decisions.* Working paper, University of Oregon, Regional Resource Center for Handicapped Children, Eugene.

Liberty, K. (1985). Enhancing instruction for maintenance, generalization, and adaptation. In K. C. Lakin & R. Bruininks (Eds.), *Strategies for achieving community integration of developmentally disabled citizens* (pp. 29-71). Baltimore: Paul H. Brookes.

Lloyd, J. W. (1984). How shall we individualize instruction—or should we? *Remedial and Special Education, 5*(1), 7-15.

McGreevy, P. (1983). *Teaching and learning in plain English* (2nd ed.). Kansas City, MO: Plain English Publications.

Neel, R. S., Billingsley, F. F., & Lambert, C. (1983). IMPACT: A functional curriculum for educating autistic youth in natural environments. In R. B. Rutherford, Jr. (Ed.), *Monograph in behavior disorders: Severe behavior disorders of children and youth* (Series No. 6, pp. 40-50). Reston, VA: Council for Children with Behavior Disorders.

Nietupski, J., & Hamre-Nietupski, S. (1979). Teaching auxiliary skills to severely handicapped students. *American Association for the Education of the Severely/Profoundly Handicapped Review, 4*(2), 107-124.

Reichle, J., & Karlan, G. (1985). The selection of an augmentative system in communication intervention: A critique of Decision Rules. *Journal of the Association for the Severely Handicapped, 10*(3), 146-156.

Renzaglia, A., & Aveno, A. (1986a). *Curriculum assessment forms for: An individualized, functional curriculum assessment procedure for students with moderate to severe handicaps.* (Available from Curry School of Education, University of Virginia, Charlottesville, VA.)

Renzaglia, A., & Aveno, A. (1986b). *Manual for the administration of: An individualized, functional curriculum assessment procedure for students with moderate to severe handicaps: Domestic, leisure, and community domains.* (Available from Curry School of Education, University of Virginia, Charlottesville, VA.)

Sailor, W., Guess, D., Goetz, L., Schuler, A., Utley, B., & Baldwin, M. (1980). Language and severely handicapped persons: Deciding what to teach to whom. In W. Sailor, B. Wilcox, & L. Brown (Eds.), *Methods of instruction for severely handicapped students* (pp. 71-105). Baltimore: Paul H. Brookes.

Seay, M. B., Suppa, R. J., Schoen, S. F., & Roberts, S. R.(1984). Countercontrol: An issue in intervention. *Remedial and Special Education, 5*(1), 38-42.

Snell, M. E., & Smith, D. D. (1978). Intervention strategies.In M. Snell (Ed.), *Systematic instruction of the moderately and severely handicapped* (pp. 74-99). Columbus, OH: Charles E. Merrill.

Sternberg, L., Ritchey, H., Pegnatore, L., Wills, L., & Hill, C. (1986). *A curriculum for profoundly handicapped students.* The Broward County Model Program. Rockville, MD: Aspen.

Tawney, J. W., Knapp, D. S., O'Reilly, C. D., & Pratt, S. S.(1979). *Programmed environments curriculum.* Columbus, OH: Charles E. Merrill.

Voeltz, L., & Evans, I. (1983). Educational validity: Procedures to evaluate outcomes in programs for severely handicapped learners. *Journal of the Association for the Severely Handicapped, 8*(1), 3-15.

White, O. R. (1984). Selected issues in program evaluation: Arguments for the individual. In B. Keogh, (Ed.), *Advances in special education: Volume 4*. New York: JAI Press.

White, O. R. (1985). The evaluation of severely mentally retarded populations. In D. Bricker & J. Fuller (Eds.), *Severe mental retardation from theory to practice*. Reston, VA: Division on Mental Retardation, The Council for Exceptional Children.

White, O. R. (1986). Precision teaching-precision learning. *Exceptional Children*, *52*(6), 522-534.

White, O. R., & Haring, N. G. (1976). *Exceptional teaching: A multimedia training package*. Columbus, OH: Charles E. Merrill.

White, O. R., & Haring, N. G. (1980). *Exceptional teaching* (2nd ed.). Columbus, OH: Charles E. Merrill.

White, O. R., & Haring, N. G. (1982). Data based program change decisions. In M. Stevens-Dominguez & K. Stremel-Cambell, (Eds.), *Ongoing data collection for measuring child progress* (pp. 129-150). Seattle, WA: Western States Technical Assistance Resource (WESTAR).

York, J., Nietupski, J., & Hamre-Nietupski, S. (1985). A decision-making process for using microswitches. *Journal of the Association for Persons with Severe Handicaps*, *10*(4), 214-233.

As we learned in Chapter 2, researchers have identified strategies which are effective in promoting generalization, but research might not always translate into classroom application. Our research with decision rules convinced us that a system for selecting among strategies could be developed and would help classroom teachers. So, we developed the Decision Rules for Generalization and conducted a study involving nine teachers to determine whether their application of generalization strategies would be effective in increasing generalization and whether decision rules would increase the effectiveness of the teachers. This chapter describes that study.

Chapter 4

IMPACT OF GENERALIZATION STRATEGIES AND DECISION RULES IN PUBLIC SCHOOL SETTINGS

Kathleen Liberty, Owen White, Felix Billingsley, Norris Haring, Valerie Lynch, and Mary Anne Paeth

Research has indicated that students with severe handicaps may not generalize skills unless special instructional strategies are used. Strategies which are effective in facilitating generalization by students with severe handicaps include: altering the location of training to the setting where responding is desired (Neef, Iwata, & Page, 1978; Neel, Billingsley, & Lambert, 1983); altering the contingencies available in the training setting to duplicate those in the desired generalization setting; altering the contingencies available in nontraining situations (Billingsley & Neel, 1986; Thompson, Braam, & Fuqua, 1982); using general case methodology to select training exemplars which represent the class of stimuli to which responding is desired (Horner & McDonald, 1982); increasing response proficiency to ensure that natural reinforcers are accessed (Burned, Russel, & Shores, 1977); training in self-control techniques (Ackerman & Shapiro, 1984; Liberty, 1987); and training to generalize by reinforcing only generalized responses (Warren, Baxter, Anderson, Marshall, & Baer, 1981).

However, most research has relied on experimenters to implement the strategies which were the subject of the research. Little information is available on the effectiveness of strategies when applied by public school teachers. That is, once strategies are selected and implemented by teachers, does skill generalization by students with severe handicaps increase?

Another question concerns how teachers are to determine which strategy to implement during the process of individualization of instruction. Liberty (1985) and Horner, Bellamy, & Colvin (1984) have suggested methods of selecting strategies, but no empirical tests of any decision-making strategies have been reported. That is, do decision-making strategies or rules result in increased levels of generalization when compared with that achieved when strategies are selected without use of decision-making rules?

It was the purpose of this study to investigate the impact of the application of generalization-facilitating strategies, with and without the use of decision-rules to select a particular strategy, by public school teachers of students with severe handicaps.

Method

Three school districts with cooperative arrangements with the University participated in the study. The procedures and goals of the study were explained at staff meetings, and eight teachers and one occupational therapist volunteered to participate. These service providers are referred to collectively as "teachers;" fictional names have been used for teachers and students in this report.

Teachers. Three teachers (Alma, Brenda, and Cathy) taught seven students each in classrooms located in a regular elementary school. Each had a Bachelor's Degree and an average of three years of experience. Donna had a Master's Degree, and her classroom of seven students was located in a regular junior high school. Alma, Brenda, Cathy, and Donna taught in one school district.

Holly, Gretchen, and Frances taught in the second school district. Holly, an occupational therapist, along with Gretchen and Frances, taught in a school serving primarily students with handicaps ranging in age from 3 to 21, although some regular preschool classes were located in the building. Each had a Master's Degree. Gretchen's and Frances' classrooms included 7 and 10 pupils, respectively. Holly's case load was 35 pupils.

Ingrid and Jane taught at a school located on a university campus. The campus school primarily served pupils with handicaps, with the exception of a preschool program. Ingrid and Jane each had a Master's Degree, and 5 and 6 students, respectively, were enrolled in their classrooms.

Pupils. Each teacher selected between 2 and 6 students for the project and district personnel sought consent for participation in the study. The age, handicapping conditions, test scores, and medication of each of the 31 participating pupils are shown in Table 4-1. Chronological ages at the start of the study ranged from 6 years 10 months to 20 years 7 months. Thirty of the 31 pupils were classified with severe or profound mental retardation, and each had additional handicapping conditions. Eighteen lived with parents or guardians in homes or foster homes, while some lived in group homes or nursing homes (see Table 4-2).

Target skills. Each teacher selected functional skills from their students' IEPs to serve as the focus of the experimental procedures (Table 4-3). Functional skills were defined according to Billingsley (1984; in press) as those which increase the autonomy of an individual in the performance of a skill which can be used in extrainstructional situations to achieve some naturally desired, required, or demanded outcome by: (a) gaining access for the individual to a wider range of environments and/or natural maintaining contingencies within an environment; and/or (b) increasing the reinforcing value to others for interacting with the individual; and/or (c) reducing the need for others to engage in activities on behalf of the individual which might be considered burdensome or effortful; and/or (d) permitting the individual to engage in culturally normative, age appropriate leisure or recreational activities. Where a skill was included as part of a sequential instructional program or behavior chain, it was required that it be a necessary part of the chain in order to be considered functional. By "necessary," it is meant that if the behavior was removed, the functional impact of the behavior was lost. Also, assurances had to be provided that enough parts of the chain would be acquired within a reasonable period to achieve a functional outcome during the study, or that accomplishment of that single part would represent a meaningful outcome in and of itself, including the accomplishment of partial participation.

The number of IEP objectives per student ranged from 8 to 28, with a mean of 15.75 (Table 4-4). The number of target programs selected by each teacher ranged from Gretchen's 6 to Donna's 22 (Table 4-4). The number of programs per pupil ranged from 1 to 11, with a median of 3 (Table 4-4) and a total of 104.

Experimental Design

There were two experimental phases to the study. During Baseline, teachers were taught to write objectives which specified functional skills expected to generalize to specific situations. The teachers then implemented instructional programs and collected data on pupil performance. The experimenters periodically assessed skill performance in the nontraining situations which were the generalization targets. An experimenter met with each teacher to review student progress twice a month for each program, spending an average of 10 minutes per program.

The Intervention Phase involved different training content. In order to prevent the possibility

Table 4-1

Participating Students

Pupil	Chronological Age[1]	Sex	Primary Handicapping Condition	Secondary Handicapping Condition	Most Recent Psych. Test		Medication
					Chronological Age (at time of test)	Score	
Strategies Group							
Lee	9 yrs. 1 mo.	M	Severe/profound retardation	spastic quadriplegia, anoxic encephalopathy	7 yrs. 4 mo.	2-6 mo.[2]	Valium
Pat	12 yrs. 1 mo.	F	Severe/profound retardation	cerebral palsy, autism, Rett syndrome	9 yrs. 7 mo.	4-12 mo.[2]	Depakene, Tegretol
Sarah	17 yrs. 2 mo.	F	Severe retardation	cerebral palsy	16 yrs. 3 mo.	4-12 mo.[2]	Phenobarbital
Robert	14 yrs. 0 mo.	M	Profound retardation	cerebral palsy, blindness, seizure disorder	not available	not available	not available
Janet	15 yrs. 2 mo.	F	Severe retardation	autism, Rett syndrome	6 yrs. 6 mo.	6 months[3]	Depakene, Meberal, Valproic acid
Amy	19 yrs. 5 mo.	F	Severe retardation	not available	18 yrs.11 mo.	6-11 mo.[3]	none
Kate	19 yrs. 4 mo.	F	Profound retardation	Trisonomy 18	not available	not available	not available
Peter	17 yrs. 4 mo.	M	Profound retardation	cerebral palsy, epilepsy, degenerative neurological disease	not available	not available	not available
Scott	13 yrs. 11 mo.	M	Profound retardation	spastic quadriplegia, cerebral palsy, scoliosis, blindness, static encephalopathy, kyphosis	not available	not available	Mylicon, Tegretol
Julie	10 yrs. 1 mo.	F	Severe retardation	blindness	9 yrs.	3.8-6.4 mo.[4] 8-26 mo.[2]	Tegretol Mebaral
Laura	18 yrs. 11 mo.	F	Severe/profound retardation	static encephalopathy, Rett syndrome, spastic quadriparesis	16 yrs. 6 mo.	4-12 mo.[2]	Tegretol, Dilantin Phenobarbital, Depakote

Table 4-1 (continued)

Pupil	Chronological Age[1]	Sex	Primary Handicapping Condition	Secondary Handicapping Condition	Most Recent Psych. Test		Medication
					Chronological Age (at time of test)	Score	
Jeff	15 yrs. 10 mo.	M	Profound retardation	athetoid cerebral palsy	not available	not available	none
Dennis	15 yrs. 11 mo.	M	Severe retardation	static encephalopathy, seizures	10 yrs. 10 mo.	35 mo.[5]	none
Ellen	13 yrs. 9 mo.	F	Moderate retardation	spastic quadriplegia	11 yrs. 3 mo.	36-44 mo.[2]	Mebaral, Tridione, Depakene, Zarontin
Jim	14 yrs. 11 mo.	M	Severe retardation	Down syndrome	12 yrs. 11 mo.	IQ = 24[6]	none
Strategies + Rules Group							
Karen	11 yrs. 0 mo.	F	Severe/profound retardation	multiply handicapped health impaired	not available	not available	not available
Betsy	8 yrs. 6 mo.	F	Severe/profound retardation	cerebral palsy, seizures, tuberous sclerosis	not available	not available	Depakene, Zarontin, Mysoline, Tegratol
Cheryl	8 yrs. 0 mo.	F	Severe/profound retardation	cerebral palsy, Cri-du-chat syndrome	not available	not available	Cephulac
Candy	10 yrs. 3 mo.	F	Severe retardation	cerebral palsy, seizures	7 yrs. 5 mo.	12-20 mo.[2]	Phenobarbital, Tegretol, Imodium
Gordon	6 yrs. 10 mo.	M	Severe retardation	neuroectodermal tumor, spasticity, seizures	5 yrs. 4 mo. / 5 yrs. 5 mo.	7 months[7] / 6-12 mo.[1]	Tegretol, Dilantin, Phenobarbital
John	8 yrs. 8 mo.	M	Severe/profound retardation	cerebral palsy hypotonic quadriplegia	6 yrs. 1 mo.	10-12 mo.[2]	Phenobarbital
Hal	13 yrs. 1 mo.	M	Severe retardation	autism	12 yrs. 10 mo.	10-42 mo.[8]	none
Barbara	9 yrs. 10 mo.	F	Severe retardation	static encephalopathy, hypotonia	7 yrs. 9 mo.	6-48 mo.[8]	none
Mark	7 yrs. 1 mo.	M	Severe retardation	autism	4 yrs. 7 mo.	16-24 mo.[2]	none
Jenny	20 yrs. 7 mo.	F	Profound retardation	cerebral palsy, post Reyes syndrome w/static encephalopathy spastic quadriplegia, microcephaly	15 yrs. 9 mo.	0-6 mo.[2]	Phenobarbital, Valium, Dilantin

Table 4-1 (continued)

Pupil	Chronological Age[1]	Sex	Primary Handicapping Condition	Secondary Handicapping Condition	Most Recent Psych. Test		Medication
					Chronological Age (at time of test)	Score	
Tracy	18 yrs. 7 mo.	F	Profound retardation	cleft palate	15 yrs. 3 mo.	0-24 mo.[8]	none
Lily	17 yrs. 7 mo.	F	Severe/profound retardation	scoliosis	14 yrs. 3 mo.	0-17 mo.[8]	Phenobarbital, Valium
David	8 yrs. 0 mo.	M	Severe/profound retardation	tuberous sclerosis seizures	7 yrs. 5 mo. 7 yrs. 6 mo.	14-30 mo.[3] 0-22 mo.[2]	Tegretol Phenurone
Sharon	15 yrs. 3 mo.	F	Profound retardation	cerebral palsy, scoliosis, Rett syndrome	12 yrs. 2 mo.	4 months[4]	Depakene, Meberal, Valproic acid
Jerry	16 yrs. 8 mo.	M	Severe retardation	athetoid cerebral palsy	11 yrs. 10 mo.	0-14 mo.[2]	none

1 As of 11-1-85
2 Developmental Profile II (Alpern-Boll)
3 Vineland Social Maturity Scale
4 Bayley Scale of Infant Development
5 Merrill-Palmer Scale of Mental Tests
6 Stanford-Binet Intelligence Scale
7 Peabody Picture Vocabulary Test
8 Uniform Performance Assessment System (UPAS)

Table 4-2

Student Placements

Teacher	Pupil	Placement	Residence
Strategies			
Alma	Lee	Mixed Cross-level	Group Home
	Pat	Mixed Cross-level	Home
	Sarah	Mixed Cross-level	Group Home
	Robert	Mixed Cross-level	NA
	Janet	Mixed Cross-level	Home
Brenda	Amy	Mixed Cross-level	Group Home
	Kate	Mixed Cross-level	Group Home
	Peter	Mixed Cross-level	Nursing Home
Cathy	Scott	Mixed Cross-level	Group Home
	Julie	Mixed Cross-level	Home
	Laura	Mixed Cross-level	Group Home
	Jeff	Mixed Cross-level	Group Home
Donna	Dennis	Mixed Cross-level	Home
	Ellen	Mixed Cross-level	Home
	Jim	Mixed Cross-level	Home
Strategies + Rules			
Frances	Karen	Primary	NA
	Betsy	Primary	Home
Gretchen	Cheryl	Primary	Home
	Candy	Primary	NA
	Gordon	Preschool	Home
Holly	Gordon	Preschool	Home
	John	Primary	Home
Ingrid	Hal	Intermediate	Home
	Barbara	Intermediate	Home
	Mark	Intermediate	Home
Jane	Jenny	Mixed Cross-level	Nursing Home
	Tracy	Mixed Cross-level	Home
	Lily	Mixed Cross-level	Home
	David	Mixed Cross-level	Home
	Sharon	Mixed Cross-level	Home
	Jerry	Mixed Cross-level	Home

Table 4-3

Target Skills

Phases During Which Instruction Occurred				
Baseline	Treatment	Student	Skill	Description

Strategies Group

Baseline	Treatment	Student	Skill	Description
Yes	No	Lee	a	Holds head up (with computer setup)
Yes	Yes		b	Swallows without spilling
No	Yes		c	Holds head up while seated in wheelchair
Yes	Yes	Pat	a	Walks on knees
Yes	Yes		b-1	Chooses food by looking at pictures then signs
No	Yes		b-2	Chooses food by touching picture
Yes	No	Sarah	a-1	Complies with "come here"
No	Yes		a-2	Complies with "stand up," "sit down"
No	Yes		a-3	Complies with "step around"
Yes	Yes		b	Signs 'eat' and 'drink' to answer question
Yes	Yes	Robert	a	Positions hand before scooping food
Yes	Yes	Janet	a	Walks w/walker
Yes	Yes	Amy	a	Pushes w/walker over bumps & obstacles w/o asst. or falling
Yes	Yes		b	Actuates buzzer for attention
Yes	Yes		c-1	Stands to walker from chair
No	Yes		c-2	Pulls walker to chair
Yes	No	Kate	a-1	Drinks w/straw
No	Yes		a-2	Grasps cup and drinks w/straw
Yes	Yes		b	Indicates 'I want...walk,' '...dance,' '...brush'
Yes	Yes		c-1	Climbs stairs
Yes	Yes		c-2	Descends stairs
Yes	No		d-1	Actuates buzzer for attention at meals
No	Yes		d-2	Actuates buzzer for help off toilet
Yes	Yes		e-1	Says 'mck' for milk
No	Yes		e-2	Says 'ooo' for juice
Yes	Yes	Peter	a	Actuates buzzer; raises arm w/o cue for help out of chair
Yes	Yes		b	Touches picture/object to request item or activity
Yes	Yes	Scott	a	Reaches w/in 3 sec., grasps, and holds object for 1 minute
Yes	Yes		b	Takes glass and holds to drink
Yes	Yes	Julie	a	Follows directions and answers questions (meals)
Yes	Yes		b	Holds head up
Yes	Yes		c	Asks for object with word approx. when falls from grasp

Table 4-3 (continued)

Phases During Which Instruction Occurred				
Baseline	Treatment	Student	Skill	Description

Strategies Group

Baseline	Treatment	Student	Skill	Description
Yes	Yes	Laura	a	Eats finger food
Yes	Yes		b	Eye contact after verbalization by other
Yes	Yes	Jeff	a-1	Puts object in container to clear tray table (with help)
No	Yes		a-2	Puts object in container to clear tray table (without help)
Yes	Yes		b	Reaches for picture on comm. board and gazes for 3 sec.
Yes	No	Dennis	a	Moves clothes from washer to dryer
Yes	No		b	Puts on t-shirt w/o help
Yes	No		c	Puts toys away
Yes	No		d-1	Points to word hamburger, coke, or fries
No	Yes		d-2	Says 'burger, coke, fries' when shown word
Yes	Yes		e	Touches/hands manager requested coins
Yes	Yes		f-1	Gets in wheelchair safely
Yes	No		f-2	Gets out of wheelchair safely
Yes	No		g	Complies
No	Yes		h	Puts dirty clothes in washer
No	Yes		j	Says answer to "What do you want ____? or ____?"
No	Yes		k	Gets items out of refrigerator
Yes	Yes	Ellen	a	Points to words/pict. on comm. board to answer where, what, or how questions
Yes	Yes		b	Applies underarm deodorant
No	Yes		c	Washes upper body with towel
Yes	Yes		d	Gives requested coins
No	Yes		e	Washes tables in cafeteria
No	Yes		f	Points to picture of burger/fries/shake/coke
No	Yes		g	Given request/picture, retrieves kitchen items from fridge/shelf
No	Yes		h	Makes peanut butter and jelly sandwich
No	Yes	Jim	a	Fold clothes (from dryer) and put on shelf
No	Yes		b	Read and say restaurant words
No	Yes		c	Point to word and say "Go," "Fire," "Gentlemen"

Strategies + Rules Group

Baseline	Treatment	Student	Skill	Description
Yes	Yes	Karen	a	Walks w/walker
Yes	Yes		b	Eats w/spoon (opens mouth, bites)
Yes	Yes		c	Points to picture on comm. board to request activity
Yes	Yes	Betsy	a	Dresses
Yes	Yes		b	Initiates initial sounds of words
Yes	Yes		c	Undresses

Table 4-3 (continued)

Phases During Which
Instruction Occurred

Baseline	Treatment	Student	Skill	Description
Strategies + Rules Group				
Yes	No	Cheryl	a	Touches picture on communication board to choose food/drink
Yes	Yes		b	Touches picture on communication board to choose item/activity
Yes	No	Candy	a	Touches picture to choose food/drink
Yes	Yes		b	Touches picture to choose activity
Yes	No		c	Follows directions
Yes	No	Gordon	a-1	Eats w/spoon; grasp, bring to mouth, return to plate (assisted)
No	Yes		a-2	Eats w/spoon (independent)
Yes	Yes		b-1	Drinks from cup; grasps/brings to mouth (assisted)
No	Yes		b-2	Drinks from cup (independently)
Yes	Yes		c	Touches object/pictures to indicate choice on comm. board (instructed by Gretchen)
No	Yes		d	Scoot, crawl, roll to destination (before lunch or spontaneously) (instructed by Gretchen)
No	Yes	John	a	Eats w/spoon
No	Yes		b	Drinks from cup
Yes	Yes	Hal	a	Sustains tooth brushing
Yes	Yes		b	Initiates requests w/ comm. board
Yes	Yes		c	Lifts tongue on shoe to put on
Yes	No	Barbara	a-1	Retrieves comm. board & requests items/activities with prompt
No	Yes		a-2	Retrieves comm. board & requests items/activities spontaneously
Yes	Yes		b-1	Scoops with spoon
Yes	Yes		b-2	Pokes with fork
Yes	Yes		c	Puts on pants (shorts)
Yes	Yes	Mark	a	Delivers items (runs errand)
Yes	Yes		b	Says noun + verb phrase to request objects
Yes	Yes		c	Says 'no' to protest
Yes	Yes	Jenny	a	Initiates scooping, phy. asst. scoop, support elbow, brings to mouth
No	Yes		b	Swallows without spilling (while head supported)
Yes	Yes	Tracy	a	Puts spoon in bowl, scoops, brings to mouth
Yes	Yes		b	Takes off coat (assisted)

Table 4-3 (continued)

Phases During Which Instruction Occurred				
Baseline	Treatment	Student	Skill	Description

Strategies + Rules Group

Baseline	Treatment	Student	Skill	Description
Yes	Yes	Lily	a	Transfers from eating to drinking
Yes	Yes		b	Grasps & pulls poncho over head (phy. assist)
Yes	Yes		c	Grasps cup & to mouth
Yes	Yes		d	Grasps, scoops, to mouth w/spoon
Yes	Yes	David	a	Walks down stairs w/alternating feet
Yes	Yes		b	Sets table (w/prompts for placement of items)
Yes	Yes	Sharon	a	Sits down in chair (assist to turn & bend)
Yes	Yes		b	Walks up stairs (assist to grasp rail)
Yes	Yes	Jerry	a	Pulls t-shirt down from under arms
Yes	Yes		b	Sits down in chair

Table 4-4

Characteristics of Teacher Participation

Teacher	# Pupils Served	Pupils Participating	Total IEP Objectives	Experimental Objectives
Strategies				
Alma		Lee	9	3
		Pat	14	3
		Sarah	6	4
		Robert	NA	1
		Janet	12	1
Total	7	5	41	12
Brenda		Amy	20	4
		Kate	14	9
		Peter	16	2
Total	7	3	50	15
Cathy		Scott	16	2
		Julie	16	3
		Laura	11	2
		Jeff	14	3
Total	7	4	57	10
Donna		Dennis	24	12
		Ellen	13	8
		Jim	9	3
Total	7	3	46	23
GROUP TOTAL	28	15	194	60
Average Per Pupil			14	4

Table 4-4 (continued)

Teacher	# Pupils Served	Pupils Participating	Total IEP Objectives	Experimental Objectives
Strategies + Rules				
Frances		Karen	NA	3
		Betsy	28	3
Total	10	2	28	6
Gretchen		Cheryl	26	2
		Candy	21	3
		Gordon	2	2
Total	7	3	49	7
Holly (OT)		Gordon	6	4
		John	26	2
Total	35	2	32	6
Ingrid		Hal	17	3
		Barbara	13	5
		Mark	15	3
Total	5	3	45	11
Jane		Jenny	16	2
		Tracy	14	2
		Lily	12	4
		David	25	2
		Sharon	14	2
		Jerry	12	2
Total	6	6	93	14
GROUP TOTAL	63	15*	247	44
Average Per Pupil	18	3		

*One student (Gordon) in class with both Gretchen and Holly.

of teachers exchanging information from training, and thus possibly confounding the intervention, it was decided that all teachers in one district would receive identical training. Alma, Brenda, Cathy, and Donna were assigned to the "Strategies Only" Group by a toss of the coin. Frances, Gretchen, Holly, Ingrid, and Jane formed the Strategies + Rules" Group. Characteristics of the groups are shown in Table 4-5. Both groups received training in instructional strategies designed to improve the skill generalization of their students, and in the assessment of the student's generalization performance. The "Strategies + Rules" Group was also trained to use a set of rules to guide the selection of strategies based on pupil performance (see Chapter 9). The total training time for each group was the same—approximately 6 hours over 2 separate training days. Both groups received an implementation manual, with descriptions of the strategies and examples of their application (see Chapter 8), and the rule group received a written description of the performance-based rules and examples of their use (see Chapter 9).

During this phase, teachers continued implementing programs and collecting performance data,

Table 4-5

Characteristics of Treatment Groups

Characteristic	"Strategies" Group	"Strategies + Rules" Group
N = teachers	4	5
N = target pupils	15	15
Age range	8 yrs. 11 mo. to 19 yrs. 3 mo.	6 yrs. 10 mo. to 20 yrs. 5 mo.
Median age	15 yrs. 4 mo.	10 yrs. 0 mo.
Handicapping Condition		
N = with moderate retardation	1	0
N = with severe retardation*	9	10
N = with profound retardation	4	3
N = diagnostic classification not available	1	2
Residence		
N = living at home	6	11
N = living at nursing home	1	1
N = living at group home	7	0
Skills		
Average IEP objectives/pupil	14	18
N = target skills	60	44
Average target skills/pupil	4	3

*Included students identified as falling in the "severe/profound" range by their districts (see Table 4-1)

and teachers in both groups joined the experimenters in probing pupil performance in generalization situations. As during Baseline, an experimenter met with each teacher twice per month for each program, spending an average 10 minutes per program. Student progress was discussed and probe data were reviewed. Strategies for facilitating generalization were discussed and teachers selected which, if any, generalization strategy to implement. In addition, the "Strategy + Rules" group was guided through the rules prior to strategy selection.

Following the process of obtaining consent for teacher and pupil participation, the remaining 8 months of the school year were divided in half, so that approximately 4 months each would be available for Baseline and Intervention Phases. Each training phase was completed across all sites within a period of approximately 1 week. As a result of difficulties encountered in the scheduling of pre-Baseline training, however, the Baseline phase was somewhat shorter than the Intervention phase. The most extreme difference occurred at one "Strategies + Rules" site where the Baseline phase lasted slightly less than 3 months.

Procedures

Training to write objectives for generalization. All participating teachers were provided with 2 hours of group training in writing objectives which specified generalization of a functional skill as a desired outcome.

Objectives which specify a generalized outcome were defined as those which (a) specify performance of the skill in multiple situations (e.g., across settings, managers, or materials), or (b) indicate the need for the behavior on a "spontaneous," "as needed," or "as appropriate basis" (cf. Billingsley, 1984).

Training, provided by three members of the project staff, included a lecture on the specification of generalization within objectives as well as participant activities in which objectives provided by the project staff, and by the participants themselves, were rewritten to specify generalized outcomes (see Chapter 6).

Teachers who were later assigned to the "Strategies + Rules" Group were trained at the teachers' home school. For teachers who were later assigned to the "Strategies" Group, training was conducted at a single school which was conveniently located for all participants. Training time was 3 hours for each group.

Baseline. One of the experimenters met with teachers individually on a biweekly basis. The meetings were conducted in order to discuss teachers' concerns about each program. No advice was offered concerning strategies specifically designed to facilitate skill generalization. Teachers were responsible for the implementation of all programs using whatever resources were normally available to them. During Baseline, teachers used the instructional and generalization data which they collected; however, teachers were not shown any performance data on generalization collected by project staff.

Generalization strategy training. All of the teachers received 6 hours of training (3 hours on each of 2 days) provided by three of the experimenters. During training, strategies for facilitating generalization were explained to the teachers, and examples were provided and discussed (see Chapter 8). Participants were told that the strategies were likely to be most useful in situations where the student had acquired the skill and then failed to generalize the skill. Strategies presented included: (a) those which involved changing conditions in target generalization situations and (b) those which involved changing practices in the instructional setting (Table 4-6).

Next, participants were trained to develop generalization probes (see Chapter 7). Participants received a booklet that contained detailed descriptions of each strategy and examples of the types of situations in which those strategies might be useful (an earlier version of Chapter 8).

The training for the five teachers in the "Strategies + Rules" Group also included rules for selecting among the strategies based on characteristics of the generalization situation and student performance in generalization probes. General training methods were the same as those applied to the "Strategies" Group; however, as training time remained constant, the "Strategies + Rules" Group received less instruction on strategies. In addition, these teachers received a copy of a manual containing the decision rules and examples of their application (an earlier version of Chapter 9).

Intervention. Following training, the biweekly meetings with the experimenter continued. As during Baseline, a maximum of 10 minutes was allotted for discussion of each program. However, during this phase, generalization probe data collected by project staff was shared with the teacher. As during Baseline, teachers could choose whether or not to change a program, including use of any of the trained strategies. Once a strategy was selected by a teacher, guidance regarding its application was offered. The relationship of strategies to probe data was never mentioned in meetings with Strategies teachers. "Strategies + Rules" teachers were guided through the rules in order to determine which type of strategy should be most effective in facilitating generalization. The teachers then decided whether or not to use the strategy suggested by the rules, a different strategy of their own choosing, or no strategy at all.

Generalization Performance Data

Situations targeted for generalization were identified by the teachers. The most common targets were for the skill to be performed at school in the presence of a manager other than the program instructor, in a nontraining situation, and/or at home. In addition, generalization to community situations was selected for some skills.

Generalization probes were conducted by trained observers or by other persons in the target situation who were not instructional managers in the program. Probe managers were generally told what the skill was, and any prompts that were permitted by the objective. Consequation was determined by the probe manager. In addition, unplanned opportunities for generalization (e.g., when visitors came to the room or the class went on a field trip) were recorded if observers were present.

Table 4-6

Strategies for Promoting Generalization

I.   Strategies Involving Conditions in the Generalization Situation

1. **Train-on-site**. Conduct instruction in generalization situation (if possible).
2. **Alter contingencies**. Train persons in the generalization situation, or arrange the generalization situation so that (a) an opportunity to perform the skill is available often, and/or (b) natural reinforcers are available only for performance of the skill.

II. Strategies Involving Altering Instructional Practices in the Instructional Situation

3. **Increase skill proficiency**. Provide instruction to improve the fluency of the skill.
4. **Amplify instructed behavior**. Provide instruction in a skill related to the target skill.
5. **Program natural reinforcers**. Use the reinforcers during instruction that are naturally available in the generalization situation.
6. **Eliminate training reinforcers**. Fade any reinforcers during instruction that do not occur in the generalization situation.
7. **Use natural schedules**. Identify the schedule for reinforcement in the generalization situation, and use that schedule during instruction.
8. **Use natural consequences**. Identify the reinforcers and consequences for errors which would normally occur for performing/not performing the target skill, and program those into instruction.
9. **Teach self-reinforcement**. Train the student to monitor and/or reinforce own behavior in generalization situation.
10. **Teach to solicit reinforcement**. Train the student to seek reinforcement for performing the skill in generalization situations.
11. **Reinforce generalized behavior**. During instruction, provide reinforcement only for generalized skills.
12. **Vary stimuli**. Vary the antecedent stimuli which affect responding, including stimuli which should prompt (S+), those which should signal that responding would be inappropriate (S-), and those which occur at the same time as the response, but which are irrelevant to responding (Si). Variation can be introduced by including all of the stimuli in the generalization situation in instruction, or by including stimuli common to all situations in which generalization is desired, or by including multiple exemplars of stimuli, or by conducting an analysis of the universe of stimuli, and selecting representatives of the general case of the stimulus classes.
13. **Eliminate training stimuli**. Remove from instruction any stimuli which are not found or available in the generalization situation.

Observers recorded student performance and then compared performance with the criteria specified in the IEP objective written by the teacher during initial training. If performance met or exceeded criteria, generalization in that probe situation was coded as "Good." If the student did not respond or performed some other behavior or responded at extremely low levels, probe performance was characterized as "Poor." Performances which fell between these classifications were categorized as "Some."

For home probes, parents were telephoned and asked to assess their child's performance. A follow-up call was then made to determine the child's performance. In these probes, the parents assessed the child's performance as "Good," "Fair," or "Poor." For students who did not live at home, observers visited the living situation, and asked persons involved in the home-care situation to serve as probe managers.

Probes were scheduled to occur at the beginning and ending of each of the two experimental phases. In addition, probes were scheduled when the teachers' indicated that the student had met his/her instructional aim at a particular skill level or when a particular generalization strategy was in effect.

Results

Reliability

Reliabilities were assessed throughout the study. Two observers were assigned to observe students during school and community probes, and the ratings given by observers were compared. Reliability data were collected on 51 probes, with an average agreement of 87.6%. For home probes, a phone call probe report was followed by a visit for 20 programs in which observers recorded student performance at home. Agreement between parents and observers on the rating of student performance was 92%.

Training Time

Training time for each group was 2 hours for initial training in writing objectives and 3 hours in using strategies or strategies with rules. The individual meetings were conducted biweekly with each teacher, and were limited to 10 minutes per program. The length of the individual meetings was determined by the number of programs covered at that meeting. During Baseline, three meetings per program were held with each teacher, and during Intervention, four meetings per program.

Impact on Generalization

A total of 60 skills for 15 students in the "Strategies" Group, and 44 skills for 15 students in the "Strategies + Rules" Group were targeted for instruction during the study. A discriminate analysis of generalization probe data showed skills fell into one of four groups: generalization prior to first probe; generalization during baseline or experimental phases; no generalization or acquisition; and no generalization although acquired. Each group is discussed below.

Prior generalization. Generalization probes were conducted at the beginning of the study. A generalization rating of "Good" was recorded on the first probe for 27 programs (26%) (Table 4–7). These probes indicated that generalization had possibly occurred prior to the study.

For example, Brenda had decided to teach Kate to activate a buzzer for attention at meals (skill d-1). Initial probes showed that Kate used the buzzer whenever it was available, if Brenda was not present but other managers were (Figure 4-1). The student also used the buzzer at home when it was made available. Brenda did not probe the skill during Baseline. Following the strategy training, however, she did conduct a probe which showed good generalization. In accord with the training, she decided to expand the skill by teaching Kate to use it to signal the need for help to get off of the toilet (skill d-2). Initial probes for this expanded skill showed good generalization for this as well.

Sixteen programs were from the "Strategies" Group and seven students were involved; Dennis and Kate each contributed five programs. Eleven programs from the "Strategies + Rules" Group fell into this category. Six students were involved and Gordon and Mark each contributed three programs.

Achieved generalization. Programs in which the first generalization probe in a given situation showed "poor" or "some" generalization, followed by a later probe in which performance was "good" in the same type of probe situation, were categorized as "achieved generalization." For example, Brenda instructed Amy to push her walker over bumps. Amy met the aim for skill acquisition during Baseline, but did not generalize during the Baseline phase (Figure 4-2). During the Intervention Phase, Brenda implemented strategies to promote generalization and Amy's skill generalized. However, the summer school staff carried Amy; with no opportunity to use her walker, Amy's skill was not maintained (Figure 4-2). Fortunately, this type of problem did not occur often. In many cases generalization was achieved and maintained (e.g., Figure 4-3).

Table 4-7

Skills at Aim for Generalization at Time of First Generalization Probe

Student	Skill		Generalization Situation
Strategies Group			
Amy	c-2	pulls walker to chair	School (no chance at home)
Kate	b	indicates "I want walk/dance/brush"	Home
	d-1	uses buzzer for attention at meals	School & Home
	d-2	uses buzzer for attention on toilet	School & Home
	e-1	says "mek" for milk at meals & snack	School (no chance at home)
	e-2	says "ooo" for juice	School & Home
Peter	a	actuates buzzer for help out of chair	School & Home
	b	touches picture/object to request item or activity	School (no chance at home)
Scott	b	takes glass and holds to drink	Home
Jeff	a-1	puts item in container (assisted)	School (no chance at home)
Dennis	a	moves clothes from washer to dryer	School ("too slow" at home)
	c	puts toys away	Home & School
	f-2	gets out of wheelchair safely	Home
	g	complies with commands	Home
	j	says answer to "what do you want?"	Home & School
Jim	a	folds clothes and puts on shelf	Home
Strategies + Rules Group			
Gordon	a-1	eats with a spoon (assisted)	School (no chance at home)
	c	touches pictures to choose	School (not used at home)
	d	crawls/scoots/rolls	School & Home
John	b	drinks from cup	Home
Barbara	a-1	retrieves and uses communication board w/prompt	School
	a-2	retrieves and uses communication board spontaneously	School & Home
Mark	a	delivers items on errands	School & Home
	b	says noun & verb to request	Home
	c	says 'no' to protest	School & Home
Lily	d	grasps spoon, scoops, brings to mouth	School (no chance at home)
David	a	walks downstairs alternating feet	Community

Forty programs fit into this category (Table 4-8). Eighteen of the programs were from the "Strategies" Group and 22 from the "Strategies + Rules" Group.

Skills not generalizing: Instructional aim not met. The first two steps in the discriminate analysis included all programs where good generalization was achieved. The remaining skills were analyzed to identify programs in which good generalization did not occur during the study. Thirty-seven programs fell into this category. Twenty-seven (73%) of these skills were not acquired: the instructional aims were not met. These skills were not expected to generalize. For example, Lee was instructed to hold his head up; he did not meet his instructional aim and did not generalize well. However, some generalization was shown (Figure 4-4).

Twenty of the 27 programs were from the "Strategies" Group and represented 33% of the target programs. Seven (16%) of the "Strategies + Rules" Group's programs fell into this category.

Skills not generalizing: Instructional aim met. However, students did acquire skills in 10 programs which did not generalize (Table 4-10). In the example shown in Figure 4-5, Holly's student John met the instructional aim, but generally did not eat with a spoon in nontraining

Table 4-8

Skills Which Achieved Generalization

Student		Skill	Generalization Situation	Phase Generalization Aim Met
Strategies Group				
Pat	b-1	chooses food by looking and signing	School (no opportunity at home)	Intervention
Sarah	b	signs eat & drink	Home & School	Intervention
Amy	a	pushes walker over bumps	Home & School	Intervention
	c-1	stands to walker from chair	School & Home	Intervention
Kate	a-1	drinks with a straw	School (no opportunity at home)	Intervention
	a-2	grasps cup and drinks with a straw	School (no opportunity at home)	Intervention*
	c-1	climbs stairs	School & Community (no opportunity at home)	Intervention
	c-2	descends stairs	School (no opportunity at home)	Intervention*
Scott	a	reaches, grasps, & holds object	School & Home	Intervention
Julie	a	follows directions, answers questions at meals	Home & School	Intervention
	b	holds head up	School	Baseline
			Home	Intervention
	c	asks for object fallen from grasp	School (not useful at home)	Intervention
Laura	a	eats finger food	Home & School	Intervention
Dennis	k	gets items out of refrigerator	Home	Intervention*
Ellen	a	points to words/pictures on comm. board	Home & Community	Intervention
	b	applies underarm deodorant	School & Home	Intervention
	c	washes upper body	Home	Intervention*
	f	points to picture of burger/fries/shake/coke	Community & School (no opportunity at home)	Intervention*
Strategies + Rules Group				
Karen	c	points to picture to request activity	Home	Intervention
Cheryl	a	touches pictures to choose food/drink (communication board)	School (not used at home)	Baseline
Candy	a	touches picture to choose food/drink	Community & Home	Intervention
	b	touches picture to choose activity	Home	Intervention
	c	follows directions	Community (not probed at home)	Baseline
Gordon	a-2	eats with spoon independently	School & Home	Intervention
	b-1	drinks from cup (with assistance)	Home	Intervention
	b-2	drinks from cup (independently)	Home	Intervention*
Hal	b	initiates requests with communication board	School (no opportunity at home)	Intervention
Barbara	b-1	scoops food with spoon	School & Home	Intervention
	b-2	pokes food with a fork	Home	Baseline
			School	Intervention
	c	pants on	School (no chance at home)	Intervention
Jenny	a	initiates scooping	School (no chance at home)	Intervention
Tracy	a	puts spoon in bowl, scoops, brings to mouth	School (no chance at home)	Intervention
	b	takes off coat (assisted)	Home	Intervention
Lily	b	grasps & pulls poncho off (assisted)	School & Community	Intervention
	c	grasps cup & brings to mouth	School, Home, & Community	Intervention
David	b	sets table (with prompts)	Home	Intervention
Sharon	a	sits down with assistance	School (no opportunity at home)	Intervention
	b	walks up stairs grasping rail	Home & School	Intervention
Jerry	a	pulls shirt down from under arms	School	Intervention
	b	sits down	Home	Intervention

*Not instructed during Baseline

Figure 4-1. Kate's use of a buzzer to get attention at meals (skill d-1) during Baseline generalized well at school (probes shown as squares) and at home (probes shown as circles) on the first probes, as did her use of the buzzer to request help in the bathroom (skill d-2) during the Intervention Phase.

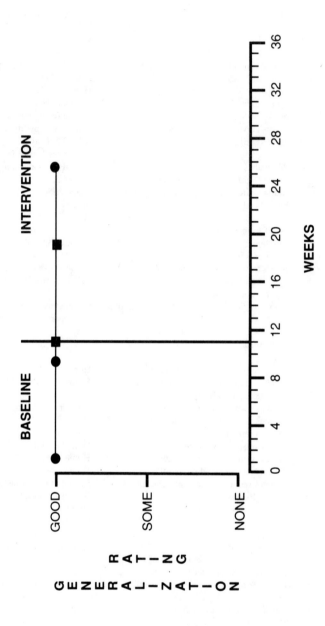

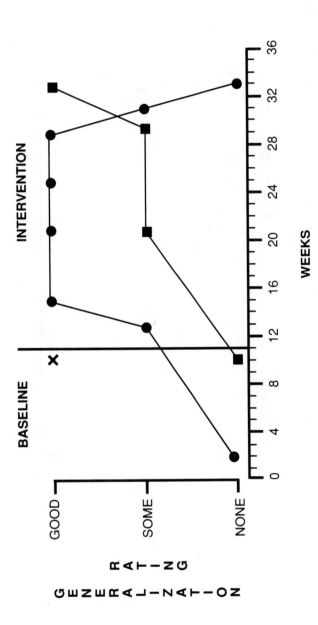

Figure 4-2. Amy's skill at pushing her walker over bumps (skill a) in generalization situations in the school (circles) and at home (squares) is shown. The instructional aim for acquisition was during the eighth experimental week (star). Amy's generalization did not maintain during summer school, when her new teacher carried her and she had no opportunity to walk.

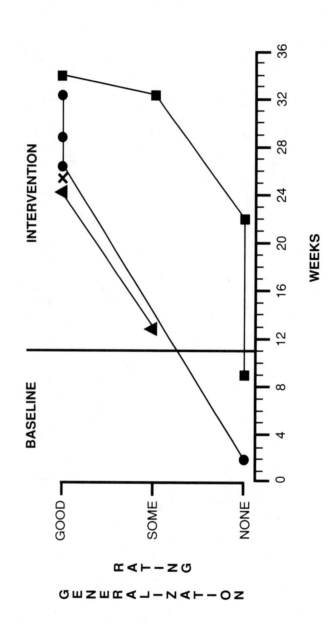

Figure 4-3. Lily's skill at independently grasping a cup and bringing it to her mouth (skill c) in untrained situations at school (circles), home (squares), and in the community (triangles) is shown. A probe during the 3 week June vacation indicated generalization had occurred; however, the instructional aim was not "met" until instruction was reinstituted during summer school (star).

Figure 4-4. Lee's skill at holding his head up when a computer provides feedback for head-down (skill a) during Baseline, and when he is in his wheelchair and instructed to hold his head up in natural situations (skill c) during Intervention, with varied classroom activities to watch and different managers providing feedback. Generalization to untrained school (circles), home (square), and community (triangle) situations is shown. Lee did not meet the instructional aim for this skill.

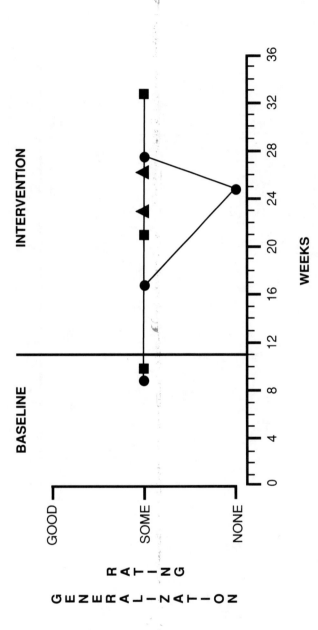

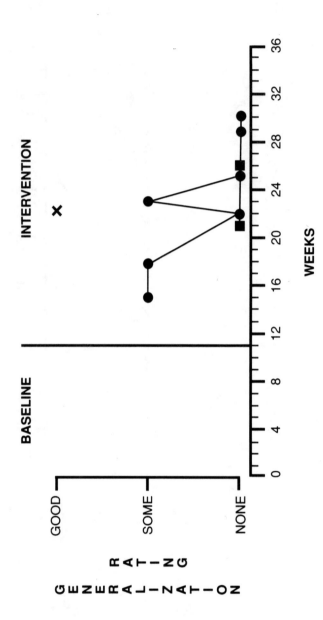

Figure 4-5. John met the instructional aim for eating (skill a). Probes in school (circles) and at home (squares) show generally poor skill generalization.

Table 4-9

Skills Which Did Not Generalize and Did Not Meet the Instructional Aim

Student		Skill
Strategies Group		
Lee	a	holds head up (with computer setup)
	b	swallows without spilling
	c	holds head up while seated in wheelchair
Pat	a	walks on knees
	b-2	chooses food by touching picture
Sarah	a-2	complies with "stand up" & "sit down"
	a-3	complies with "step around"
Robert	a	positions hand before scooping food
Janet	a	walks w/walker
Jeff	a-2	puts object in container (independently)
Dennis	d-2	says "hamburger, coke, fries" (shown word)
	e	touches/hands manager requested coins
	f-1	gets in wheelchair safely
	h	puts dirty clothes in washer
Ellen	d	gives requested coins
	e	washes tables in cafeteria
	g	retrieves items from fridge/shelf
	h	makes peanut butter & jelly sandwich
Jim	b	read and say restaurant words
	c	read and say "go," "fire," "gentleman"
Strategies + Rules Group		
Karen	a	walks w/walker
	b	eats w/spoon (opens mouth, bites)
Betsy	a	dresses
	b	imitates initial sounds of words
	c	undresses
Jenny	b	swallows without spilling (while head supported)
Lily	a	transfers from eating to drinking

situations. On one probe, he repeatedly dropped his spoon; on another he ate seven bites perfectly but dropped his spoon on the rest. Except during probe situations, John was fed at home, so he actually had only limited opportunities to use the skill. This was also true for 9 of the 10 skills (i.e., all *except* Laura's eye contact).

Six of the ten programs were from the "Strategies" Group and four were from the "Strategies + Rules" Group.

Skill generalization by students. Twelve students generalized all skills, either on the first probe or on later probes. Kate, Peter, Scott, and Julie were from the "Strategies" Group and Barbara, Mark, Tracy, David, Sharon, Jerry, Candy, and Gordon were from the "Strategies + Rules" Group. Four students never generalized a skill and never met the acquisition aim for a skill: Lee, Robert, and Janet from the "Strategies" Group and Betsy from the "Strategies + Rules" Group. The other 14 students generalized some of the skill targeted for the study.

Table 4-10

Skills Which Did Not Generalize and Which Met
the Instructional Aim

Student	Skill	
Strategies Group		
Sarah	a-1	complies with "come here"
Amy	b	actuates buzzer for attention
Laura	b	eye contact after greeting by other
Jeff	b	reaches for picture on communication board
Dennis	b	puts on t-shirt
	d-1	points to "hamburger, coke, fries" (comm. board)
Strategies + Rules Group		
Cheryl	b	touch picture to choose item/activity
John	a	eats with a spoon
Hal	a	sustains tooth brushing
	c	lifts tongue on shoe to put on (when stuck)

Table 4-11

Summary of Results

	Strategies Group	Strategies + Rules Group
Total Skills	60	44
Generalized at first probe (from Table 4-7)	16	11
Instructional aim not met (from Table 4-9)	20	7
Net Skills[1]	24	26
Generalized (from Table 4-8)	18	22
Not generalized (from Table 4-10)	6	4
Percent Skills Generalized	75%	88%
Total Students	15	16
No Generalized Skills[2]	3	1
Some Generalized Skills	8	7
All Generalized Skills	4	8
Percent Students Who Generalized All Target Skills	27%	50%

[1] Skills which generalized at first probe are excluded from the final analysis of impact because the skill may have generalized prior to the study. Skills which did not meet instructional aim for acquisition are excluded because generalization is not expected until after the skill has been acquired.

[2] All students in this category failed to meet instructional aims for acquisition on any of their target programs during the study.

Strategies Alone v. Strategies + Rules

Twice as many students in the "Strategies + Rules" Group generalized all of their skills, as compared to the "Strategies" Group (Table 4-11). A larger proportion of skills in the "Strategies + Rules" Group generalized (75% v. 88%), however, this result must be cautiously interpreted because of the small number of skills in each group.

Discussion

Twenty-seven programs (26% of the skills) had already generalized before the first probe was conducted. This indicates that teachers may be identifying skills for instruction that the student can already perform. The percentage was similar in both groups, so any difference between the students in each group is probably not the cause of this problem. It is possible that the problem is student noncompliance in the school setting. Studies have indicated a high proportion of students with severe handicaps may be noncompliant, and fail to follow instructional cues or commands for previously mastered skills (Haring, Beebe, & White, 1983; Haring, Liberty, & White, 1980). A noncompliant student who failed to perform during the teacher's in-class assessment is likely to be indistinguishable from students who can't perform. If a skill can be performed in another setting before the teacher begins instruction, it indicates that skill acquisition is not the problem—compliance is the problem. In a sense, the problem is generalization *to* the classroom or training situation from the situation in which the student already performs the skill. Probing skill use in nonclassroom situations prior to instruction will identify these skills before a heavy investment of instructional time and resources is made. If 2 out of 10 skills are mistargeted for instruction, early probing can save significant costs—up to 20% of the instructional resources.

About 26% (27) of the skills did not reach instructional aim during the study, and none of these skills generalized. There were twice as many programs in this category from the "Strategies" Group as from the "Strategies + Rules" Group. Three students from the "Strategies" Group failed to meet aim in any program. This indicates that the teachers' basic instructional methods were not effective, possibly because instructional aims were not appropriate, or possibly because of the students' special learning problems. This result may indicate an important difference between the groups.

Overall, 50 of the skills were ones in which generalization could be expected, and about 80% did generalize. Ninety percent of the students generalized at least one skill, and 40% generalized *all* of their target skills.

The results of this study support the use of generalization strategies for students with severe handicaps, since only 8% of the skills generalized during Baseline, and 92% of the skills generalized once teachers were trained to use strategies. Of course, these results are confounded by the AB nature of the design. Perhaps skills would have generalized without strategies if the "Baseline" condition had been extended. It is possible that the train and hope approach can be effective (see discussion in Chapter 2). It is also possible that writing objectives which specify generalization criteria, coupled with train and hope, can produce generalization without the need for special strategies. This hypothesis was one which we tested in our next study, described in Chapter 5.

The results also demonstrate that application of special strategies by public school teachers can facilitate generalization after only 5 hours of total training in a group, and an average of 10 minutes every 10 days of follow-up. One minute per day per program seems a very cost-effective method to ensure generalization.

References

Ackerman, A. M., & Shapiro, E. S. (1984). Self-monitoring and work productivity with mentally retarded adults. *Journal of Applied Behavior Analysis, 17*(3), 403-407.

Billingsley, F. F. (1984). Where *are* the generalized outcomes? (An examination of instructional objectives). *Journal of the Association for Persons with Severe Handicaps, 9*(3), 186-192.

Billingsley, F. F. (1988). Writing objectives for generalization. In N. G. Haring (Editor), *Generalization for students with severe handicaps: Strategies and solutions.* Seattle: University of Washington Press.

Billingsley, F. F., & Neel, R. (1986). Competing behaviors and their effects on skill generalization and maintenance. *Analysis and Intervention in Developmental Disabilities, 5,* 357-372.

Burney, J. D., Russel, B., & Shores, R. E. (1977). Developing social responses in two profoundly retarded children. *American Association for the Education of the Severely/Profoundly Handicapped Review, 2*(2), 53-60.

Haring, N. G., Beebe, R., & White, O. R. (1983). *Field initiated research studies of compliance and educational progress in severely and profoundly handicapped students: Final report.* (U.S. Department of Education, Contract No. G008001915). Seattle: University of Washington, College of Education.

Haring, N. G., Liberty, K. A., & White, O. R. (1980). Rules for data-based strategy decisions in instructional programs: Current research and instructional implications. In W. Sailor, B. Wilcox, & L. Brown (Eds.), *Methods of instruction with severely handicapped students.* Baltimore, MD: Paul H. Brookes.

Horner, R. H., Bellamy, G. T., & Colvin, G. T. (1984). Responding in the presence of nontrained stimuli: Implications of generalization error patterns. *Journal of the Association for Persons with Severe Handicaps, 9*(4), 287-295.

Horner, R. H., & McDonald, R. S. (1982). Comparison of single instance and general case instruction in teaching a generalized vocational skill. *Journal of the Association for Persons with Severe Handicaps, 7*(3), 7-20.

Liberty, K. (1987). Behaver-control of stimulus events to facilitate generalization. In N. Haring (Principal Investigator), *Investigating the problem of skill generalization: Literature review III.* (U.S. Department of Education, Contract No. 300-82-0364). Seattle: University of Washington, College of Education. (ERIC Document Reproduction Service No. ED 287 270)

Neef, N. A., Iwata, B. A., & Page, T. J. (1978). Public transportation training: In vivo versus classroom instruction. *Journal of Applied Behavior Analysis, 11,* 331-344.

Neel, R. S., Billingsley, F. F., & Lambert, C. (1983). IMPACT: A functional curriculum for educating autistic youth in natural environments. In R. B. Rutherford, Jr. (Ed.), *Monograph in behavior disorders: Severe behavior disorders of children and youth* (Series No. 6, pp. 40-50). Reston, VA: Council for Children with Behavioral Disorders.

Stokes, T. F., & Baer, D. B. (1977). An implicit technology of generalization. *Journal of Applied Behavior Analysis, 10*(2), 349-367.

Thompson, T. J., Braam, S. J., & Fuqua, R. W. (1982). Training and generalization of laundry skills: A multiple probe evaluation with handicapped persons. *Journal of Applied Behavior Analysis, 15*(1), 177-182.

Warren, S. F., Baxter, D. K., Anderson, S. R., Marshall, A., & Baer, D. M. (1981). Generalization of question-asking by severely retarded individuals. *Journal of the Association for the Severely Handicapped, 6*(3), 15-22.

*As we learned during the study reported in the previous chapter, teachers **can** apply generalization strategies and improve their pupils' rate of skill generalization. As a group, the teachers in our study were more effective than the gaggle of researchers we reviewed in Chapter 2—the teachers' success rate was 88%, as opposed to the overall 52.5% success rate we found in the published literature. However, we were still unsure about whether decision rules were an advantage in selecting strategies. In this chapter, we describe a study we conducted to determine if strategies matched to student performance via decision rules would result in more generalized skills than strategies selected counter to decision rules.*

Chapter 5

EFFECTIVENESS OF DECISION RULES FOR GENERALIZATION

Kathleen A. Liberty, Owen R. White, Felix F. Billingsley, and Norris G. Haring

In the last decade, it has become widely recognized that skill generalization should be considered a critical outcome of educational programs. The responsibility of educators to ensure that students are capable of reliably performing functional skills under the varying conditions that characterize nontraining environments, and the necessity of active planning to facilitate generalization, are pervasive themes in current literature (e.g., Alberto & Troutman, 1986; Horner, McDonnell, & Bellamy, 1986; Liberty, 1985). Striefel and Cadez (1983) have noted that, "The need for generalization of acquired skills and behaviors is unquestionably one of the major emphases of education . . . particularly for severely handicapped children who may not generalize learned behavior as easily as normal children" (p. 104).

The recognition that successful skill generalization substantially affects the quality of life has been accompanied by intensive research efforts that have identified a wide variety of instructional strategies that may promote generalized outcomes. Such strategies include, for example, training behaviors that will come under the control of natural maintaining contingencies or employing indiscriminable contingencies during instruction (Stokes & Baer, 1977), applying general case programming methods in order to select appropriate stimulus exemplars (Horner, Sprague, & Wilcox, 1982), and changing the relative efficiency or reliability with which trained and competing behaviors permit access to reinforcing events (Billingsley & Neel, 1985). Detailed discussions of available strategies have been provided by Stokes and Baer (1977) and others (Cooper, Heron, & Heward, 1987; Horner & Billingsley, in press; Marholin & Touchette, 1979).

Although generalization has received considerable attention, and methods for its promotion have been described and widely disseminated, little guidance is currently available to assist educators in choosing methods that are most likely to overcome failures to achieve generalization in specific instances. Some initial suggestions for decision-making have been proposed by workers such as Horner, Bellamy, and Colvin (1984), Horner and Billingsley (in press), and Liberty (1985). Those suggestions, however, have addressed a limited range of problems and remediation strategies, and are based on logical, rather than empirical, analyses. As Liberty has indicated, "Empirically derived decision rules for remediating plans to produce maintained, generalized, and adaptive responding have not yet been developed" (Liberty, 1985, p. 64).

The purpose of this study was to investigate the use of a comprehensive set of decision rules designed to help educators of students with severe handicaps select appropriate and effective techniques to facilitate skill generalization.

Empirically derived decision rules to select strategies for promoting initial skill acquisition and fluency-building do exist and have been found quite effective. Haring, Liberty, and White (1980; 1981) found that, in the absence of guidelines, interventions selected by teachers to improve skill acquisition and fluency-building by learners with severe handicaps were successful only about 33% of the time. However, it was also found that the use of the rules, which were applied using data from the programs of individual students, increased the probability of choosing an effective intervention on the first try to 86% (see Liberty, 1985; White, 1985; and White and Haring, 1982, for thorough discussions of those rules).

The present investigation represents an attempt to extend the utility of those instructional decision rules beyond the initial step of skill development within training contexts to the critical step of reliable skill application within new, untrained situations. The new rules, which address five major problem areas and associated remedial strategies, were initially developed from a logical analysis of generalization and maintenance performance errors that have appeared in the research literature, in our own work, and in student performance data that teachers have shared with us.

Method

Subjects and Setting

Six students with multiple handicaps ranging in age from 9 to 19 years 7 months served as subjects in the study. The subjects' characteristics are shown in Table 5-1. The students attended a University affiliated campus school, and were assigned to the same classroom. The classroom served as the primary training setting during the study. Other settings within the school building (e.g., gym, cafeteria, office, principal's office, and kitchen) served as secondary training sites for some programs, and as untrained probe situations for others. Two nearby cafeterias, the campus grounds, and the students' homes also served as probe sites.

Experimental Design

Within the context of a multiple baseline design, repeated measures of performance in untrained situations were conducted before and after instruction and before and after implementation of generalization strategies (Table 5-2). Skills which met instructional aims were randomly assigned to "rules," "contrary to rules," or to "both" conditions. For the first condition, rules derived from analysis of generalization data were used to identify the problem that might have impeded generalization. A strategy specifically designed to address that problem was then implemented. In the "contrary to rules" or "vs. rules" condition, generalization strategies were selected which did not match the problem identified by the rules. For the third condition, strategies were first chosen in opposition to the rules, and then followed by strategies selected in accord with the rules. All experimental phases were conducted during 6 calendar weeks.

Procedures

Skill selection. Experimenters and the classroom teacher met individually with each student and her/his parent(s) to discuss the study, to solicit parental input on desirable skills and the level of performance needed for each skill to be functional, to conduct informal assessments, and to determine which skills would be taught as part of the study. Skills selected met these requirements: agreement that the skill was functional, that it was useful in a variety of situations, that opportunities to perform the skill currently existed or would be provided by the parents, that the skill was not currently in the student's repertoire, and that there was good reason to believe that the skill could be acquired during the course of the study. The target skills are listed in Table 5-3.

Generalization probes I. Procedures for probing generalization were developed for each target skill. Three classifications of stimuli were evaluated to determine patterns of responding to trained and untrained stimuli present during each response opportunity (i.e., stimuli associated with the person(s) present during skill use, stimuli associated with the setting in which the skill is performed, and stimuli preceding or concurring with the response, such as verbal directions or objects presented). Four different configurations of these stimuli were developed as representative

Table 5-1

Participating Students

Pupil	Chronological Age[1]	Sex	Primary Handicapping Condition	Secondary Handicapping Condition	Most Recent Psych. Test Chronological Age (at time of test)	Most Recent Psych. Test Score	Medication
Donna	16.17 years	F	Severe retardation	autism, Rett syndrome	6.5 years	6 months[2]	Depakene, Meberal, Valproic acid
Ruth	19.58 years	F	Profound retardation	cleft palate	15.25 years	0-24 mo.[3]	none
Mary	18.58 years	F	Severe/profound retardation	scoliosis	14.25 years	0-17 mo.[3]	Phenobarbital, Valium
Larry	9.00 years	M	Severe/profound retardation	tuberous sclerosis seizures	7.42 years / 7.5 years	14-30 mo.[2] / 0-22 mo.[4]	Tegretol Phenurone
Amy	16.25 years	F	Profound retardation	cerebral palsy, scoliosis, Rett syndrome	12.17 years	4 months[5]	Depakene, Meberal, Valproic acid
George	17.67 years	M	Severe mental retardation	athetoid cerebral palsy	11.83 years / 11.00 years	0-14 mo.[4] / 14-53 mo.[3]	none

1 As of 11-1-86
2 Vineland Social Maturity Scale
3 Uniform Performance assessment System (UPAS)
4 Developmental Profile II (Alpern-Boll)
5 Bayley Scales of Infant Development

Table 5-2

Program of Experimental Conditions for Each Student

Student	Skill	Probe I	Acquisition Training	Generalization Probe II	Training I	Probe III	Generalization Training II	Probe IV
							Sessions Covered By Experimental Phases	
Larry	dry hands	1-3	4-16	17-19	20-42 rule	32-34	43-45	
	use radio	1-3	4-16	17-19	20-31 vs rule	32-34	35-42 rule	43-45
	pincer grasp	1-3	4-16	17-19	20-42 vs rule	32-34	43-45	
	wipe mouth	1-3	4-16	17-19	20-42 vs rule	32-34	43-45	
Mary	take object	1-3	4-16	17-19	20-37 rule	32-34	43-45	
	extend arm	1-3	4-16	17-19	20-31 vs rule	32-34	34-42 rule	43-45
	wipe mouth	1-3	4-34	34-35	36-42 vs rule	43-45		
	use straw	1-3	4-16	17-19				
Amy	take food	1-3	4-23	25-27	28-42 rule	33-34	43-45	
	to knees	1-3	4-23	25-27	28-32 vs rule	33-34	34-42 rule	43-45
George	take object	1-3	4-24	25-27	28-42 rule	33-34	43-45	
	touch picture	1-3	4-24	25-27	28-42 vs rule	33-34	43-45	
Ruth	yes/no	1-3	4-24	25-27	28-42 rule	36-37	43-45	
Donna	walk	1-3	4-24	25-27	28-35 vs rule	36-37	38-42 rule	43-45

Table 5-3

Skills Selected for Participating Students

Student & Skills	Description and Instructional Aim	Days of Instruction to Meet Aim
Donna		
Walks	Takes steps with someone holding her hand and walking next to her; 80% of trials without additional support at 80 steps/min.	5
Takes object	Reachs for and grasps object on request without physical assistance; 80% of requests.	not met
Wipes mouth	Independently wipes mouth clean with a napkin or tissue; 80% of requests within 6 seconds.	dropped at parent request
Ruth		
Answers yes/no	Touch symbol for yes or touch symbol for no following a question, without physical assistance; 85% of questions answered without assistance.	20
Sits down	Sits down from walker following request when chair positioned behind knees without physical assistance; 80% of requests.	not met
Wipes nose	Independently wipes nose with a tissue when requested; 80% of requests.	not met
Larry		
Dries hands	Dries hands without prompting on request 5 of 6 trials without assistance; completed within 15 seconds.	11
Turns on radio	Turns on radio on request, 4 of 5 trials without assistance.	4
Pincer grasp	Uses pincer grasp instead of palmar grasp or other behaviors to pick up flat, thin objects without assistance; 8 of 10 objects correct within 3 seconds.	9
Wipes mouth	Independently wipes mouth clean with a napkin following a request to do so; 80% of requests followed within 5 seconds.	10
George		
Answers yes/no	Touches symbol for yes or touches symbol and/or shakes head for no following a question; 80% of questions answered without assistance.	not met
Takes object	Independently reaches for and grasps object on request; 2 of 3 objects within 6 seconds.	10
Selects activity	Touches photo to select activity; 5 of 6 trials within 15 seconds.	12
Amy		
Answers yes/no	Touches symbol for yes or touches symbol for no following a question, without physical assistance; 80% of questions answered.	not met
Takes finger-food	Reaches for and grasps finger food on request without physical assistance; 80% of requests.	19
Rises to knees	Rises to two-point position on knees from sitting position on floor with verbal request and physical prompt in armpits; 80% of requests followed within 5 seconds.	11
Touches switch	Touches switch to activate tape recorder; 80% of trials.	not met
Mary		
Takes object	Independently reaches for and grasps object on request; 80% of objects taken within 6 seconds of request.	1
Extend left arm	Extends left arm on request (active range of motion); 6 of 8 sessions, arm extended within 15 seconds without physical prompt.	5
Wipes mouth	Independently wipes mouth clean with a napkin following a request to do so; 80% of requests followed within 6 seconds.	27
Uses a straw	Independently drinks liquid from a straw without prompting; 80% of trials without assistance.	10

Table 5-4

Generalization Probe Stimuli

Stimuli Clusters Associated with Responding

	Person managing the student	The setting	The stimuli (cues, prompts, materials)
Situation # 1	person instructing the target skill	the classroom setting where instruction occurred	both instructed and uninstructed
Situation # 2	classroom staff excluding instructor	instructional setting and uninstructed settings in the school	both instructed and uninstructed
Situation # 3	persons relatively unfamiliar to the student	community settings (uninstructed)	natural stimuli (may include instructed and uninstructed)
Situation # 4	parent or other family member	the home	natural stimuli (may include instructed and uninstructed)

of "situations" where generalized responding would be desirable (see Table 5-4).

Consequences for correct and incorrect responding, if any, were selected and arranged by the probe manager, who was encouraged to provide the "natural" consequences he or she would normally provide. However, in probe situations 1 and 2, the probe manager was cautioned against providing specific consequences programmed during instruction that were not available in natural situations. During instruction, for example, a failure to respond after 5 seconds might have been followed by physically molding the response. In the probe situation, a failure to respond after a time determined by the probe manager might be followed by a repetition of the verbal direction, by redirection to another task, by verbal feedback, by the manager leaving, or by some other combination of relatively "natural" circumstances. Probe trials were generally scheduled over a 2 to 3 day period, and occurred during normal school hours (probes 1-3) or at the parent's convenience (probe 4). Each target behavior was probed in all four situations prior to the initiation of instruction. As outlined in Table 5-4, probe 1 was conducted by the instructional manager, probe 2 by a member of the classroom or research staff who was not the instructional manager, probe 3 was conducted by a person unfamiliar with the student and her/his programs (e.g., University professor, project secretary, cashier in restaurant), and probe 4 was conducted by the parents or another family member. Except for probe 1, persons conducting probes were usually involved only once in a probe for a particular skill.

Instruction for skill acquisition. Instructional procedures were developed for each target skill using the practices generally prescribed for facilitating skill acquisition (e.g., Gaylord-Ross & Holvoet, 1985; Snell, 1983), but avoiding any specific strategies known to facilitate generalization. Two or three instructional sessions for each target skill were conducted each morning by a research assistant. Previously validated rules for determining when to change instructional procedures and the type of strategy most likely to facilitate learning were applied to the performance data collected during acquisition programming (Haring, Liberty, & White, 1980, 1981; Liberty, 1972; White, 1986; White & Haring, 1980, 1982)[6].

Instruction continued on a frequent basis until the student reached the aim set in the pre-experimental parent-teacher meeting for instructional performance on two or more target skills

---

[6] In some cases, procedures were adapted so that performance was evaluated on a session-by-session basis instead of a day-by-day basis.

Figure 5-1. The sequence of decision points and procedures for determining the nature of the generalization strategy to be implemented[7]. Examples of strategies for each category are shown in Table 5-5.

Decision Rule Question Sequence

	QUESTION	PROCEDURES	ANSWER	NEXT STEP
1a.	Is generalization desired to only one situation?	Analyze function of behavior objective, and current and future environments available to student.	yes	CONTINUE with question 1b.
			no	CONTINUE with question 2.
1b.	Is it possible to train directly in that situation?	Determine if accessibility and frequency of training is likely to be adequate.	yes	Train on site until aim is met. [EXIT sequence]
			no	CONTINUE with question 2.
2.	Has skill generalized at the desired level in all target situations?	Probe for generalization in all desired situations, then compare performance with aim.	yes	Identify next target skill, set aim, probe for generalization and use this sequence to determine next step for that skill. [EXIT sequence]
			no	CONTINUE with question 3.
3.	Has skill been acquired?	Compare performance in instruction with performance aim for acquisition.	yes	CONTINUE with question 4.
			no	Continue instruction until acquisition aim is met, reprobe for generalization, and repeat question sequence at step 1. [EXIT sequence]
4a.	Does the student access events likely to be reinforcers even when he does not perform the target skill?	Observe events during probes and note events which follow appropriate, inappropriate, target, and nontarget skills. Determine if the reinforcers are those which should follow the target skill, or have been shown to reinforce other skills.	yes	CONTINUE with question 4b.
			no	CONTINUE with question 5.
4b.	Are the natural reinforcers ones that are delivered by others?	Observe events, and note how reinforcing events are delivered.	yes	Select strategy from category: COMPETING REINFORCER PROBLEM Implement strategy until aim in generalization instruction is met, reprobe for generalization, and repeat question sequence at step 1. [EXIT sequence]
			no	Select strategy from category: COMPETING BEHAVIOR PROBLEM Implement strategy until aim in generalization instruction is met, reprobe for generalization, and repeat question sequence at step 1. [EXIT sequence]

(continued on next page)

---

[7] These rules were used during the study. However, the rules were consequently revised, as shown in Chapter 9.

Figure 5-1 (continued)

5.	Did the skill generalize once at aim? (but not as well in other situations/ trials)	Analyze how the student responded to each trial opportunity in each probe situation.	yes	Select strategy from category: REINFORCING FUNCTION PROBLEM Implement strategy until aim in generalization instruction is met, reprobe for generalization, and repeat question sequence at step 1. [EXIT sequence]
			no	CONTINUE with question 6
6.	Did the student respond partially correctly during at least one response opportunity?	Analyze anecdotal data and observational notes from probes	yes	Select strategy from category: DISCRIMINATION FUNCTION PROBLEM Implement strategy until aim in generalization instruction is met, reprobe for generalization, and repeat question sequence at step 1. [EXIT sequence]
			no	Develop new instructional plan, using: GENERALIZATION TRAINING FORMAT Implement strategy until aim in generalization instruction is met, reprobe for generalization, and repeat question sequence at step 1. [EXIT sequence]

(Table 5-3). Acquisition instruction was then terminated, in accord with the rules for acquisition instruction. If the aim was reached on one skill before another, instruction ceased for that skill. In those situations, instruction was reinstated once the remaining target skill(s) reached aim at the end of the phase, to ensure that aim levels had been maintained during the no-instruction period.

Generalization probes II. Once the student met the aim for instructional performance on two or more skills, generalization was again evaluated. Probes were constructed as previously described, and stimulus conditions where the student had previously demonstrated good generalization were eliminated as probe situations.

Instruction for skill generalization I. Following the second probe set, skills which had not generalized were assigned to either a "Rule" or "Versus Rule" condition. A coin flip procedure was used to assign one skill for each student to the "Rule" condition; the other skills for each student were then automatically assigned to the "Versus Rule" condition.[8] Rules for identifying any problems with generalization were applied to the probe data for each target skill. An abbreviated version of these rules is shown in Figure 5-1. For skills in the "Rule" condition, experimenters selected a strategy type according to the problem category defined by the question sequence (Figure 5-1), and modified instructionalprocedures for that skill in accord with the strategy recommendations. Strategies for each category type are shown in Table 5-5. For skills in the "Versus Rule" condition, experimenters identified a strategy in one of the other problem areas that seemed likely to improve performance (e.g., if the rule procedure identified a reinforcing function problem, in the "Versus Rule" condition, the experimenter might identify the strategy of programming multiple managers and varying the situations in which the target behavior was consequated).

Generalization probes III. When the "Rule" or "No Rule" skill reached the aim in the new instructional program, each of the target skills identified for that student was probed in the four generalization situations.

Instruction for skill generalization II. Following the third probe set, "Rule" procedures were instituted for the skills previously assigned to "No Rule" condition. If skills assigned to the

---

[8]   Donna and Ruth reached aim in acquisition instruction on one skill each. Donna's parents requested that her wipe mouth program be discontinued. The two skills at acquisition aim, Donna's walk and Ruth's answer yes/no, were linked, and the coin flip was used to determine which condition would apply.

"Rule" condition had not generalized, rule procedures were repeated, using the third probe set data, and another strategy was selected in accord with the rules.

Generalization probes IV. Each of the target skills was probed at the end of study in each of the four probe situations.

Data Collection

The primary measure of generalization was a rating of the skill's usefulness as judged by the person managing the student during a probe situation.[9] Generalization probes for situations 1-2 were conducted in the school, and the probe managers were asked by an experimenter at the conclusion of the preset probe procedures to rate the student's performance of the skill as: "poor or no response," "somewhat functional or useful," or as "good/functional/useful." No additional information or definition of the terms was provided, except for the phrase, "Whatever you think." Probe managers for community probes were asked to rate the student's performance in an identical manner as soon as possible after the student's return to the classroom. Home probes were conducted in two parts. Parents were first telephoned and asked if they were providing routine opportunities to perform the target skill. If they were, the experimenter proceeded to the second part of the probe. If there were no regular opportunities, the parents were asked to provide several response opportunities for the target skills, and the parents were telephoned again on the following day. After opportunities for the skill had been provided, parents were asked to describe how their child had responded to the opportunities, and then asked in an identical manner as other probers to rate the target skill. Parents who were difficult to contact by phone were mailed letters. Once their written reports were returned, they were called and asked to rate the target skill.

Reliability

The reliability of performance ratings was determined by assigning a research assistant or one of the experimenters to observe the performance of the student during a probe conducted by another manager. This second observer was then asked to independently rate the student's performance. Reliability checks were conducted for 12 of the 89 probes. There were no disagreements; inter-rater reliability was 100% across all probes.

Results

Skill Acquisition

Fourteen of the 21 skills met aim for skill acquisition (Table 5-3). A mean of 11 (range 1-27) instructional days were required to meet aim for the 14 skills. Generalization probes proceeded with the 14 skills meeting instructional aim.

Skill Generalization

Probes were not conducted in the community for three skills, since the probe situations could not be contrived to occur as they might occur in some other setting (i.e., Larry's "turn on the radio;" George's "touch picture;" Amy's "rise to knees"). George's parents never replied to probes, and student absences prevented some probes. A total of 89 probes were conducted during the study. The results for individual students are shown in Figure 5-2.

---

[9] During instruction, the research assistant instructional manager collected data on the accuracy of responding to each training opportunity (i.e., whether the response was correct, incorrect, or if no response had occurred) and a measure of fluency. Types of fluency data collected included: rate (walking, drinking, activating switch), latency (take object/finger food; answer yes or no; wipe nose/mouth; pick up object; sit down; touch picture; rise to knees), and duration (dry hands; sit down; extend arm). The instructional manager collected data identical to those collected during instruction when s/he administered the generalization probes in Situation 1 (see Table 5-4). Research assistants (other than the one acting as instructor) and/or classroom staff conducted the probes in Situation 2. During those probes, data similar to instructional data were also collected. However, the collection of such data during community situations (Situation 3) was not always possible since a visible data collector might have produced reactive effects, and since it was not always possible for the data collector to be hidden from the student and still be able to observe the behavior.

Table 5-5

Generalization Categories and Strategies

	Competing Reinforcer	Competing Behavior	Reinforcing Function	Discrimination Function	Teaching Format
DESCRIPTION	Persons are reinforcing other behaviors, or no responses, with events which either should be available only for the target behavior, or with events which compete with the natural reinforcers for performing the target behavior.	The student performs another behavior and accesses the same reinforcers available for performing the target behavior.	The type or schedule of consequences available in natural situations for performing the target behavior does not function to reinforce the target behvior.	Relevant and/or irrelevant stimuli in the generalization situations are discriminated from those in the training situation. Stimulus control of trained stimuli is too "tight" for generalization to untrained stimuli to occur.	None of the other problems can be identified; either rules followed incorrectly or other problem in teaching situation.
EXAMPLE OF PROBLEM	Ruth stands by her chair after being asked to "sit down." After a few minutes, the manager physically guides Ruth to sit, and says "Thank you." Ruth is then given a new activity.	Larry is asked to wipe his mouth, and is handed a napkin. He shreds the napkin and wipes his mouth on the hem of his shirt.	At the Center Restaurant, Mary is told "Hey, you've got a milk moustache!" Mary picks up a napkin and wipes her mouth. Meanwhile, her new friend has started chatting with another neighbor. A few minutes later, she says, "Hey, Mary, wipe your mouth," Mary doesn't respond.	Amy quickly takes trained and untrained types of food from her teacher when they are held out to her and she is asked to "Take" the food. However, when the school principal holds out a sucker, and says, "Here, try this," she doesn't respond. When the principal holds out a hairbrush and says "Take," however, she reaches for the brush but does not actually grasp it.	
STRATEGIES	-alter contingencies in generalization situation -amplify the target behavior	-increase proficiency of target behavior (so it is a faster way to get the reinforcer) -amplify the target behavior -alter contingencies in generalization situation	-program natural reinforcers in the training situation -fade training reinforcers -program natural schedules -program natural consequences -teach self-reinforcement -teach to solicit reinforcement -reinforce generalized behavior -alter contingencies in generalization situation	-stimuli that should control/ not control the target behavior are systematically varied in training, determine the stimuli by using: -general case stimuli -multiple exemplars -common stimuli	-check format to see if other relevant factors may be impeding generalization. -eliminate any other training stimuli.

Prior to instruction, three skills generalized well to one situation but none generalized across more than one. Overall, 5.8% of the probes showed "good" generalization prior to instruction. Following instruction, six skills generalized well to one situation, but none generalized well to two or more situations. Two skills which had previously shown good generalization to a single setting no longer showed generalization in that setting. One program was dropped from the study during this phase: Mary's functional drinking with a straw increased from 0 out of 4 to 3 out of 4 situations with "good" ratings following instruction, and the skill difficulty was increased. Since the instructional target had changed, this skill was not included in further experimental phases. Overall, 9 of the 52 (17.3%) probes administered following instruction showed good generalization.

For the 13 skills meeting aim, excluding Mary's straw drinking program, strategies were selected contrary to the rules for four skills, in accord with the rules for five skills, and four skills were scheduled for both types of interventions. For each skill, the results of the second probe set were used in conjunction with the rules to determine which types of generalization problems existed. Appropriate or inappropriate strategies for the problem(s) were then selected for inclusion in the instructional program. Similar strategies were selected for both groups when possible, as shown in Table 5-6. For example, if "vary stimuli" was selected on the basis of the rules for one program, an attempt was made to use the same strategy in another program for which the rules would not recommend that approach.

Decisions were made contrary to the rules for eight skills (four times in programs where contra-rule strategies were used alone, and four times in programs where they were followed by the use of strategies in accord the rules). In the 35 probes conducted following "contrary" interventions, good generalization was shown in nine (25.7%). When strategies selected in accord with the rules were implemented after the "contrary" phase, "good" generalization increased from 14.3% (2 of 14 probes) to 42.9% (6 of 14 probes).

Strategies selected in accord with the rules were implemented for four skills immediately following instruction. Of the 39 probes conducted during this phase, 18 (46.2%) of the student performances were rated good. When the results for the "rules" phase from skills which had both "contrary" and "in accord" phases are included, "good" generalization was rated in 24 of 53 probes (45.3%). A summary of these and other results is shown in Table 5-7.

Generalization was not uniform across probe situations. Prior to the interventions, students were most likely to transfer good performance to a situation similar to training or to the home (Table 5-8). This pattern maintained after a "contrary" strategy. However, good generalization to the two least familiar situations was more likely following implementation of a strategy selected in accord with the rules.

Of the five skills programmed with interventions selected to follow the rules, four generalized well to one or more settings during the treatment phase (80%), although generalization strategies were in effect for an average of only 14.2 days. Of the four skills programmed with rule-based strategies after a "contrary" intervention, three generalized well to one or more settings during the "follow rules" treatment phase (75%), even though rule-based strategies were in effect for only 7 days. Overall, seven (78%) of nine skills programmed according to the rules generalized within two weeks. In contrast, only one of the four skills in the "contrary only" group and none of the four skills in the "both" group (12.5%) generalized to a new setting during the "contrary" treatment phase, although implemented for an average of 14.5 and 8.3 days, respectively.

Rule Validity

If strategies are implemented in accord with the rules, and if the rules are effective, generalization should improve. Of the 53 probes conducted while rule-followed strategies were in effect, 30 (56.6%) showed an improved rating over the prior probe[10] (Table 5-9). In addition, if the rules are valid, performance should not improve when the rules are not followed. Of the 35 probes conducted while strategies contrary to the rules were in effect, 25 showed no improvement (71%). If all probes are summarized, 55 (30 in accord with rules and with improvement, and 25 contrary with no improvement) of the 89 (62%), match the prediction of the rules. If one looks only at

---

[10]   Probe III better than Probe II or Probe IV better than Probe III; if Probe III was "good," then Probe IV could not improve, so if Probe IV was also "good," it was included in this analysis.

Figure 5–2. The percent of probe situations where student performance was rated as good generalization. The dotted lines indicate the lowest non-zero score obtainable (i.e., 4 probe situations, 25% is lowest possible non-zero score; 3 situations, 33% is lowest; 2 situations, 50% is lowest).

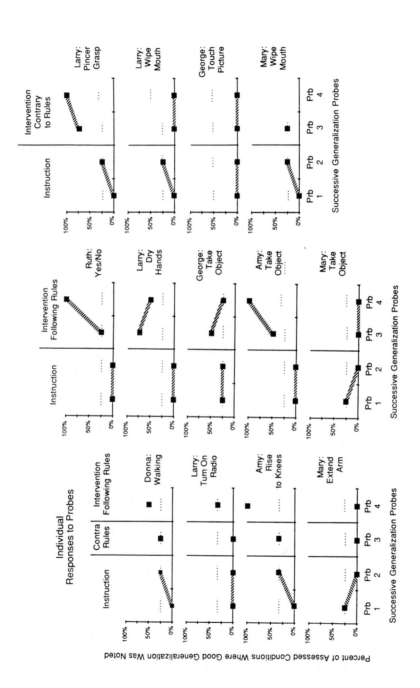

Table 5-6

Strategies Applied in Experimental Phases

Rule Category	Number of Programs Applied	Strategies	
		Contrary to Rule	Accord with Rule
Competing proficiency Reinforcer contingencies	2	Vary stimuli Program natural reinforcers	Increase Alter generalization
Competing contingencies Behavior	3	Vary stimuli Cease instruction	Alter generalization
Reinforcing reinforcers Function	5	Vary stimuli Reinforce generalized behavior	Program natural
Discrimination Function	2	Program natural reinforcers Increase proficiency	Vary stimuli
Format stimuli	1	Vary stimuli	Eliminate training

Table 5-7

Effects of Interventions

Probe Performance Ratings	Experimental Phase			
	A Prior To Instruction	B After Met Instructional Aim	C Strategies Contrary To Rules	D Strategies In Accord With Rules
	N = 52	N = 52	N = 35	N = 53
Rated "Good"	5.8%	17.3%	25.7%	45.3%
Rated "Some"	28.8%	55.8%	22.9%	25.9%
Rated "Poor"	65.4%	26.9%	51.4%	27.8%

Table 5-8

Generalization Across Situations

% Probes Rated "Good Performance"	Experimental Phase			
	A Prior To Instruction	B After Met Instructional Aim	C Strategies Contrary To Rules	D Strategies In Accord With Rules
"Training" Situation 1	14.3%	21.4%	27.3%	35.7%
"School" Situation 2	0.0%	0.0%	20.0%	50.0%
"Community" Situation 3	0.0%	18.2%	25.0%	58.3%
"Home" Situation 4	7.7%	30.7%	33.0%	42.9%

Table 5-9

Rule Validity

	Generalization Rating Improved or Continued Good	Generalization Rating Did Not Improve
Decisions in Accord With Rule (N = 53)	56.6%*	44.4%
Decisions Contrary To Rule (N = 35)	28.9%	71.0%*
Program Changes in Accord with Rule (N = 14)	64.3%*	35.7%
Program Changes Contrary to Rule (N = 12)	25.0%	75.0%*

* Support rule application

general changes in the number of situations to which generalization occurs, the pattern of overall results is very similar, with 69% of the changes supporting the validity of the rules (see Table 5-9).

Discussion

The selection of strategies according to the rules was associated with an increased number of skills generalizing well to new situations. When similar strategies were applied to programs in contradiction to the rules and instruction without specific generalization strategies, much lower levels of generalization were obtained. The rules correctly predicted the effects of intervening in about 62%-69% of the instances where skill performance was evaluated in nontraining settings. These results suggest that the decision rules may be an effective aid in selecting the type of strategy to apply when generalization does not occur following skill acquisition.

Since the rules were applied in only nine programs, with six different students, these results must be viewed as only the first step in an empirical analysis of the effectiveness of decision rules. Not only must the overall impact of the rules be tested repeatedly, but additional questions regarding the rules must be carefully examined. For example, are there student or ecological characteristics which affect rule validity? All three of Mary's programs failed to support the rules, and performance was consistently poor in nontraining situations. Each of the skills involved moving either her left arm ("extend arm") or her right arm ("take;" "wipe mouth"), and it is possible that Mary's handicapping conditions, resulting from an accident, affected her skill generalization and thus rule applicability, in a unique manner. Alternatively, the strategies may need to have been implemented for longer periods of time, or Mary's passive physical therapy for left arm movement occurring concurrently with the interventions may have affected the impact of the strategies. It is certainly possible that prior/concurrent programs and/or conditions within the training situation may affect generalization and, therefore, rules governing the selection of strategies designed to solve generalization problems. Further research, involving different students and skills, will help resolve such questions.

Decision rules and matrices have become an increasingly common component of instructional and curricular guides over the past few years (e.g., Bailey & Wolery, 1984; Deno & Mirkin, 1977; Evans & Meyer, 1985; Fredericks et al., 1979; Gaylord-Ross, 1980; Lent & McLean, 1976; Renzaglia & Aveno, 1986; Sailor, Guess, Goetz, Schuler, Utley, & Baldwin, 1980). The tremendous increase in information and strategies related to the education of students with handicaps and the concurrent philosophical, legal, and ethical trends have added impetus to this proliferation, because of their utility in aiding complex decision-making. However, if decision rules are to be truly useful, they must provide more than a short cut—they must improve education of students with handicaps. In this study, 78% of the skills programmed in accord with the rules generalized to at least one new untrained setting within two weeks of strategy implementation, as compared with only 12.5% of skills programmed contrary to the rules. The present study is the first step in providing an empirical basis for decision rules to facilitate generalization.

References

Alberto, P. A., & Troutman, A. C. (1986). *Applied behavior analysis for teachers* (2nd ed.). Columbus, OH: Charles E. Merrill.

Bailey, D. B., Jr., & Wolery, M. (1984). *Teaching infants and preschoolers with handicaps*. Columbus, OH: Charles E. Merrill.

Billingsley, F. F., & Neel, R. S. (1985). Competing behaviors and their effects on skill generalization and maintenance. *Analysis and Intervention in Developmental Disabilities, 5*, 357-372.

Cooper, J. O., Heron, T. E., & Heward, W. L. (1987). *Applied behavior analysis*. Columbus, OH: Charles E. Merrill.

Deno, S. L., & Mirkin, P. K. (1977). *Data-based program modification: A manual*. Reston, VA: Council for Exceptional Children.

Evans, I. M., & Meyer, L. H. (1985). *An educative approach to behavior problems: A practical decision model for interventions with severely handicapped learners.* Baltimore: Paul H. Brookes.

Fredericks, H., Baldwin, V., Moore, W., Templeman, V., Grove, D., Moore, M., Gage, M., Blair, L., Alrick, G., Wadlow, M., Fruin, C., Bunse, C., Samples, L., Samples, B., Moses, C., Rogers, G., & Toews, J. (1979). *A data-based classroom for the moderately and severely handicapped* (3rd ed.). Monmouth, OR: Instructional Development Corporation.

Gaylord-Ross, R. (1980). A decision model for the treatment of aberrant behavior in applied settings. In W. Sailor, B. Wilcox, & L. Brown (Eds.), *Methods of instruction for severely handicapped students.* Baltimore: Paul H. Brookes.

Gaylord-Ross, R. J., & Holvoet, J. (1985). *Strategies for educating students with severe handicaps.* Boston: Little, Brown.

Haring, N., Liberty, K., & White, O. (1980). Rules for data-based strategy decisions in instructional programs: Current research and instructional implications. In W. Sailor, B. Wilcox, & L. Brown (Eds.), *Methods of instruction for severely handicapped students* (pp. 159-192). Baltimore: Paul H. Brookes.

Haring, N. G., Liberty, K. A., & White, O. R. (1981). *Field initiated research studies of phases of learning and facilitating instructional events for the severely/profoundly handicapped* (Final project report). (U.S. Department of Education, Contract No. G007500593.) Seattle: University of Washington, College of Education.

Horner, R., Bellamy, G. T., & Colvin, G. T. (1984). Responding in the presence of nontrained stimuli: Implications of generalization error patterns. *Journal of the Association for the Severely Handicapped, 9*(4), 287-295.

Horner, R. H., & Billingsley, F. F. (in press). The effect of competing behavior on generalization and maintenance of adaptive behaviors in applied settings. In R. H. Horner, G. Dunlap, & R. L. Koegel (Eds.), *Generalization and maintenance: Lifestyle changes in applied settings.* Baltimore: Paul H. Brookes.

Horner, R. H., McDonnell, J. J., & Bellamy, T. (1986). Teaching generalized skills: General case instruction in simulation and community settings. In R. H. Horner, L. H. Meyer, & H. D. B. Fredericks (Eds.), *Education of learners with severe handicaps: Exemplary service strategies* (pp. 289-314). Baltimore: Paul H. Brookes.

Horner, R. H., Sprague, J., & Wilcox, B. (1982). General case programming for community activities. In B. Wilcox & G. T. Bellamy (Eds.), *Design of high school programs for severely handicapped students* (pp. 61-98). Baltimore: Paul H. Brookes.

Lent, J. R., & McLean, B. M. (1976). The trainable retarded: The technology of teaching. In N. Haring & R. Schiefelbusch (Eds.), *Teaching special children.* New York: McGraw-Hill.

Liberty, K. A. (1972). *Decide for progress: Dynamic aims and data decisions* (Working paper No. 20). Eugene: University of Oregon, Regional Resource Center for Handicapped Children.

Liberty, K. A. (1985). Enhancing instruction for maintenance, generalization, and adaptation. In K. C. Lakin & R. Bruininks (Eds.), *Strategies for achieving community integration of developmentally disabled citizens* (pp. 29-71). Baltimore: Paul H. Brookes.

Marholin II, D., & Touchette, P. E. (1979). The role of stimulus control and response consequences. In A. Goldstein & F. Kanfer (Eds.), *Maximizing treatment gains* (pp. 303-351). New York: Academic Press.

Renzaglia, A., & Aveno, A. (1986). *Domestic skills assessment forms: An individualized functional curriculum assessment procedure for students with moderate to severe handicaps.* (Available from University of Virginia, Curry School of Education, Charlottesville, VA)

Sailor, W., Guess, D., Goetz, L., Schuler, A., Utley, B., & Baldwin, M. (1980). Language and severely handicapped persons: Deciding what to teach to whom. In W. Sailor, B. Wilcox, & L. Brown (Eds.), *Methods of instruction for severely handicapped students.* Baltimore: Paul H. Brookes.

Snell, M. E. (Ed.). (1983). *Systematic instruction of the moderately and severely handicapped* (2nd ed.). Columbus, OH: Charles E. Merrill.

Stokes, T., & Baer, D. (1977). An implicit technology of generalization. *Journal of Applied Behavior Analysis, 10*, 349-367.

Striefel, S., & Cadez, M. J. (1983). *Serving children and adolescents with developmental disabilities in the special education classroom: Proven methods.* Baltimore: Paul H. Brookes.

White, O. R. (1985). Decisions, decisions . . . *British Columbia Journal of Special Education, 9*, 305-320.

White, O. R. (1986). Precision teaching-Precision learning. *Exceptional Children, 52*(6), 522-534.

White, O. R., & Haring, N. G. (1980). *Exceptional teaching* (2nd ed.). Columbus, OH: Charles E. Merrill.

White, O. R., & Haring, N. G. (1982). Data based program change decisions. In M. Stevens-Dominguez, and K. Stremel-Campbell, (Eds.), *Ongoing data collection for measuring child progress.* Seattle: University of Washington, College of Education, Western States Technical Assistance Resource (WESTAR).

II. STRATEGIES AND SOLUTIONS FOR THE CLASSROOM

Cindy is apprehensive her first day on the job at the Pacific Oyster Bar. She failed so badly at the Seattle Hotel. She looks carefully at the dishwasher, and loads the bowls and cups. She closes the door. She searches and finds the buttons on the side of the machine. They are strange, but the little stickers just below them are just like the ones at school. She confidently pushes the series, and smiles when the dishwasher hums into action. At the end of the day, the kitchen supervisor says, "Good work today, Ms. Burchart." He smiles as Cindy gets her coat and leaves. Still smiling, he looks again at the little stickers the trainer from the Seattle Training Center had put on each of the dishwashers. He thinks, "Well, you learn something new every day."

Richard leaves the office of the head housekeeper. As he wheels himself toward the chain of pink cabins of the Sunset Motel, he repeats to himself, "Knock. Then say, 'Housekeeping here.'' Over and over he says these instructions, just as Mr. White taught him to do when he was teaching him to say his name and address, all those years ago. He is pleased that he can practice by himself. At Cabin 1 he stops, squares his shoulders, and knocks briskly. "Housekeeping here." He unlocks the door and goes in to earn his first wage.

Jody is screaming so loudly that his face is eggplant purple again. Mrs. Loomis smiles to herself, and walks out the door to join the rest of the family waiting in the car, leaving Jody's shoes on the floor where he threw them. She gets in the car. "Now where's Jody?" asks Mr. Loomis. "Just wait," she replies. In 30 seconds, Jody comes flying out the door. "Don't forget to shut the door," cries his mother. She thinks with satisfaction of Jody's teacher—she was right, after all! Jody does know how to put on his own shoes.

Cindy, Richard, and Jody have generalized the skills they learned in school—their problems have been solved. In the second section of this book, we describe the procedures involved in facilitating generalization.

The first step is to identify the importance of generalization. If you are teaching a skill which should be useful to the student in a variety of situations, the IEP objective should so specify. We must begin to promote generalization by identifying it as the target of our instruction. In the following chapter, we describe how to write objectives for generalization.

Chapter 6

WRITING OBJECTIVES FOR GENERALIZATION

Felix F. Billingsley

Since the enactment of PL 94-142 in 1975, the development of instructional objectives has become a familiar part of the professional life of most special educators. Although variations may exist in practice, the structural components of a "good objective" seem generally agreed upon. Those components include identification of (a) the learner and the behavior to be taught, (b) the conditions under which the behavior will be assessed, (c) performance criteria including a date for completion, and (d) the person(s) responsible for assessing the behavior. Thorough discussions of those components can be found in many sources (e.g., Mager, 1975; Snell & Grigg, 1986). However, the following guidelines are provided for quick reference.

Overview of Basic Components of Objectives

The Learner and the Behavior

Objectives are written for a specific student. Although a number of students may be working on the same general goal, objectives should be tailored to meet individual needs. The particular student for whom the objective was developed, therefore, should be identified. It is especially important to note that instructional objectives are written for learners, not for teachers, and that the objective should indicate behaviors that will be acquired as a result of instruction, not experiences or instructional activities that the teacher provides. The behavior must be observable, must possess a definite beginning and end, and must be defined in specific terms. In the absence of observable behaviors, assessments of pupil performance must, at best, be based on inferences and/ or vague impressions.

Example 1.	"Jerome will transfer garments from the clothes hamper to the washing machine . . . " specifies the learner and a specific observable behavior.
Example 2.	"Jerome will be given the opportunity to participate in . . . " does not specify behaviors that will be acquired; rather, it indicates only the activities that will be provided.
Example 3.	"Jerome will transfer objects . . . " is not specific.
Example 4.	"Jerome will develop his knowledge of clothes washing procedures . . . " is not observable.

The Conditions

The objective should state those conditions under which the target behavior will be demonstrated and measured. As Snell and Grigg (1986) have noted, "This will include factors such as the physical setting, people present, the instructional materials and cues to be provided, and any other relevant variables that are expected to influence the student's performance" (p. 82).

Example 5. "When wearing pants pulled up to the knees after toileting in the bathroom at school, Jerome will independently . . . " states the conditions.

Example 6. "Given physical assistance at the forearm during lunch periods in the cafeteria, Jerome will scoop . . . " also states the conditions.

Example 7. "Jerome will pull up his pants . . . " does not state the conditions.

Example 8. "Jerome will scoop . . . " does not state the conditions.

The Criteria and Aim Date

Objectives must contain criteria for success which state exactly what level of performance is expected of the learner. Criteria should indicate, for example, how accurately the behavior must be performed, how rapidly the behavior must be performed, how quickly it must be initiated, and/or how long it must continue in order for mastery to be presumed. In addition, an aim date should be established which specifies when criterion levels of performance should be achieved.

Example 9. "Given a verbal direction by the teacher, Jerome will independently complete 8 of 10 steps in his hand washing program before lunch by June 10, 19__. Total time to complete the sequence should not exceed 3 minutes." This objective contains the criteria and aim date.

Example 10. "Jerome will walk independently using his walker at a rate of 150 feet per minute . . . by March 23, 19__," contains the criteria and aim date.

Example 11. "Jerome will independently wash his hands before lunch by June 10, 19__ . . . " does not adequately specify criteria.

Example 12. "Jerome will walk using his walker . . . " contains neither criteria nor the aim date.

Person(s) Responsible for Determining Success

Individuals responsible for determining successful completion of the objective should be specified. Traditionally, the classroom teacher has taken this responsibility. As the educational team mode of service delivery has gained widespread acceptance, however, and as it has become increasingly apparent that instructional success must be based largely on performance in nontraining situations, input from a variety of sources has become appropriate.

Example 13. "Jerome will have eaten his lunch at school consuming all items within 20 minutes on at least 5 consecutive occasions by December 4, 19__ as determined by the teacher. By that same date, Jerome will consume meals at home within a time period satisfactory to his parents as determined by weekly parental reports . . . " indicates the responsible individual(s).

Example 14. "Jerome will eat meals at school and at home within a satisfactory amount of time . . . " does not indicate the responsible individual(s).

Functional Behavior and Generalized Outcome

Although many educators may have become quite proficient in developing objectives which are "technologically adequate" (i.e., which contain components specified above), the value of those objectives may be diminished if target behaviors do not serve a useful function or fail to be performed under nontraining conditions. In other words, objectives should usually specify both functional skills and generalized outcomes.

Functionality

Behaviors are functional if they are demanded by or used in community, domestic, vocational, or recreational settings which are or will be accessed by the student and will permit at least partial participation in naturally occurring activities (Billingsley, 1984). Behaviors that are functional benefit the individual, and allow him or her to contribute meaningfully to the community, by at least:

- gaining access for the individual to a wider range of environments and/or natural reinforcers within an environment; and/or
- increasing the reinforcing value to others for interacting with the individual; and/or
- reducing the need for others to engage in activities on behalf of the individual which might be considered burdensome or effortful; and/or
- permitting the individual to engage in culturally normative, age-appropriate recreational activities

To be considered functional, then, a behavior must serve some current or future extrainstructional purpose of value to the individual and/or community. However, functionality does not always imply completely independent performance (see Example 19). For a more thorough discussion of the principle of partial participation, see Brown et al. (1979).

Example 15. "Jerome will floss his teeth . . . " could be functional.

Example 16. "Jerome will turn on the television . . . " could be functional.

Example 17. "Jerome will take out the garbage . . . " could be functional.

Example 18. "Jerome will shop for 15 specific brand grocery items . . . " could be functional.

Example 19. "Given support at the elbow, Jerome will wave the school colors at appropriate times during pep rallies . . . " could be functional for a student who experienced severe motoric impairment.

Example 20. "Jerome will verbally label words on flash cards . . . " is not functional because it specifies a skill that is not required in natural environments. On the other hand, objectives related to the ability to respond appropriately to exit or restroom signs and to vending machine cues could be very functional (Brown et al., 1979).

Example 21. "Jerome will touch his wrist, nose, knee, leg, foot, hair, and ear upon request . . ." is not functional because touching one's own body parts upon request is not required within nontraining environments. The activity is not useful to either the individual or the community.

Generalized Outcomes

It appears obvious that if a skill is to be truly functional it must be performed in those situations in which it would normally be demanded, not simply in a classroom simulation setting in the presence of a particular teacher. In other words, it is critical that performance of target skills *generalize* to nontraining environments. Because a major function of objectives is to act as guides to the selection of appropriate instructional methods and evaluation procedures, generalized outcomes should be specified in order to ensure that performance generalization receives consideration in both the planning of instructional programs and the assessment of student performance. Unfortunately, it has been found that a great many objectives written for students in special education programs specify performance of target behaviors in only a single training situation (Billingsley, 1984; Kayser, Rallo, Rockwell, Aillaud, & Hu, 1986).

An objective specifies a generalized outcome if it requires the student to perform the behavior in a situation or situations other than the one in which the student was trained. The new situation(s) could involve new locations, new people, different times, different materials, different examples of a concept, and so on.

Behaviors are generalized when they occur:

1. Across settings and/or time

Example 22. "Jerome will put on his pants after swimming (in gym) and after toileting . . . " is generalization if acquisition training occurred in the classroom.

Example 23. "Jerome will put on his pants . . . " does not specify generalization, although it could occur.

2. Across people

Example 24. "Jerome will say 'hi' to peers when visiting other classrooms or on the playground . . . " is generalization, if the peers were not involved in training.

Example 25. "Jerome will say 'hi' to his teacher when entering the classroom . . . " is not generalization across people if the teacher provided the training.

3. Across relevant objects

Example 26. "Jerome will turn pages on a variety of books and magazines . . . " is generalization, assuming some of the "variety" includes untrained materials.

Example 27. "Jerome will turn pages . . . " does not specify generalization.

4. As needed, as appropriate, spontaneously

Example 28. This is generalization: "Jerome will spontaneously request food using his communication board . . ."

Example 29. This is also generalization: "Jerome will wash his hands as appropriate (e.g., before eating, when dirty, after toileting) . . . " assuming that all such situations were not directly trained.

Example 30. "Jerome will use his communication board when asked by the teacher at language time . . . " is not generalization.

Example 31. "Jerome will wash his hands at the classroom sink when directed to do so . . . " is not generalization, assuming that other appropriate situations exist for the skill.

There are, of course, an infinite number of generalization possibilities. The relevant type of generalization should be determined by the nature of the skill and the environment(s) available to the student. Nontraining situations that are indicated in the objective should be representative of the range of situations in which the student will actually have the opportunity to perform the behavior outside of training. In other words, if shopping skills are being taught under simulation conditions, generalization situations specified in the objective should require assessment of the student's behavior in one or more of the types of stores which are likely to be accessible to the student in the community.

Here are some objectives that specify a generalized outcome:

Example 32. "By the end of the school year, Jerome will demonstrate the ability to shop independently at three different supermarkets on two occasions each: Joe's Market (6754 15th Avenue), Alice's Grocery (3508 Remington), and Fred's Quick Market (4449 15th Avenue) for 15 specific brand grocery items. Picture cards will be used as the grocery list. Performance includes travel to the store, selecting items, paying for the purchases, and transporting purchases back to school. Shopping must be completed without error within 1 hour and 15 minutes, and success will be determined by the teacher." (This example drawn from Wilcox & Bellamy, l982.)

Example 33.   "Following lunch, Jerome will independently clean the table of all crumbs and liquids with a sponge within 2 minutes on three consecutive occasions by May 9 as assessed by the teacher. By that same date, Jerome will have cleaned the dining room table at home to the satisfaction of his parents (in terms of duration and quality) at least once. Determination of success will be based on biweekly parental reports of acceptable skill performance."

Example 34.   "Provided verbal praise upon task completion, and using his right hand for assistance along the railing, Sam will ascend stairs (at home and at school) containing at least 12 steps at a rate of 40 steps per minute on one occasion in each setting by December 15. Success will be judged by the teacher."

Criteria for Generalized Performance

In example 32 above, it may be noted that differences in criteria for successful performance may exist within training and generalization situations. Such differential criteria may exist, and be entirely appropriate, for various reasons.

First, criteria selected for training may be dictated by constraints which exist only in the instructional environment. An objective might specify that, in training, a pupil will finish his snack within 15 minutes. Fifteen minutes may, of course, be a reasonable period of time for eating a snack, but—in this case—that particular duration was used for training purposes because the maximum length of time allotted for the classroom snack period was 15 minutes. Depending on conditions within the home, the generalization criterion could be less specific and indicate that the pupil could complete his after-school snack within a duration that was satisfactory to his mother or father.

Second, it may be beneficial to build "superfluent" performance within training settings to increase the ease with which the pupil can perform a new skill and thereby contribute to use of the skill in new situations (White, 1985). In other words, criteria for skill mastery may need to surpass normal demands in nontraining situations to ensure that the new skill will actually be used, particularly where competing behaviors exist (see Chapter 8 for discussion of competing behaviors). Generalization criteria in these cases might either be less precise than training criteria (e.g., stated in terms of satisfaction with performance by parents, co-workers, waitresses, or other significant individuals) or, where specific, absolute level of performance is desirable, they might be precise, but less stringent. For example, generalization criteria specifying precise minimum levels of performance might be included for a street crossing program or where significant individual (e.g., parent, employer) indicated a required performance level.

Third, it may be that it is extremely difficult or awkward for the teacher to obtain first hand information concerning the generalized performance of a skill within the natural setting in which the skill should be performed (e.g., taking off clothes in the bathroom before taking a shower in the evening). In such cases, generalization data may have to be collected by other individuals such as the parents (see Chapter 7, "Probing Skill Use," for a discussion of the assessment of generalized performance). Once again, depending on the specific situation and individuals involved, generalization criteria might best be stated in terms of satisfaction of other with the learner's performance.

Must Every Objective Include Generalization?

It should be noted that it is not necessarily desirable that all objectives specify a generalized outcome. It could be, for example, that independent eating skills are being trained using a backward chaining format in which a number of steps are taught one at a time and where considerable physical assistance is first provided and then systematically faded as training progresses. In such a case, the initial objectives in the instructional sequence might permit such a relatively small amount of independent behavior on the part of the student, and include such large amounts of manager assistance, that performance of the skills specified in the objectives would be of little value in natural settings. Generalization, then, might reasonably be excluded from such objectives until such time as enough of the steps in the chain have been learned to a level of mastery that makes the skills proficiently useful outside of training situations.

References

Billingsley, F. F. (1984). Where *are* the generalized outcomes? (An examination of instructional objectives). *Journal of the Association for Persons with Severe Handicaps, 9*(3), 186-192.

Brown, L., Branston, M. B., Hamre-Nietupski, S., Pumpian, I., Certo, N., & Gruenewald, L. (1979). A strategy for developing chronological-age-appropriate and functional curricular content for severely handicapped adolescents and young adults. *Journal of Special Education, 13*, 81-90.

Kayser, J. E., Rallo, P., Rockwell, G., Aillaud, W., & Hu, F. (1986). Review of IEPs. In W. J. Schill (Principal Investigator), *Institute for Transition Research on Problems of Handicapped Youth. Annual Report, 1985-86.* Washington, DC: U.S. Department of Education, Contract No. 300-85-0174.

Mager, R. F. (1975). *Preparing instructional objectives.* Belmont, CA: Fearon.

Snell, M. E., & Grigg, N. C. (1986). Instructional assessment and curriculum development. In M. E. Snell (Ed.), *Systematic instruction of persons with severe handicaps* (3rd ed., pp. 64-109). Columbus, OH: Charles E. Merrill.

White, O. R. (1985). Aim*star wars: Episodes II and III. *Journal of Precision Teaching, V*, 86-96.

Wilcox, B., & Bellamy, G. T. (1982). *Design of high school programs for severely handicapped students.* Baltimore, MD: Paul H. Brookes.

In Chapter 4, we saw that about 20% of the skills targeted for instruction had already generalized before instruction began. The time and effort spent on skill acquisition would better have been spent on figuring out why the student performed the skill other places and not at school! We have found that there is simply no substitute for direct assessments of generalization—before, during, and after the instructional program. It's not always obvious how to assess generalization, however, since a highly structural probe might effectively change that situation into a training situation. How do we establish "new" situations to make sure we are testing generalization? What types of performance are we looking for? The procedures for assessing generalization are explained in the following chapter.

Chapter 7

PROBING SKILL USE

Owen R. White

Good teachers monitor the instructional progress of each student on a frequent basis. Those evaluations are vital for making timely and appropriate instructional decisions. Presumably, however, teachers don't just want good *instructional* performance, they want their students to *use* their skills *outside the instructional situation* during the course of their daily lives. To find out whether that goal is achieved, special probes will have to be conducted.

General Probe Characteristics

Students should be prepared for the "real world," and skill-use probes should reflect that world as closely as possible. That has several implications for the way in which our probes should be conducted.

Probes Should be Conducted in a Representative Sampling of "Natural" Settings

Probes should be conducted in at least a sampling of the situations in which the skill might and/ or should prove useful. Occasionally a skill will be useful even if it is practiced in only one situation. If so, then that situation should be given the highest priority for evaluation, but every effort should still be made to evaluate the skill in as many different situations as possible.

> **Example 1:** Dressing is most important in the home, so a home probe should be given the highest priority. Dressing skills might also be useful outside the home, however, like before and after PE or swimming, or when spending the night with friends. Probes should also be conducted in those situations if at all possible.

> **Example 2:** Saying names of food items may be most useful in the school cafeteria or at home, but a really complete set of probes would also include restaurants and supermarkets, to see if the student is able to ask where an item is located.

Try to select situations which collectively represent a broad range of the situations in which the skill will eventually prove useful.

> **Example 3:** Dressing might be probed in "private" areas like the student's own bedroom and "public" areas like the locker room at the school or local swimming pool.

Example 4:   Shopping should be probed in both large and small stores which use different methods for labeling prices, different ways of displaying goods, and different check-out systems.

Of course, when trying to find a variety of different situations, it is still important to keep the real world in mind. Don't set up a meaningless situation simply to have something different.

Example 5:   Dressing behind a screen in the back of the classroom is *not* a good example of the situations in which the skill will be typically used.

Example 6:   Identifying important signs (e.g., "men," "women," "exit") would be appropriate in the school halls or the community, but after instruction is over, the student would *not* typically use those skills in a small communication-therapy room down the hall from the classroom.

Finally, probes should be conducted in situations which are noticeably different from the situation in which instruction took place. If instruction takes place in one or more of the situations in which the skill will be used, *something* about the way the probe is conducted should still be changed (e.g., the people involved, or perhaps the levels of assistance and cues used). Those other variables will be discussed later in this chapter.

Probes Should be Conducted at Natural Times and Upon Natural Opportunities

The general "setting events" or circumstances leading up to the probe should be as similar as possible to those which should eventually control the behavior.

Example 7:   Dressing in the classroom at precisely 11:00 each day just because it is convenient for the teacher is *not* natural. Dressing in the morning at home or after PE at school *is* natural.

Example 8:   Ordering fast food at lunchtime is natural, but going to a fast food restaurant and ordering food just after eating lunch at school is *not* natural.

The Number and Distribution of Opportunities Should Be Natural

Some behaviors occur only once or a few times each day while other behaviors will occur many times. Also, some behaviors will occur several times during a short period, while the occasions to use another skill might be distributed throughout the day. The number and distribution of opportunities to use a skill during a probe should be as natural as possible.

Example 9:   When a person has finished one dressing sequence, that's generally the end of it for a while. It is *not* natural to have a student get dressed, undressed, and dressed again several times in a row. To get at least two dressing sequences completed in a relatively short period, special activities might be scheduled (e.g., a trip to the swimming pool, a clothes shopping trip, or a dress rehearsal for a class play).

Example 10:   When people take bites to eat, they generally take several bites before the meal is finished. It *would* be natural, therefore, to assess several bites all in one short period. It would *not* be natural to let the student have only one chance to take a bite independently, and then remove the meal or immediately begin to feed the student yourself.

Example 11:   Using a communication board to answer questions could occur almost anywhere and at any time. However, it would *not* be natural to ask a student 105 questions during a 10-minute period, and then never ask another question all day.

People Who Would Naturally Be Involved Should Conduct the Probe

If the behavior involves interaction with a person, or people are at least likely to be present when the skill is employed, every attempt should be made to involve those people who would be most naturally involved.

Example 12: Most dressing tasks will be performed in the privacy of one's own home. If other people are involved to assist or are "just around," like a sibling who shares the same room, they are likely to be members of the family. It would not be natural for an unknown person or even the student's teacher to invade the student's bedroom to conduct a dressing probe. It might be natural for strangers to be around while a student gets dressed in a public locker room, but a stranger should *not* provide any direct assistance. If assistance is required in a task like dressing, it should be offered by someone the student knows.

Example 13: Under certain circumstances, virtually anyone might ask a student a question. In a communication program, therefore, a real mix of familiar and unfamiliar people would be appropriate. The nature of the question should be appropriate.

Example 14: Almost anyone might be around when a student is eating in a public place, or even in the home if the family has a visitor. However, it would generally *not* be appropriate for an unknown person to provide assistance to the student during the meal.

Natural Cues and Assistance Should Be Used

The cues or signals within the environment which tell the pupil when it is appropriate or inappropriate to behave in a certain way should be as natural as possible. That does not mean that cues cannot be enhanced a bit, if it is appropriate for the student's level of expertise, but such enhancements should be reasonable and the type of thing a person might do naturally to help someone out.

Example 15: Ideally, a student would automatically get dressed after getting out of bed in the morning, or following a shower. The probe should be constructed to allow the student the opportunity to demonstrate the skill given only those natural conditions. If the student does not begin to get dressed in a reasonable period, however, it is *also* natural for a parent or coach to nag a bit, "Come on, it's time to get dressed." When the student has not yet completely mastered all the steps in a dressing sequence, it might also be natural for parents or other familiar people to provide a little assistance like reminders about what to put on next, help in pulling up socks, or assistance in buttoning. Dramatic or elaborate forms of assistance like graduated guidance, molding, continuous tapping, or gesturing would *not* be natural in the typical dressing situation, and should be avoided.

Example 16: A host of natural cues could control requesting food at a fast food restaurant, including moving to the front of the line and hearing the person behind the counter say something like, "May I help you?" or "What would you like?" It might also be natural for a waitress to ask something very specific like, "Would you like a hamburger?" or for a friend or parent to provide alternatives—"Would you like a hamburger or chicken chunks?" It would *not* be natural for a person to hold up a picture card for the student to read, or to shout at the student, "HAMBURGER, say HAMBURGER!!!"

Example 17: Pointing to a picture on a communication board in response to a question should be prompted solely by the question itself. Many people would understand the purpose of a communication board, however, and might well add extra prompts like, "Point to a picture," or "Can you tell me by using your picture board?" It would be especially appropriate for a parent or friend to add such cues. It would *not* be natural for a relative stranger to take the pupil's hands and make the student touch each picture in turn while chanting, "Show me the answer, point. . . ."

Example 18: Walking should be prompted simply by the desire to get somewhere. Given a choice of walking, crawling, or being carried, if all three modes of locomotion are possible, the best probe for walking would be to simply see which way the student chooses to travel. To ensure proper motivation, special incentives might be provided (e.g., "Come to the kitchen and I'll fix you a snack"). If the student consistently chooses some other form of locomotion, like crawling, it could be forbidden, but if the student only walks when someone is there to prevent crawling, walking could not be considered as useful a skill as it might be, at least from the standpoint of the student. Some support might also be given, like holding the student's hand, or offering the student your arm. That would reduce the usefulness of walking, but being able to walk under those circumstances would still be better than not being able to walk at all. However, it would *not* be natural for the parent to crawl behind the child, tapping the back of each knee in turn to prompt each step; and it would *not* be useful for a helper to offer so much support that the student is virtually being carried.

Natural Consequences and Feedback Should Be Used

If a skill is to be truly useful, it must be maintained by natural consequences and feedback. As with cues and assistance, however, some exceptions might be made for a person who has not fully mastered a skill.

Example 19: The consequences for dressing are usually warmth and the avoidance of nasty (or lecherous) stares from other people. Children are sometimes also threatened with cost contingencies (e.g., "You won't get any breakfast unless . . ."), and they might also be praised if they get dressed nicely. It is not natural, however, to consequate each correctly performed step in a dressing sequence with a bit of Fruit-Loops, or following errors with "a physical mandate, an undoing of the step, and a request for the student to try again." A hurried parent is much more likely to consequate errors by scowling and doing it him/herself.

Example 20: The consequence for street crossing is usually getting closer to some destination. Special incentives could be provided for getting somewhere (e.g., "Let's go to the park and get an ice cream cone"), and it might also be appropriate to provide a little praise for crossing quickly and safely, or a sharp reproval for crossing when it was not safe. It would *not* be natural, however, to have a child cross a street just so he can turn around and cross back.

Example 21: The natural consequence for scooping food is getting it ready to bring it to one's mouth, even if we need some help getting it there. It helps if the food is something the student likes. Praise for good eating is not too unnatural, as long as it comes from a familiar person, and rebukes for slopping or slow scooping might also be in order. Occasionally it would even be natural to have one's food taken away for making too much of a mess, but it is *unlikely* that a parent or friend would naturally consequate errors with 50 trials of overcorrection or precisely 15.6 seconds of time out.

If a "Natural Probe" Doesn't Seem Reasonable . . .

As illustrated above, skill-use probes should attempt to emulate as closely as possible the conditions which are most likely to occur in the real world. If a "natural probe" doesn't seem reasonable, perhaps the usefulness of the skill should be questioned. Perhaps other skills in some hierarchy must be developed before skill-use probes make sense, or maybe the skill will *never* be useful and should just be dropped from the student's curriculum. In any event, if a natural probe doesn't make sense, *something* needs to be done.

When Should a Skill be Probed?

Most people only think to probe for skill use after the student has mastered the skill in an instructional setting. In fact, however, probing before instruction begins and frequently during the instructional sequence can be very useful.

Probe Before Instruction Starts

Students, even students with severe handicaps, are often much more capable than we think. Even after careful assessments of the student's skills in the classroom, surprises often abound.

Example 22: One teacher worked long and hard to get a student with severe handicaps to speak in two-word phrases, only to find out later that the child had been speaking in six- and seven-word phrases in the home for several years! Luckily, the student did not generalize his "school-skill" to the home, and regress to using shorter phrases there.

Example 23: Special therapists in a residential facility "taught" an adult with severe handicaps to eat with a spoon, only to discover that he had already been using that skill in other environments since he was very young. He had been transferred into a cottage where most of the other residents ate with their fingers, and he just decided to "do as the Romans do." Had they *asked* the resident to eat with a spoon before starting to shape it, . . .

Example 24: One parent decided to teach the alphabet to her young daughter with mild handicaps. Her special preschool instructors hadn't gotten to that skill in class, and it seemed a good idea to give her daughter a head start. When the mother began, however, her daughter rambled off the whole alphabet without a single error, and could even name the letters when shown to her at random. Why she wouldn't do it at school yet was a mystery.

Example 25: One teacher worked out a careful sequence of steps that would allow a youngster with multiple handicaps to transfer independently from his walker to the toilet. When stepped through the sequence during an initial assessment, the student started to make many errors (i.e., do something other than what was on the task analysis) and had to be corrected before things got out of hand. During the next few weeks he seemed to progress nicely in the program, but still forgot some of the steps, and had to be brought back to the right step in the sequence over and over again. Finally the teacher decided to just sit back and see what happened. The student made the transfer quickly and easily, without help—he just left out those steps in the sequence that seemed to be giving him trouble, and substituted a few other steps which worked just fine. The student probably had a better plan in mind all along.

The lesson should be clear. Just because a student hasn't been "taught" a skill, and just because the student doesn't "share" the skill when formally assessed, doesn't mean that the student can't apply the skill, or a useful alternative, in the real world where it really counts! In addition to traditional pre-instruction assessments therefore, it helps to *ask other people* (e.g., parents, friends, former teachers) what the student does, and to *observe the student in natural situations* to see what happens. Otherwise, one might expend a great deal of time and energy to develop and implement a program that might not be needed at all.

Probe as Often as Possible While the Skill is Being Developed

Assuming that the skill really does need to be taught, there still remains the question of *how well* the student must learn to perform the skill before it becomes useful. Suggestions for performance aims can be found in many books and curriculum guides, along with strategies for establishing individualized standards, but one never really knows how good is good enough until the usefulness of the skill is probed in a natural situation.

Example 26: The student with multiple handicaps in Example 25 who wrote his own task analysis" for transferring from the walker to the toilet might not have known how to perform that task before instruction began. Since his teacher did not try a "hands off" skill-use probe before starting the program, we'll never know. Because his teacher did probe for skill use before the student reached the instructional aim, however, at least the program was terminated before too much time was wasted.

Example 27: A therapist working on dressing skills with a young child with handicaps established a "buttoning" aim which seemed reasonable given the child's physical limitations. Since she did not really know how fast one should button before the skill is useful, however, she also asked the child's parents to pause each morning in the dressing sequence when it was time to button their daughter's blouse. They didn't have to say anything, just wait a moment or two. When the child was only halfway to her instructional aim she began to button her own buttons at home without any prompts or assistance. The parents said she was quick enough to make it worth their while to let her do it, and it was obviously worthwhile to the girl. Needless to say, the school program was terminated, with a likely savings of several weeks of instructional time and effort.

Probe After Instruction Ends

Skill-use probes before and during instruction can be very helpful and often result in better programs and/or a savings in time. Even if "before and during" probes are not conducted, however, it is absolutely essential to probe for skill use when a pupil has reached the instructional aim and the program is terminated. Quite simply, unless the child actually begins to use the skills we teach by the time we stop instruction, there is a very good chance that the skill never will be used, and all our efforts will have been wasted.

Example 28: A teacher in a class for elementary school children with mild handicaps worked a little each day to help one student overcome a minor speech impairment. She wanted to bring the student's fluency in saying the sounds correctly up to a level that was equivalent to the fluency of her nonhandicapped peers. After reaching the aim the program was terminated, but the teacher noticed that the girl slipped back into her old habits whenever she was engaged in conversation with one of the other children. The program was reinstated and kept in place until the child was able to say the sounds at normal fluency with no errors for nine days in a row. More probes revealed that the child still slipped back into her old habits, however, so the program was begun once again. This time the teacher doubled the fluency aim ("Now, Patsy, you have a problem, so you must be twice as good as most children . . ."). After reaching aim, Patsy began to use the correct speech patterns in all her conversations without being reminded. The extra week it took to reach the new aim was certainly well worth the effort.

Example 29:   When students with severe handicaps were evaluated in the fall at a secondary school, they could no longer perform several of the skills they had "mastered" the preceding spring. Before reteaching the skills, however, the parents were interviewed and it was discovered that in almost every case, the students remembered the skills they had been given opportunities to use over the summer, and forgot the skills they did not have the opportunity to practice. The students who had been given the opportunity to ride a bus, for example, remembered how to ride buses; the students who had no opportunity to ride buses over the summer had forgotten. After discussing the problem with the parents, some of the programs were dropped as being essentially meaningless for some students, and other programs were reinstated with assurances from the parents that opportunities to practice the skill would be provided. In both cases, time was saved and the individual curricula became more meaningful. Of course, if the issue of opportunities had been raised before the initial programs were implemented, even more time would have been saved.

It makes sense to probe immediately after the instructional aim has been reached, and again much later. Unless assurances are provided that the skills we teach are actually being used and continue to be used, a great deal of instructional time can be wasted.

Probe Whenever It is Practical

Ideally, skill-use probes would be conducted every day, or at least as often as instruction is provided. In some cases that is not difficult to arrange, like the buttoning program where the parents were simply asked to pause each day and give their daughter a chance to do it herself. It would also have been relatively easy for the teacher working with the speech impaired child to simply note how the child conversed with her peers for a few minutes during each lunch or recess.

In other cases it might be difficult or impossible to conduct skill-use probes very often. Some skills may be expensive, like shopping or ordering food in restaurants. In addition to the cost in dollars, however, it is also a good idea to consider the time and good will of people involved in the probes. Parents might not object to occasional trips to the library to give their child the opportunity to practice his skills, but they are not likely to feel very good about a request that they do that every day.

Finally, if the same people conduct essentially the same probe too often, the student might learn to perform well in that situation, but still not be able to perform the skill with other people or in slightly different situations. It's a good idea to rotate people and situations as often as possible, both to reduce the effort required of any given person, and to provide more information about a wider range of skill-use situations.

How Should a Probe be Conducted?

Three basic strategies are available for probing skill use. (1) asking people who know; (2) asking people to find out; and (3) directly observing the behavior yourself.

Just Asking—Retrospective Reports

The easiest and least expensive way to evaluate skill use is simply to ask one or more people who are in a natural position to know. To learn if a child is toilet trained, for example, one might only have to ask the parents how many times they had to clean up after accidents over the last few days. Accidents are hard to miss, so parents could generally be relied upon to know. Of course, if the parents have the child on a schedule, going to the bathroom at regular intervals and helping the child undress and eliminate, the parents might not know if the child was already trained, and they would have to be asked to give the child more opportunities to act independently before an accurate assessment could be made.

Simply asking someone whether a skill is being used is a good strategy when . . .

(1) One or more people can be identified who are in a good position to be aware of skill usage.

Parents are an obvious choice, but depending upon the skill, school personnel, friends, or even strangers might be appropriate. After a student has made a purchase and left a store, for example, the clerk might be asked whether there had been any difficulty in the transaction and whether the student had used certain "key behaviors" he had been taught.

(2) Natural opportunities exist for the behavior in sufficient number to allow the observer to make an accurate assessment.

Behaviors which are truly self-initiated (i.e., the child can begin the skill without any assistance) are probably the best candidates for evaluations by simple reports. Expressive communication, assuming that all necessary materials are available, would be good, but responsive communication like "answering questions" might pose a difficulty if no one ever thinks to ask a question. Reliable reports could also be obtained for behaviors like toileting and walking, but as noted above, parents might inadvertently restrict the opportunities for even those behaviors. Before relying on any report, therefore, be sure to ask whether the opportunity to use the skill really exists.

(3) The consequences of the behavior or failing to behave are dramatic.

If the behavior or the consequences of failing to behave appropriately are dramatic and hard to overlook, people are much more likely to make accurate reports. If a child had always scooted on the floor to get around and suddenly started to walk, that would be hard to overlook. On the other hand, if the behavior is rather subtle, people might simply not notice whether it occurs or not. For example, most parents really don't know if their young children use a palmar grasp or a pincer grasp, even if they know the difference between the two grasps. That sort of behavior is simply too easy to overlook, unless we are specifically asked to assess it.

To get reports from informed people . . . It is best to solicit reports in person or by telephone. It will then be possible to follow up immediately on unexpected statements and to engage in a conversation to elicit the specific information desired.

(1) Prepare a list of questions ahead of time.

Prepare a list of key questions before beginning your interview. There is nothing wrong with ad-libbing somewhat, but you must have a clear idea of the critical issues to be addressed. The items outlined below should provide some ideas for that list.

(2) Describe the skill of interest and ask if they have seen the student use it.

Generally, it's best to keep things simple. Instead of asking whether a child performs each step in a self-feeding program correctly, for example, it's best to simply ask the parent if the child eats without assistance. If the answer is "yes," then you might want to know a bit more about the specifics—does he serve himself, does he scoop, does he spill food on the way to his mouth, and so on. If the answer is "no," then you might have to focus on more specific substeps in the task. Still try to keep questions rather general, however, so you have the chance to discover whether the student uses variations in the skill different from those which you are teaching. If you ask whether the child scoops his food from the right-to-left side of the plate, for example, you might never discover that he does perfectly well at home scooping from the front-to-back.

It may also be useful to ask about a broader behavior than you have really been teaching or plan to teach. Even though you might only be working with scooping in an eating program, for example, you might begin by asking about "independent eating" in general. Broad questions can sometimes reveal many surprises, and if they don't, you can always ask more specific questions about the actual subskill of interest.

Finally, there are times when you will need to be very specific. After asking whether the child picks up small objects, for example, you might need to describe the difference between a palmar grasp and a pincer grasp in order to get an accurate report from the parents concerning that important variation in the skill. Leave those detailed questions for the last, however.

(3) Establish whether there are sufficient opportunities for the behavior to occur.

If the person reports that the skill is not used, be sure to ask whether there are any opportunities for the skill to occur. If they report, for example, that the child does not eat without assistance, ask them if they ever give the child the chance, or whether they simply feed the child without letting him try. Even if the person reports that the skill is used, be sure to find out how often they have seen it. Occasionally a person will report that a skill is being used, but can only remember seeing it once, several months ago. Reports of skill use more than a few days old should not be trusted too much.

(4) Establish the conditions under which the skill is used.

If the skill is used, try to determine the conditions under which it occurs. Does the student use the skill "spontaneously," or only "after a little nagging"? Are special cues or prompts necessary? Is any special assistance provided? What happens after the skill has been performed—is the child consequated in any special fashion, or does he simply get whatever the natural outcome of the skill would be? Often the answers to such questions can be useful in identifying ways of making the instructional program more effective, and until the skill is used under conditions which can really be called at least an approximation of "natural conditions," the program cannot be considered a complete success.

(5) Ask for a summary statement of "satisfaction."

Before closing the conversation, ask for an overall evaluation of the skill—if, of course, it is being used at all. It sometimes helps to provide a little structure to the question, like asking whether the behavior is "just fine," or "o.k., but it could still improve," or "pretty bad, and not worth the effort." A parent might report that the child can eat independently, but that the time necessary to clean up the mess after letting him try makes it unlikely that many opportunities will be provided. That would be very important information for determining whether a program can be considered a success.

Getting Someone to Look—Direct Observations by Someone Else

If a person who could be expected to have seen this skill already, if and when it is used, cannot be identified, it may be necessary to ask someone to look for it.

Asking someone to look for skill usage is a good strategy when . . .

(1) The behavior is "private" or easily overlooked.

Some behaviors may go relatively unnoticed, like recreational or leisure skills which are generally performed alone, or whether the child consistently says "thank you" after being helped in the community. In such cases, it might be necessary to ask someone to make a specific effort to observe the skill.

(2) Key features of the behavior are subtle.

It is often unreasonable to expect even concerned persons to make subtle distinctions about certain key features of a skill. Parents might not notice certain speech patterns, for example, or exactly how their child manipulates objects. In addition to asking a person to be more vigilant, therefore, it might be necessary to provide a little training in how the skill can be identified and evaluated.

(3) Good opportunities for the skill to be used do not occur often enough for a meaningful evaluation.

Opportunities might have to be created for the proper evaluation of a skill. If parents are used to feeding their child, they might be asked to provide at least some opportunity for the child to eat independently. Or perhaps special equipment, like a communication board or walker, must be sent to the new situation before the skill can be assessed. It might also be necessary to provide guidance concerning the way in which those opportunities should be provided. If placing a normally wheelchair-bound student in a walker doesn't seem to produce results, the parents might be told to provide a gentle push on the back (i.e., the cue used in instruction) to get things going.

To solicit direct observations by other people . . .

(1) Prepare a small packet of necessary materials.

Unlike retrospective reports, it is generally a good idea to provide people with a prepared set of materials when asking them to make a special effort to observe a skill. Those materials might include a brief description of the skill to be observed, examples or illustrations (e.g., a drawing of the way in which the child should be sitting), suggestions as to how the observation might be conducted (e.g., the time of day; general activity; allowable cues, assistance, or consequences), and perhaps a special form for recording the results of the observation. Of course, any necessary equipment (e.g., communication boards or arm splints) should also be provided if it is not already available in the situation where the observation will take place.

Any suggestions concerning when and how the observation should be conducted should stress the idea that conditions should be kept as natural as possible. The observer should be directed to terminate the observation if it appears necessary to provide so much assistance or guidance that the skill would no longer serve any reasonable purpose. If possible, the observer should be asked to try and observe the skill on several occasions before making a final evaluation.

Special materials should be brief and simple—no more than a page or two, if at all possible. The procedures which you ask the observer to employ should also work from the general to the specific, just as in the case described above for retrospective reports. That is, observers should first try to elicit the most general skill in the least intrusive manner possible (e.g., simply placing a student near the walker and seeing what happens). If that fails to elicit the skill, the observer can become more and more specific in setting up or guiding the activity.

(2) Provide special training, if necessary.

When the target skill has one or more "key features" which might be difficult to evaluate, it might be necessary to provide the observer with a little training. Frequently that can take the form of having the person come into the school and observe several children who do and do not display the skill in question. Alternatively, the teacher might visit the observation site and demonstrate to the observer how to set up and conduct probes.

As with materials, training should be as brief and simple as possible. Training should involve some active participation on the part of the new observer, however. Don't just demonstrate the skill to the observer, ask the new observer to demonstrate it as well. Don't just show how the probe should be conducted, ask the new observer to practice it while you are still there to provide feedback.

(3) Follow up the activity with an interview.

After the observer has had the opportunity to probe the skill, meet with or call the observer to find out what happened. That interview would generally take the same form described earlier for retrospective reports.

Looking—Conducting Direct Observations Yourself

If other willing people cannot be found, or the skills necessary to observe and evaluate the skill are too sophisticated for other people to employ, you will have to conduct the observation yourself. That can be a disadvantage in many cases, not only because of the added effort required on your part, but also because you might know too much about the conditions under which the behavior might occur and/or have become too much a part of the conditions which signal the student to use the skill. To avoid those problems, you should:

(1) Avoid using special conditions or cues associated strongly with instruction.

Being familiar with the instructional program will make it difficult for you to be "natural." Out of habit, there will be a tendency for you to use the special cues, prompts, levels of assistance, and consequences that are used during instruction. Even if those events are reasonable approximations of "natural events" (e.g., providing some praise after a correct application of the skill), you must strive not to use them extensively, and to intermix them with other events which are not used during instruction, but which are likely to occur outside instruction.

(2) Be as unobtrusive as possible.

In some cases you will not have to work directly with the individual in order to conduct the observation. To evaluate shopping skills, for example, you need only be "around" when the shopping expedition takes place. That reduces the threat of using "unnatural events," but it doesn't necessarily mean that you won't influence the outcomes. Just being there, as you are during instruction, can serve as a special "signal" to the student to behave in a particular way. The student might perform the shopping skills just fine, as long as he knows you are looking, but fall to pieces the minute you're out of sight. Unless you always plan to take him shopping, that poses a problem.

To minimize the effects of your presence, you should try to be as unobtrusive as possible. If you can, conduct the observation covertly, so the student has no idea that you are there at all. If a completely covert observation is impossible, then at least be as "natural" as you can. Stroll casually around the store, keeping the student in sight; don't hover within inches of his back with a stopwatch and clipboard in hand, madly recording his every move.

A Summary Checklist

Probes for skill use can provide very important information for deciding what to teach, how to teach, and when instruction can be safely terminated. Probes can often be quite easy and simple to conduct, but they must be carefully planned to provide the most meaningful information possible.

Be Natural

It is most important to construct probes that reflect the natural conditions under which the skill will be used. That includes:
- Natural settings
- Natural times and opportunities
- Natural number and distribution of opportunities
- With people who would naturally be involved
- Natural cues and assistance
- Natural consequences

If it seems difficult to think of the natural conditions under which a skill would be used, then perhaps the skill isn't really important and shouldn't be taught.

Probe Often

Whenever possible, skill-use probes should be conducted:
- Before an instructional program is developed
- During the instructional process
- After the instructional aim has been reached, but before the program is terminated
- Long after the program is terminated to see if skill-use has maintained

If it's not possible to check for skill use at least after the student has reached the instructional aim, then you're taking a great risk that all the instruction will have gone to waste.

Probe Efficiently

- Just ask someone who should know if the skill is being used. If that's not possible,
- Ask someone to make a special effort to see if the skill is being used, or as a last resort,
- Conduct direct observations of the skill yourself.

In any event, conduct the probe as efficiently and unobtrusively as possible.

An analysis of the learner's behavior and interactions with the generalization situation is vital to matching generalization strategies to the specific problems of a learner. In this chapter, we describe the critical problems encountered in generalization, and how strategies can work to solve those problems. We also provide specific examples of how strategies may be individualized for each skill situation.

Chapter 8

STRATEGIES TO IMPROVE GENERALIZATION

Kathleen A. Liberty and Felix F. Billingsley

This chapter provides descriptions and examples of the types of problems which can prevent generalization, and explanations and descriptions of strategies that can remediate the problem and facilitate generalization. Additional applications and information about the strategies may be found in Chapter 2. The decision rules presented in the next chapter will guide the identification of the type of problem experienced by a learner in a particular generalization situation and thus the selection of a category of strategies from which a specific technique may be selected.

The first category is designed for skills which are to be generalized to only a few situations. Subsequent categories include strategies designed to remediate problems caused by noncontingent reinforcers, competing behaviors and competing reinforcers; problems with the nature of reinforcement or other consequences, problems affecting the discrimination of appropriate stimuli in the generalization situation; and problems with the general format used to program for generalization.

Limited Generalization Situations

Generalization may occur across many different dimensions (see Chapter 1), although generalization across settings is the term often described in the professional literature (e.g., Falvey, 1986). Some skills are very setting-specific. For example, you may target grocery shopping, which involves skills specifically appropriate for grocery stores.

Generalization is therefore "limited" to grocery stores, but a great many other dimensions of generalization must be considered—to new items on the shopping list, to items in different sections of the store, to different checkers, to different stores. So, you can see that although the *general setting* is specific, there are many *situations* to which generalization may be desired. It may be possible to train generalized skills in a few representative settings, but training in one or two "natural" settings may not result in generalization across all of the desired situations (see Chapter 2). However, it is possible to identify some skills which are applicable in only a very few situations, and which have very few dimensions across which generalization is desired. The strategy of "train in desired situation" is designed to avoid generalization problems for the latter class of skills.

If you desire the behavior to be performed in many different untrained situations, as when expressive communication of "yes" and "no" is desirable in the classroom, the home, and the community, and with all the people, question-types, inflections, etc. the student will ever encounter, this strategy is not appropriate. It is improbable that you would be able to provide instruction in *all* of these situations—so strategies which facilitate generalization across situations (as those discussed in subsequent sections of this chapter) are likely to be more efficient than trying to teach all of the settings and dimensions of generalization where the skill is desired.

If the behavior is desirable in only a limited number of situations, it may be most efficient to simply train the behavior in the situation(s) in which it is desired—if it is possible to provide training in those situations.

Strategy: Train in the Target Situations

This will be efficient if the behavior itself is appropriate only in one situation, or in a very small number of situations, and if it is possible to conduct training in those situations. This strategy can be applied to behaviors which are designed for only two or three situations by training first in one situation, then in a second, then in a third. Stokes and Baer (1977) called this "sequential modification." Articles which describe training in the desired situation are listed in the bibliography at the end of this chapter.

If it is not possible to train in a particular situation, or if it is impossible to train in *all* situations, you can provide instruction in one setting, *probe* for generalization in other situations, and use the other strategies described in this chapter to facilitate generalization.

Problem and Solution, Example 1. Doug moved into the Ravenna Avenue Group Home when he turned eighteen. The director has requested that Doug learn how to operate the washer and dryer. Ms. Anderson, Doug's teacher, looks over Doug's current schedule. Most of his time is spent in vocational training—Doug has been progressing well as a bakery trainee, and now works part-time at the Tastee Bakery. It looks like Doug will eventually be living in the group home and working full-time at Tastee Bakery after he graduates from high school. Ms. Anderson decides that the most efficient way to teach Doug to use the washer and dryer at the group home is to provide instruction there. She visits the group home and inspects the washer and dryer, talks with the director, and several of the residents. A young man from a local church volunteers to teach Doug and several other residents how to wash and dry their clothes. Ms. Anderson and the director develop the program and assist the volunteer in learning how to run it. Doug is trained directly in the situation in which the skills will be applied, so in this case skill mastery will mean skill application in the desired setting.

Noncontingent Reinforcer, Competing Behavior, and Competing Reinforcer Problems

Sometimes reinforcers that are naturally available for performing new, instructed behaviors are provided whether the pupil performs those behaviors or simply does nothing. When that happens, we refer to noncontingent reinforcement. A frequent result of noncontingent reinforcement is that the pupil will fail to perform the instructed behavior in a reliable manner, if at all. In other cases, competing behaviors may be reinforced in generalization settings. Competing behaviors are those which exist in a pupil's repertoire prior to instruction which function to access the reinforcers which are naturally available for performing the new, instructed behavior. The maintenance of competing behavior may result in pupils performing those behaviors rather than the instructed behavior outside of the training situation. A similar outcome may occur when attention or other consequences follow undesirable behavior and thereby compete with the reinforcer available for the target behavior. If a reinforcer which follows an undesirable behavior is different from and stronger than that which follows an instructed behavior, a competing reinforcer problem exitst and the undesirable behavior may be the one which is performed.

The following examples illustrate either noncontingent reinforcer, competing behavior, or competing reinforcer problems, as identified at the end of each example. Interventions designed to facilitate generalization in each case are described later in this section.

The function of strategies described in this section is to ensure that the instructed behaviors emitted by pupils result in more effective reinforcement than (1) the absence of such behaviors or (2) other, undesirable behaviors.

Problem, Example 2. Robert is learning to hold his head up. During instruction, his teacher sits next to him and praises him and talks to him as long as his head is up. When his head is down, she moves away. Although Robert will now keep his head up whenever his teacher is near, the rest of the day his chin is on his chest. The teacher notices, however, that other people and classmates come up and talk to Robert anyway.

Because the attention and activity are available whether or not Robert has his head up, this is a noncontingent reinforcer problem.

Instructed Behavior:	head up
Natural Reinforcer:	see people, attention, activity
Noncontingent Reinforcer:	attention, activity

Problem, Example 3. Sally's teachers are delighted that she has learned how to answer yes/no by pointing to large colored figures taped to her wheelchair tray table. Despite her severe cerebral palsy, Sally answers her teachers quickly and consistently. However, she is answering her peers and other adults more slowly and much less consistently.

Observation of the natural consequences for Sally's answers showed that the adults with whom she interacted tended to either ignore her answers (e.g., Sally was given popcorn even after she answered "No" to the question, "Do you want some popcorn?"), ask questions where Sally really had no choice (e.g., "Do you want to go home?"—asked as she was being put on the bus), or to ask questions without waiting for an answer.

Because the attention and activity are available whether or not Sally answers questions, this is a noncontingent reinforcer problem.

Instructed Behavior:	answer question
Natural Reinforcer:	objects and events provided by others
Noncontingent Reinforcer:	objects and events provided by others

Problem, Example 4. Todd is 8 years old and has spina bifida. For the last several years, his primary means of locomotion when out of his wheelchair has been to scoot along the floor in a sitting position. Last year, his teacher and his parents agreed to work on alternatives for independent locomotion more closely approximating normal styles of locomotion, since Todd was getting pretty big to scoot around. The teacher implemented a 10-step instructional program to teach him to walk with crutches. After 7 months, he could get around on crutches without assistance. When she reported his progress to his parents, they purchased crutches for Todd to use at home.

Todd has a new teacher this year, and he assessed Todd's walks-with-crutches behavior. Todd's rate had slipped considerably from where it was at the end of the previous year. His teacher instituted a program that required Todd to use the crutches frequently, and within a few weeks Todd met his previous aim. In preparation for the IEP meeting, the teacher called Todd's parents, who reported that Todd never used his crutches at home. According to his father, "Todd just loves to scoot."

Because the reinforcer of getting from one place to another is natural to both walking and scooting this is a competing behavior problem.

Instructed Behavior:	walks with crutches
Natural Reinforcer:	gets quickly to desired place
Competing Behavior:	scoots on fanny

Problem, Example 5. Sharon, who is nonverbal, grabs for what she wants—rather than indicating her desires with a more appropriate request behavior whenever food is served family style. Her teacher decides to teach Sharon to point for desired food items at lunch rather than to grab for them. The teacher wants Sharon's pointing to generalize to other situations, so she also assesses Sharon's behavior at morning snack time in another room with a different manager. Sharon grabs there, too.

After four days of the program, she was pointing all but once or twice during lunch. During snack, however, Sharon didn't do so well. She continued to grab much more than she pointed, even after she met her aim in training.

Because the natural reinforcer of getting what one wants is available for both pointing and grabbing, this is a competing behavior problem.

Instructed Behavior:	point for food
Natural Reinforcer:	food
Competing Behavior:	grabs food

Problem, Example 6. Chris learned to dress himself as a result of his teacher's systematic dressing program. At the end of the program, he could put on his shirt, pants, socks, and loafers.

At home, he screams rather than gets dressed; ear-splitting, nerve-shattering screams. And he continues screaming until his mother dresses him. Whenever his mother tries to encourage Chris to dress himself, his screams escalate into full-scale tantrums, complete with clothes-tearing and breath-holding, and getting him dressed takes forever.

Because Chris's mother dresses him, the reinforcement is available even if he does not dress himself. This is probably a competing behavior problem.

Instructed Behavior:	puts on shirt, pants, socks and shoes
Natural Reinforcer:	gets dressed/goes on to next activity
Competing Behavior:	screams and tantrums

In this example, a competing reinforcer for tantrums in the form of attention from Chris's mother may also be present. Obviously, more than one problem can exist at a time.

Problem, Example 7. Colin, who is 4 years old and nonverbal, enjoys being hugged and cuddled by his parents. To get what he wants, he has learned to walk up to his mother or father and bang his head on the most convenient object—the refrigerator produces an excellent deep tone, and the floor is always available. When he emits this dramatic behavior, his parents almost always pick him up and cuddle him, regardless of what else they might have been doing.

His teacher realizes that head-banging brings attention, so he decides to teach Colin an alternative behavior. He instructs him in the use of the Exact English manual sign for "hug" and, very soon, whenever he wants a cuddle at school, he signs "hug" for it.

At home, however, his parents sometimes ignore or miss seeing the sign. Before long, Colin begins to bang his head again at home, although maintaining the more desirable communicative behavior in the classroom.

Because the natural reinforcer for the "hug" sign (attention and cuddling) also follows head banging, this is a competing behavior problem.

Instructed Behavior:	signs "hug"
Natural Reinforcer:	attention, cuddling
Competing Reinforcer:	head-banging

Problem, Example 8. Where undesirable behaviors are maintained by their own, particular reinforcers, it is common that systematic behavior deceleration programs are developed and implemented in training settings concurrent with programs designed to build new, functional behaviors. Typical behavior deceleration strategies might include, for example, differential reinforcement of other behaviors (DRO), response cost, and time out. This example, and the associated solution, reflect the presumption that many failures of skill generalization due to competing reinforcers are actually failures to obtain generalized suppression of the undesired behavior.

Terry's rather dramatic stereotypic behaviors (hand flapping and "light filtering") have been brought under control in his elementary school classroom by using DRO. Generally, he makes good progress in programs designed to teach functional skills in training situation where natural outcomes (including praise) are used as the principle reinforcers. Many of the skills he has learned, however, fail to carry over into other areas of the school, his home and other nontraining environments, even though members of the school staff and his parents compliment Terry's efforts on appropriate occasions. Large amounts of Terry's time outside of the classroom are spent engaging in stereotypic behavior.

Because Terry performs an activity other than the instructed behavior and the consequences for that activity appear to differ from those which follow instructed behaviors, this could be a competing reinforcer problem.

Instructed Behavior:	various functional skills
Natural Reinforcer:	verbal praise
Undesirable Behavior:	hand flapping, light filtering
Competing Reinforcer:	sensory stimulation

Table 8-1

Example of Observation to Determine Natural
Schedule of Reinforcers

Response: Lifts head and holds head up
Aim: 100% of the time

Events shown below occurred during the generalization situation. Natural reinforcers for "lifts head" include being able to see what's going on around you, and opportunity for social contact.

Time of Day	Student Behavior	Event Following
9:00	head down	No activity near student.
9:01	"	"
9:02	"	"
9:03	lifts head	"
9:04	head down	"
9:05	"	"
9:06	lifts head	Peer says "Hi" to student.
9:07	head up	Peer and Teacher set up puppets in vicinity of student— student watches.
9:08	"	Teacher finishes setting up puppets, moves away from student.
9:09	head down	No activity near student.
9:10	"	"
9:11	lifts head	"
9:12	head down	"
9:13	"	Teacher and group of students come over to the puppets.
9:14	lifts head	Teacher/pupils play with puppets
9:15	head up	Puppet "talks" to student.
9:16	"	Puppet "talks" to student.
9:17	"	Puppet goes to another student.
9:18-9:23	"	Puppets talking to students.
9:24	"	Teacher & students put puppets away.
9:25-9:35	head down	No activity near the student.
9:36	lifts head	"
9:37-9:40	head down	"

Total Observation Time: 40 minutes

"Lifts head" was followed by a natural reinforcer twice. The reinforcing nature of these events is easy to identify, since in both cases the student continued to keep her head up until the event ceased.

    This schedule is: VR 2 (4 responses, 2 reinforced) and
                            VI 20' (40 minutes, 2 reinforcers)

How to Identify Natural Reinforcers

Reinforcers are events which immediately follow the response, and which increase the probability that the behavior will occur again. Behaviors that are reinforced either accelerate (i.e., occur with increasing frequency) or are maintained at levels sufficient to access reinforcement. To identify possible reinforcers, observe other individuals performing the target behavior in the generalization situation(s) and record all of the events which follow the performance of the desired response (an example is shown in Table 8-1).

If you have time for multiple observations, you may be able to determine which of the events you observed in the generalization situation are the actual reinforcers, but even with successive observations, it may not be clear. Therefore, it might be better to assume that all of the events act to reinforce the behavior. Remember, behavior may be reinforced by the termination of events, and even by the occurrence of events that you might think are obnoxious.

How to Identify Noncontingent Reinforcers, Competing Behaviors, and Competing Reinforcers

Observe in the generalization situation. Write down the exact behavior of the student including the instructed behavior if it occurs, and any other behavior, especially if you think it is inappropriate.

Next, write down the exact events which follow each behavior—including the activities and words of other people, changes in the environment, etc.

As a result of your observations, you should be able to identify the competing behavior and the natural reinforcers, as well as any events which might be reinforcing the competing behavior. If those reinforcing events differ from the natural reinforcers which follow the instructed behavior, they are probably competing reinforcers.

Many undesirable behaviors that may at first appear to have consequences which are different from trained behaviors ultimately result in the same consequences. For example, self-injurious behavior may result in escape from a task. Some of the consequences that follow escape may be different from those which are likely to follow task performance; however, escape may also allow access to many of the same consequences (i.e., the opportunity to engage in a more pleasurable activity). It is recommended, therefore, that a competing reinforcer problem be identified only after strategies for noncontingent reinforcers or competing behaviors have been tried with unsuccessful results.

Strategy: Increase Proficiency

Increase the relative efficiency of the instructed/desired response by increasing the performance aim for the target skill, and then reinstitute instruction in the training setting to build fluency to that level. This should insure that the new skill will access reinforcers more efficiently than the competing behavior.

How to Determine a Competitive Performance Aim

In the training situation, determine how quickly the student obtains reinforcement for the target response. With a stopwatch, measure the time from the beginning of the response or response chain until the time the reinforcer is obtained. You may need to collect data for several trials to determine the average length of time.

In generalization situations, determine how quickly the student is reinforced for the competing behavior, using the same procedures as for the target behavior. Compare those data. If the competing behavior results in faster reinforcement than does the target behavior, set the fluency aim for the target behavior to be faster than the competing behavior.

Solution, Example 4 (Competing Behavior). In Todd's situation, although he walked with crutches fast enough to satisfy his teacher, it was still more efficient for him to scoot to get what he wanted. His teacher reasoned that if Todd could crutch-walk faster than he could scoot, then he would use the crutches—so he measured the speed of Todd's scooting and established a new aim for walking which was faster than the scoot rate. Then he reinstituted the instructional procedures he had used at the first of the year until Todd met the new aim. Sure enough, when Todd found out that he could get around faster with crutches, he stopped scooting at home.

Strategy: Amplify Instructed Behavior

Determine whether the new behavior is capable of reliably securing the available natural reinforcer in the generalization setting. If it isn't, then additional instruction in the training setting to modify or augment the instructed behavior may be required.

Solution, Example 4 (Competing Behavior). In Todd's case, it was possible for the teacher to increase his crutch-walking proficiency until he met a competitive performance aim. In some mobility training programs, however, such a strategy might not be effective. For example, an objective might specify independent walking as an outcome. After considerable instructional effort, however, it might be found that the pupil is unable to achieve a faster rate of walking than crawling due to physically handicapping conditions. The "amplification" strategy under these circumstances could potentially involve the use of equipment that would facilitate efficient locomotion. Perhaps the use of a walker or crutches would do the trick.

Solution, Example 7 (Competing Behavior). The sign Colin learned was simply too easy to ignore or miss in a nontraining environment—unlike his head-banging, which was almost impossible to miss. Head-banging functioned both to get his parents' attention and to get hugged.

An appropriate intervention would be to teach Colin some behavior which would get his parent's attention; but which would be less dangerous than head-banging—like tapping his parents' arm. Once he had his parent's attention, he could then sign "hug" for his cuddle.

Strategy: Alter Generalization Contingencies

In the case of noncontingent reinforcer and competing behavior problems, ask people in the generalization situations (or train them, if necessary) to allow only the new behavior to access reinforcers. This strategy is designed to increase the reliability of the new behavior in securing reinforcers and to decrease the reliability and/or efficiency of any old, competing behavior.

In the case of competing reinforcer problems, ask a variety of people in generalization situations to use the deceleration procedure employed in training settings. Provide training as necessary. The purpose of this strategy is to both reduce the relative strength of reinforcers associated with undesirable behaviors and to establish individuals in nontraining environments as effective stimuli for the control of those behaviors. It is possible that, as the student experiences multiple examples of situations in which deceleration tactics will be applied, a more generalized reduction across additional settings and people will be observed. Where it is difficult for relevant individuals (e.g., parents) to apply the deceleration procedure in generalization settings, it may be possible to "preprogram" such individuals as controlling stimuli by inviting them to participate in administration of the procedure within the school for a short period of time each day (cf. Marholin & Touchette, 1979).

Solution, Example 2 (Noncontingent Reinforcer). Robert's teacher could either ask people to ignore him when his head is down and to talk to him when his head is up, or else put a sign on his wheelchair requesting this. As long as the reinforcer is available for doing nothing, there is no "reason" for Robert to engage in the behavior.

Solution, Example 3 (Noncontingent Reinforcer). One might alter contingencies for Sally to answer questions. Adults could be asked to pay attention to Sally's answers and to avoid asking meaningless questions—generalization probes could then be extended to untrained questioners. A small sign could be put on Sally's wheelchair requesting that questioners follow such procedures; one might probe to determine if such a procedure was effective in altering questioner contingencies, although certainly the original conditions of generalization have been altered.

Solution, Example 5 (Competing Behavior). For Sharon, the grabber, the intervention during snack consisted of two steps. First, contingencies were altered so that only pointing was successful in obtaining food—increasing the reliability of pointing. This was accomplished by a simple intervention (cf. Billingsley & Neel, 1985): if she grabbed, the food she grabbed was taken away from her for a period of time. This decreased the reliability of the old behavior.

Second, because it was highly unlikely that pointing could ever become more efficient than grabbing, a procedure was implemented in which grabbing resulted in a delay of opportunity to point—Sharon's hands were held in her lap for 15 seconds after a grab. As a result, Sharon began to point in order to request food during snack as well as at lunch.

Solution, Example 6 (Competing Behavior and, perhaps, Competing Reinforcer). For Chris, who wouldn't get dressed at home, the teacher recommended first of all that his mother ignore the screaming. Second, the teacher suggested that Chris simply not be allowed to come downstairs for breakfast until he was dressed—the usual sequence of events in the household. Third, it is recommended that his mother increase her attention to Chris for indedpendent dressing as a "replacement" for attention that would be lost when she ignores tantrums. Everyone concerned realized that this meant that Chris would probably be late to school a few times—not to mention that his screams would likely get more frequent and louder right away.

The teacher dropped by his house on her way to work during the first 3 days of this intervention to provide his mother with support, encouragement, and advice. The success of this intervention depended on ensuring that only independent dressing is reliable in permitting access to reinforcement in the form of participation in post-dressing activities.

Solution, Example 7 (Competing Behavior). Colin's teacher might have asked Colin's parents to keep a careful watch for his "hug" signs and to hug him only after he signed, allowing only the new behavior to access the reinforcer, and to briefly but firmly restrain him when he banged his head.

Solution, Example 8 (Competing Reinforcer). The DRO procedure was applied to Terry's hand flapping and light filtering by other individuals within the school (PE and music teachers, classroom volunteers) across settings (gym, band room, hallway, playground). In addition, his parents were taught to use DRO and they agreed to employ it on a consistent basis at least in their home. His grandfather, with whom Terry spent considerable time, visited the classroom for an hour a day and participated in administering the DRO program.

New Probe Situations

Chris can now dress himself at home and at school. Sharon now points for food at lunch and snack. In both cases, the natural events at the generalization situation were changed. Is generalization to other situations desired? If so, you must assess generalization in additional settings. Can Chris get dressed after swimming? Does Sharon point at the buffet line at the Royal Fork Restaurant?

It is possible that once the learner has experienced altered contingencies in several settings, generalization across other situations will be observed in the absence of additional programming. If generalization is not occurring, however, you must stop and reconsider using this particular strategy. Is it reasonable to suppose that many other people who meet Chris and Sharon in other situations will impose the altered contingencies? Can you "engineer" the application of such contingencies in a variety of situations? If not, then perhaps you may want to try an intervention strategy which does not rely on altering conditions in the generalization situation.

Reinforcing Function Problem

Behaviors are maintained by reinforcement. If reinforcement does not follow, or fails to occur often enough, the behavior will cease to occur. If the target behavior has been performed once appropriately in the generalization situation, it has transferred. If, however, the behavior does not occur again in the new situation under the same stimulus conditions, or if it occurs erratically, the problem is likely to be with reinforcement. Examples of possible problems are followed by an explanation of strategies which can be used in training to prevent, alleviate, or correct the problem. Additional examples may be found in the articles listed in the bibliography at the end of this chapter.

Problem, Example 9. The students in Ms. Zee's class operate a salad bar. During the last part of the school day, Jay has been taught to collect the salad bowls, wash and dry them, and put them away. Jay has met all of his teacher's aims for accuracy and speed, which were set to match workers in the cafeteria. Then, Jay is considered for a job with a sheltered workshop which sends out teams of housecleaners. On the first day of Jay's placement evaluation, he is asked to wash, dry, and put away dishes in the client's house. He washes and dries all of the dishes, and puts them away—searching cupboards and drawers for reasonable storage places. The evaluator records Jay's work on his placement form. The next time Jay is asked to wash, dry, and put dishes away, however, he simply runs them under a lukewarm tap (i.e., no soap, no scrubbing, no clean dishes) and stacks them in the dish drainer.

Problem, Example 10. Scott has learned to pick up and hold a variety of objects. This is a big step for him at twelve—with his severe athetoid cerebral palsy and his frequent seizures, no one had been able to teach him this skill before. Scott's teacher, however, shaped the behavior by following little increments of change with Merle Haggard's music. Now, Scott will hold the objects as long as the music's coming through his earphones! Although this program has taken quite a bit of time, the instructor is pleased—at least Scott will have something to do during the times he must work with other students.

However, once Scott's teacher started putting other objects in front of Scott during other times of the day, he was disappointed. Scott would occasionally pick up one of the objects, but then he would drop it right away—he hadn't generalized the "hold" part of the response.

Problem, Example 11. Tina is learning to fold sheets, pillowcases, and towels. In the training situation, Tina's work is checked frequently and she has to refold any misfolded items. Her teacher praises her about every 5 minutes for working and for staying on the job. At the end of the 3-hour training session in the school laundry room, Tina is given a check for $9.75. In the afternoons, Tina is learning about saving and spending the money she earns.

At the end of the school year, Tina's teacher and supervisor find a summer vocational program which provides an actual summer job like many teens have. Tina proudly goes to work at the local hospital laundry. After a week, however, Tina is fired—she is making too many mistakes, and is spending lots of time looking around instead of working.

Problem, Example 12. Anne's teachers are delighted that she has learned how to answer yes/no by pointing to large colored figures taped to her wheelchair tray table. Despite her severe cerebral palsy, Anne answers her teachers quickly and consistently. However, she is answering her peers and other adults more slowly, and much less consistently.

Strategy: Program Natural Reinforcers

Introduce the reinforcers which occur naturally in the generalization situation into the training situation to ensure that those events will functionally reinforce the instructed behavior.

Reinforcers

Reinforcers are events which immediately follow the response, and which increase the probability that the behavior will occur again. Behaviors that are reinforced either accelerate (i.e., occur with increasing frequency) or are maintained at levels sufficient to access continued reinforcement.

The events that are available as reinforcers in the generalization situation must acquire reinforcing properties with respect to the instructed behavior. Although certain general classes of events are usually considered to be reinforcers—verbal and physical attention, food when hungry, drink when thirsty, additional clothing/campfires/hot drinks when cold—reinforcers do not have universal properties. That is, an event which reinforces one behavior will not necessarily reinforce another behavior. Also, an event which reinforces a behavior in one situation may not be available in another situation, or even if it is available, it may not reinforce the behavior. Therefore, it may be necessary to introduce the student to the events which do occur naturally in the generalization situation in such a way that they acquire reinforcing properties with respect to the specific instructed behavior.

How to Identify Natural Reinforcers

Observe other individuals performing the target behavior in the generalization situation(s) and record all of the events which follow the performance of the desired response (an example is shown in Table 8-1).

If you have time for multiple observations, you may be able to determine which of the events you observed in the generalization situation are the actual reinforcers, but even with successive observations this may not be clear. Therefore, it might be better to assume that all of the events act to reinforce the behavior. Remember, behavior may be reinforced by the termination of events, and even by the occurrence of events that you might think are obnoxious.

Pairing and Fading

During training, whenever you present the training reinforcers, also present the natural reinforcers. This process is called pairing. The natural events should acquire reinforcing properties because they are associated with events already functioning as reinforcers—the events you used during training must be reinforcing—after all, the student did meet your aim!

Gradually decrease the use of the training reinforcers until the natural reinforcers alone control the behavior. The process, which is also known as "fading," should continue until the natural reinforcers produce performance identical to that desired/controlled by the training reinforcers.

Solution, Example 8. Ms. Zee used this strategy in retraining Jay. She talked to the sheltered workshop coordinator, who described the work situation. It seems that Jay will be expected to wash, dry, and put dishes away, and then ask for another job. During her earlier training, however, Ms. Zee had used extensive verbal praise, which is not available in this job situation. In retraining, she decides to continue the verbal praise, which is a known reinforcer, but to pair the praise with the opportunity for Jay to ask for and select another activity. She gradually reduces the praise (i.e., fading), until the opportunity to ask for and select another task controls the instructed behavior.

Strategy: Eliminate Training Reinforcers

Eliminate reinforcers used during acquisition and fluency-building in the training situation. First, compare your list of events which occur naturally in the generalization situation (see "How to Identify Natural Reinforcers,") with the reinforcers in effect in the training situation at the time the student met the training aim and/or at the time the generalization problem was identified. If the lists are not identical, then reinforcers that are present in training, but not available in the generalization situation, should be gradually eliminated from the training situation.

Often during acquisition and fluency-building, teachers will reinforce behavior with events which do not normally follow the behavior. When these reinforcers do not follow the student's behavior in the generalization situation, he may simply quit responding. When this happens, control of the response must be shifted from the non-natural reinforcer to the naturally occurring reinforcer by gradually eliminating (i.e., fading) the non-natural event(s). Steps similar to those described for introducing natural reinforcers into training situations may be used.

Solution, Example 9. Every time Scott picked up and held an object, he was reinforced with Merle Haggard's music. His teacher used several steps in fading the reinforcing music.

1. **Identify the natural reinforcer.** The natural reinforcer for picking up and holding an object is likely to (a) be related to the nature of the object and (b) include doing something with the object. For example, the natural reinforcer for picking up and holding a chocolate bar is being able to eat it—or see it better—or to be able to give it to Kathleen, etc. Scott hadn't learned to do much with objects, but he could feel them and look at them, and he did occasionally drop one, or bring one up to his eye level. Come to think of it, he could do things with objects, even if they weren't very sophisticated.

2. **Introduce the natural reinforcer into training.** The event which should reinforce the response was always present, so the teacher didn't have to make any special effort to include it in training.

3. **Eliminate the "teaching" reinforcer from training.** Scott's teacher realized that if he simply stopped the music all at once, Scott would probably stop picking things up, too—just as had happened in the earlier generalization probes (i.e., since there was no reinforcer, the behavior was extinguished). He thought about it—there were two simple dimensions he could use to gradually decrease the music—the length of time the music was on and the volume of the music. So he gradually decreased the length of time the music was on and gradually decreased the volume of the music. It took about two weeks—but, by that time, Scott was picking up all sorts of objects.

Strategy: Reinforce at Natural Schedules

Schedule the reinforcers used during training to occur according to the same schedule with which they occur in the generalization situation.

Schedules of Reinforcement

Schedules of reinforcement are used to describe when reinforcement is delivered or made contingent upon responding. The most typical schedules are:

1. **Continuous.** Every response is reinforced. This type of schedule is often used during acquisition, when the teacher is likely to arrange for every correct response to be followed by a reinforcer.

2. **Conjugate.** Reinforcement occurs continuously as long as the response occurs. Again, a schedule that may be used during acquisition. For example, Ms. Britainy turned on Scott's Walkman whenever he picked up an object (Problem, Example #9). The music stayed on as long as Scott held the object. When he dropped the object, or when it was taken away from him, the music was stopped.

3. **Ratio.** Reinforcement occurs after a number of responses—either a fixed number of responses or a variable number of responses. For example, if a reinforcer is delivered after every five corrects, the schedule is called a "fixed ratio five responses" (FR 5). If the reinforcer is delivered more randomly, but averages once for every five responses, the schedule is called a "variable ratio five responses" (VR 5).

4. **Interval.** Reinforcement occurs for the first response after a certain period of time has elapsed—either a fixed amount of time or a variable length of time. For example, if a reinforcer is delivered for the first response to occur every 5 minutes, the schedule is called a "fixed interval 5 minutes" (FI 5'). If the reinforcer is delivered more randomly, but averages once for every 5 minutes, the schedule is called a "variable interval 5 minutes" (VI 5').

Observation to Identify Schedule(s) of Natural Reinforcers

1. Conduct your observations in the generalization setting. Observe a peer of your student perform the target behavior.

2. Write down the exact behavior and the time of day in which it occurs.

3. Write down the exact events which follow each behavior and the time they occurred. Events include the activities and words of other people, changes in the environment, etc. Events that immediately follow a behavior are the most powerful reinforcers, so focus your attention on them first. Remember, it is likely that some behaviors are ignored. By identifying how many are followed by some overt action and how many are not, you will be able to identify the natural schedule. Do the same events follow each behavior? Each part of the behavior? A whole string of responses? When there are multiple natural reinforcers, each one may be on a different schedule.

4. You may make a chart like those shown in Tables 8-2 and 8-3, writing each event separately, to help you identify how schedules operate.

5. It is most likely that events you will observe occur on a mixed ratio/interval schedule. In order to determine the schedule, divide the total number of responses by the total number of events and divide the total time spent responding by the total number of events. This calculation should be performed separately for each potential reinforcer.

Maintenance and Generalization

The schedule with which a behavior is reinforced in training may affect both maintenance and generalization. Reinforcement delivered on a mixture of high ratios (i.e., many behaviors with few occasions of reinforcement) and long intervals (i.e., long periods of responding with few occasions of reinforcement) will help make the behavior resistant to extinction. If, however, reinforcement ceases, the behavior will probably extinguish—disappear over time. The speed with which a behavior extinguishes is usually a function of how often it has been previously reinforced. If every response has been reinforced, it will extinguish quickly when it is *not* reinforced. If a behavior has been reinforced frequently during training, and if that behavior is not reinforced the first or second time it occurs in the generalization situation, it may be extinguished in that situation. If the response has been reinforced infrequently and variably, it will maintain quite a long time before it is extinguished, and it is less likely to extinguish if the first few generalized responses are not reinforced immediately.

Table 8-2

Examples of Two Different Ratio Schedules of Reinforcement

The reinforcement, as indicated by the asterisk, immediately follows the response. Multiple responses are indicated by numerals in left column.

Response #	FR 5	VR 5
1		
2		*
3		
4		
5	*	
6		*
7		
8		
9		
10	*	
11		
12		
13		
14		
15	*	
16		*
17		
18		
19		
20	*	*
21		*
22		
23		
24		
25	*	
	reinforcement follows every 5th response	5 reinforcers, 25 responses, 5/25 = VR 5; reinforcement averages every 5th response

Implementation of Natural Schedules

In order to promote response maintenance, the schedule of reinforcement which controls responding in the training situation should resemble the natural schedule of reinforcing events in the generalization situation. The natural schedule should be gradually introduced into the training setting:

1. Identify the schedule of natural reinforcers.

2. Begin reducing the schedule of training reinforcement by increasing the criterion for reinforcement (e.g., increase the number of responses or the duration of responding required for reinforcement). Reduce the number of reinforcers delivered until it matches the natural schedule.

If you are unable to identify the schedule, then train the behavior to come under the control of a mixed variable ratio/variable interval schedule, with very high ratios and very long intervals.

Table 8-3

Examples of Fixed, Variable, Ratio, and Interval Schedules

Response #	FR 5	VR 5	Time Response Occurred	FI 5'	VI 5'
1			1:00		*
2		*	1:01		
3			1:03		
4			1:05	*	
5	*		1:06		
6		*	1:09		*
7			1:10	*	
8			1:13		*
9			1:14		
10	*		1:15	*	
11			1:18		*
12			1:19		
13			1:20	*	
14			1:25	*	
15	*		1:26		
16		*	1:27		*
17			1:29		*
18			1:30	*	
19			1:31		
20	*	*	1:32		
21		*	1:33		
22			1:35	*	
23			1:37		*
24			1:38		*
25	*		1:40	*	
Total Responses	Total Reinforcers		Total Time	Total Reinforcers	
25	5[1]	5[2]	40:00	8[3]	8[4]

Such schedules will help make the behavior resistant to extinction.

Solution, Example 10. Tina's teacher decides to visit the hospital laundry to see what goes on there. Workers in the hospital laundry are praised only occasionally, on the average of once or twice per day, and they are paid every 2 weeks. Quality control checks are made very infrequently, and usually the worker is reprimanded and loses pay for too many mistakes—or is fired. The differences in the schedule of contingencies need to be corrected.

Tina's teacher decides to gradually reduce praise until it occurs only once or twice every two work sessions, and to gradually increase the time which Tina must wait for her pay until she is paid only every 2 weeks. The teacher also gradually reduces her feedback for errors, and "fires" Tina for the day if she makes too many mistakes. This strategy helped Tina get a permanent job, even after Tina was fired from the summer laundry job.

---

[1]   Reinforcement follows every 5th response
[2]   5 reinforcers, 25 responses, 5/25 = VR5; reinforcement averages every 5th response
[3]   Reinforcement every 5 minutes regardless of number of responses
[4]   8 reinforcers, 40 minutes, 8/40 = VI5; reinforcement averages every 5 minutes

Strategy: Use Natural Consequences

In many situations, the instructed behavior is simply taken for granted—praise is not normally delivered by bystanders for appropriate table manners or for speeding through a grocery checkout stand or for crossing a street with the light. In such situations, the natural reinforcers are those provided by the event itself.

However, if behavior is not acceptable to persons nearby, the student may experience a different reaction. Unacceptable table manners in a public place may result in people turning away from the student, or making rude remarks loud enough to be overheard; stalling the grocery line might result in persons moving away, or asking the student to "hurry up," or even by cart bumping; crossing against the light might result in people yelling, grabbing the person, a jaywalking ticket, or even an accident.

These reactions, or ones similar to them, function for most of us as "socialized punishers" and decelerate the behavior they follow. Especially in the absence of more overt social reinforcers, they often have a controlling influence on our behavior. If the student performs the instructed response in the generalization situation and it is ignored, the response may extinguish—which in turn may be followed by certain "social punishers" as well as by the absence of the natural reinforcers associated with appropriate performance. It should be possible to pair those natural consequences with the ones used during training to decelerate errors in a manner similar to the first strategy described in this section.

For example, observation could identify that when Anne does not answer a question, questioners usually (a) repeat the question, (b) ask another question, (c) make some excuse for the behaver (e.g., "Maybe you're too tired today") and finally, (d) walk away or turn their attention to another student. While event (d) is effective, Anne could learn that events (a), (b), and (c) will be followed by (d) if the teacher paired those events with (d) in the training situation.

Strategy: Teach Self-Reinforcement

If reinforcement is sparse or unidentifiable in the generalization situation, or if the response is not maintained in the generalized situation by the intrinsic reinforcers, one may teach the behaver to reinforce himself/herself. In this way, the student's self-reinforcement mediates the difference between the type and frequency of reinforcement required to maintain the behavior and what is actually available in the generalization situation.

In most studies of self-reinforcement, students are taught to deliver a token to themselves contingent upon the completion of the target behavior. These tokens are then later exchanged for special privileges, money, or other items. A list of possible self-controlled reinforcers is shown in Table 8-4.

You may teach self-reinforcement in the way that you would teach any other skill, using data collected on accuracy of delivery to make decisions about the effectiveness of instruction. The student is taught the criteria for reinforcing himself following the target behavior, and for not reinforcing himself following any other behavior. One must then probe to determine if the self-reinforcement behavior generalizes to the new setting. However, teaching the student self-reinforcement as part of training may improve generalization even if the student does not generalize the self-reinforcement behavior itself.

When selecting the nature of the self-delivered reinforcer, one must consider its portability. Will the student have access to the tokens in each setting in which the target behavior might occur? Will there be a means of exchange for items if that is needed? The tokens, points, or other immediate reinforcers may acquire and maintain strength even when they are not later associated with the original reinforcers (e.g., toys, privileges, money, etc.).

Solution, Example 11. Anne's teachers have been following a consistent plan for providing consequences for answering during training, but they realize that it would be impossible to train everyone else to follow the same plan. Instead, they decided to teach Anne to reinforce herself. Every time Anne answered a question, she was prompted to actuate a button on a mechanical counter on her tray. After a while, Anne was thus able to count all of her answers. The teachers also noticed that Anne occasionally counted her answers to questions asked her by her peers and other acquaintances. Once she learned to count, Anne's answers to her peers' and to other adults' questions became quicker and more consistent.

Table 8-4

Sample Events Students Have Been Taught to Use for Self-Reinforcement

Immediate Event[5]	Backup Event[6]
Uses a pencil to mark a "/" on a piece of paper	Marks exchanged for free time; food; special privileges.
Actuates a mechanical counter (records points)	Points recorded on counter exchanged
Pushes a lever to record a count	Points recorded on counter exchanged
Pushes a lever to receive a token	Tokens exchanged
Marks a + on a piece of paper	+s exchanged
Takes a coin from a cup	Opportunity to spend money
Verbally praises self out loud	None needed

Strategy: Teach to Solicit Reinforcement

One may teach the student to follow the target behavior with an additional behavior that will normally elicit social approval. This strategy is one method of altering the reinforcement density and delivery in the generalization situation without overtly or directly changing staff behavior.

Solution, Example 8. Jay could be taught to say "I'm done" or "What's next?" or to turn and smile at the supervisor once he has finished the dishes. Such behavior should evoke attention that may serve to reinforce dishwashing behavior in the generalization situation.

Strategy: Reinforce Generalized Behavior

In training, generalized or adapted responses, or responses which occur in new, untrained situations are reinforced. When a response form is repeated, or performed a second time in the same situation, it is not reinforced.

Problem and Solution, Example 12. Susan's teachers are trying to teach her to play with other students during recess. Once Susan has played successfully with one student, she doesn't even approach other students. Of course, the natural reinforcer here should be that the play itself is fun. But, if Susan doesn't ever approach other students, she won't discover this. In order to teach Susan that playing with other students can be fun, the teachers decided to give Susan a token whenever she approaches another student for a play activity. Susan can spend the tokens to "rent" the toys of her choice. Susan only earns a token when she approaches a child whom she has not approached before—approaching previous playmates does not qualify for reinforcement. The strategy is evaluated by determining if initiations to new playmates improves, and, if it does, the tokens will be gradually faded.

---

[5]   The *immediate event* is a self-reinforcing or self-monitoring behavior performed by the student immediately after the target behavior occurs. It serves to reinforce the target behavior.

[6]   The *back-up* event may be a self-reinforcing behavior or it may be performed by the teacher or other manager. This event is designed to "strengthen" the reinforcement for the target skill and to provide additional "external" reinforcement for the "immediate event."

Strategy: Alter Generalization Contingencies

One may ask people (or train them, if necessary) in the generalization situation to reinforce the target behavior appropriately, and/or on a particular schedule.

Problem and Solution, Example 13. Walker et al. observed the playground behavior of fifth and sixth graders. Next, in a classroom situation, they trained emotionally disturbed students of the same age specific and appropriate playground social behavior, especially initiations. During training, they used the natural social interchange identified in their observations to reinforce the initiations and to signal subsequent appropriate behaviors.

Once their students met aim, they ventured onto the playground. Although the students perfectly generalized the trained social behavior, their fifth and sixth grade contemporaries met those behaviors with scorn, ridicule, or by ignoring the overtures. In short, the fifth and sixth graders treated the behavior displayed by the emotionally disturbed students differently than they treated those same behaviors when displayed by their peers.

One possible solution to this problem is to provide some form of training to the fifth and sixth graders or to selected leaders of those groups with the intention of modifying their current reactions to the emotionally disturbed youth. Once contingencies have been altered in the generalization situation, one must probe generalization in other situations if such generalization is desired. For example, if selected leaders were trained to contingently reinforce social behavior, one could probe the student's generalization to other "untrained" students.

Discrimination Function Problem

In this particular category of generalization strategies, we are concerned with the function of the events that occur before or during responding. These events evoke a particular response which will then result in reinforcement. The process by which the student learns to respond to these antecedent events in a particular situation is called discrimination learning. The following terms will be useful in our discussion.

Setting Events

Setting events include the constellation of factors which generally "set the stage" for a large class of responses. For example, a restaurant sets the stage for the class of "restaurant behaviors"—such as ordering and eating food, conversation with friends, paying the check, and so forth. It also eliminates other classes of behavior, which are usually not performed in restaurants—like "playground behaviors" (e.g., running, screaming, kicking a ball) and "religious behaviors" (e.g., praying, kneeling, singing hymns). Some behaviors, with certain modifications, are appropriate in many settings—like talking. In any case, settings events are thought to represent any and all stimulus events in a particular situation. Whether a specific behavior occurs or does not occur, however, is more precisely evoked by specific stimuli associated with the response—the discriminative stimuli.

Discriminative Stimuli

The discriminative stimuli are environmental events that occur prior to or during the response and in whose presence the behavior is either reinforced or punished (S+) or in whose presence the behavior is neither reinforced or punished (S-).

S+ is the discriminative stimulus (S^D) in whose presence a specific response is likely to be either reinforced or punished (see Table 8-5 for examples).

S- is the discriminative stimulus (S^Δ) in the presence of which a specific response is neither reinforced or punished (see Table 8-5 for examples).

Discrimination learning is the process by which the behaver learns that responding with a particular behavior in the presence of the S+ will most likely be reinforced (depending on the schedule of reinforcement) or punished and that responding with that same behavior in the presence of the S- will not be reinforced or punished.

Discrimination learning is a critical component of acquisition—the student must learn the conditions under which the response will be reinforced and the conditions under which the response will not be reinforced.

In a chain of responses, each step functions both as a discriminative stimulus for the next response in the chain, and as conditioned reinforcement for the response that preceded the stimulus change (see Table 8-6).

Si: Irrelevant stimuli are those that may or may not be present before and/or during responding (concurrent with S+s and S-s) but whose presence is not related to reinforcement (see Table 8-5 for examples).

These stimuli play an important role in the development of acquisition. In addition to discriminative stimuli, irrelevant events may interfere with generalization. When supposedly irrelevant stimuli are paired with S+s and S-s, they may come to control the behavior. For example, if a specific teacher or manager (Si) becomes associated with a response (a S+), the student will only perform the behavior for the teacher. The student who will answer his teacher but not his peers may be influenced by training in which his teacher taught him to answer her. In this case, the teacher or instructional manager (who should be irrelevant to answering questions) actually controls answering. The response occurs when the teacher or manager is present and does not occur when she is absent—the response is controlled by a stimulus which should be irrelevant to the response.

In order for generalization to occur, students need to learn to discriminate the stimuli which occur in the generalization situations as "triggers" for the behavior they have learned. Generalization problems may occur when (a) discrimination learning has been so successful that any difference between the trained S+s and those that occur in the generalization situation is sufficient to signal an S- situation (so the student does not respond), (b) discrimination learning has failed to establish control by the naturally occurring S+s and S-s, or (c) discrimination learning has failed to establish Sis as irrelevant (i.e., they act as S+s or S-s).

Strategies for solving generalization problems related to discrimination are described in the following sections. Additional examples may be found in the articles listed in the bibliography at the end of this chapter.

Problem, Example 14. Down the hall from Mel, Joanne, and Tim's high school classroom is a vending machine which dispenses a variety of snack items. One of their teachers, Mr. Ferd, decided that this would be a handy machine to use in training those students to purchase food and beverages from machines located in various community sites. After training, all three students were able to operate that machine rapidly, without errors and without any prompts from him. To find out whether his students were able to purchase items in locations where high school students normally use vending machines, Mr. Ferd conducted generalization probes on 10 machines—another one in the high school, the machines in a video game arcade, a hospital lobby, a laundromat, a movie theater, and a lunchroom in the local courthouse. He found, to his dismay, that none of the students were able to perform the skills which would allow them to purchase items from more than one of the untrained machines. On some machines, the students could not find the coin slot; on other machines, they inserted the coin, but did not make a selection.

Problem, Example 15. Prior to training, Lorraine did not greet people or respond to greetings in the usual socially acceptable manner. Instead, she would immediately begin telling a story, or asking questions, or she would simply ignore a friendly "Good Morning" or "Hi." A program was then instituted to teach Lorraine to greet people, and to respond appropriately to the greetings of others.

It wasn't long, however, until the teacher received a call from Lorraine's mother, who was unhappy (to say the least) with the results of the program. It seems that Lorraine ignores her mother's "Good morning," but now greets or will enthusiastically respond to greetings from just about everyone she sees who says "hi" or "hello," including strangers and people that she has just seen a few minutes earlier. Her mother considers this an embarrassing and potentially dangerous outcome.

Problem, Example 16. Paul is learning to pick things up. As a start, the teacher uses toys in his instructional program because (a) toys possess characteristics which might act as natural reinforcers and (b) Paul has demonstrated an interest in a variety of toys by visually attending to them. The teacher selects a wide number of toys, which vary according to the S+ characteristics relevant to the response, and a wide number of objects as exemplars of the S- characteristics.

Table 8-5

Examples of S+, S-, and S*i*

Discriminative Stimuli	Irrelevant Stimuli	Response
Example I		
(S+) screw to be tightened	(S*i*) number of threads	pick up screwdriver
(S-) nut on bolt	(S*i*) color of screw	
(S-) screw tightened		
Example II		
(S+) checkout clerk says amount owed	(S*i*) age of clerk	give clerk money
(S-) checkout clerk asks for identification	(S*i*) sex of clerk	
(S-) checkout clerk asks price of specific item	(S*i*) amount of money	
(S-) checkout clerk says "Have a nice day."		
Example III		
(S+) agreeable food + hunger + location where eating is acceptable	(S*i*) name of restaurant	eat food
(S-) inedible food	(S*i*) time of day	
(S-) not hungry	(S*i*) color of plates	
(S-) library/church service		
Example IV		
(S+) desire to walk some place + ok time to walk there + ok place to walk	(S*i*) color of clothing	walks
(S-) no place to go	(S*i*) name of companion	
(S-) too tired		
(S-) unsafe weather		
(S-) inappropriate place to walk ("No Trespassing")		
(S-) inappropriate time to walk ("Please wait for the next available clerk")		
Example V		
(S+) dirty carpet	(S*i*) color of carpet	vacuums carpet
(S-) clean carpet	(S*i*) make of vacuum	
(S-) uncarpeted floor	(S*i*) size of carpet	
(S-) grass		
Example VI		
(S+) Verbal request for 3 + 3 available	(S*i*) object asked for	gets 3 ("concept of three")
(S-) Verbal request for another number of objects.	(S*i*) color of objects	
	(S*i*) person requesting	

Table 8-6

Functions of Events/Responses in an Operant Chain[7]

Event	Function
screw on table hole empty	S+ for response: place screw in hole
screw in hole	Conditioned reinforcer for response of place screw in hole AND S+ for response: pick up screwdriver
screwdriver in hand	Conditioned reinforcer for response of picking up screwdriver AND S+ for place nose in screw head slot
screwdriver in screw	Conditioned reinforcer for response of placing nose in screwhead slot AND S+ for response of rotating head clockwise.
screw tight	Conditioned reinforcer for response of rotating clockwise AND S+ for response of putting screwdriver on table.
screwdriver on table	Conditioned reinforcer for response of putting screwdriver down AND S+ for next task or Conditioned reinforcer for finishing task.

Once training has been completed, however, she is disappointed to see that Paul rarely picks up objects.

She decides to make a list of the objects that Paul picks up and those he doesn't. After much puzzling, she realizes that Paul only picks up objects that are red, or at least predominantly red. She looks again at the objects she has trained, and discovers that all of the toys she has selected are at least partially red!

Problem, Example 17. Ms. Olson takes Penny and several other class members to the McDonald's near the school twice a week to teach the chain of skills necessary to purchase food in fast food restaurants. On the other 3 days of the week, instruction is provided in the classroom using a realistic McDonald's simulation the teacher has devised. Penny seems to love to be able to purchase her own lunch and acquires the behavioral sequence quite rapidly. Since Penny is nonverbal, she learns to use a packet of photographs of food to place her order. Once the clerk has rung up her order on the cash register, Penny hands dollar bills, one at a time, to the clerk, until the clerk stops taking the money. Penny then waits quietly until the clerk pushes a filled tray toward her, takes the tray, and goes to the condiment stand.

Ms. Olson reports to Penny's dad that she can order in a fast food restaurant. He takes her to Hank's Hamburgers. Penny selects the items she wants from her photographs and shows them to the counterperson, who takes her order and enters it in the cash register. Penny tries to give the clerk money like she does at McDonald's. But instead of taking the money, the clerk puts a receipt on a tray and slides it down the counter. At Hank's, another clerk will read the receipt and fill the tray and then a third clerk, at the far end of the counter, will accept cash and give the filled

[7] Adapted from *Vocational Habilitation of Severely Retarded Adults* (p. 72) by G. T. Bellamy, R. H. Horner, and D. P. Inman, 1979, Baltimore: University Park Press. Copyright 1979 by University Park Press and PRO-ED, Inc. Used with permission.

tray to the customer. The first clerk sees Penny's confusion, and tried to direct her down the counter, but Penny, still clutching her dollar bills, squats down on her heels and begins to rock—her usual response when she is confused and upset.

Problem, Example 18. Cheryl has just finished her vocational training program at Martin Luther King High School. Cheryl and three of her classmates have been trained to work as an industrial janitorial team. Today her team has been assigned to clean one floor of a local medical-dental building regularly serviced by Furham Sheltered Industries. The supervisor is evaluating the team for possible after-school employment. One of Cheryl's primary responsibilities is washing floors. She confidently begins work. Of course, she hasn't seen these particular floors before, or the mop, buckets, and detergent, but she does a thorough job. The supervisor is quite upset, however, when he sees that Cheryl has washed the floor of an office with wall-to-wall carpeting

A closer look at our examples will illustrate each of the kinds of problems that can occur if there is a discrimination function problem. First, problems can occur if discrimination learning has been "too successful." Key stimuli (S+) for vending machine operation include: how cost per item is displayed; location of displayed cost; location of coin slot; amount of item; item activator; whether item is visible; type of product; coin return slot. Mel, Joanne, and Tim learned these stimuli on a single vending machine. When the stimulus features were different on the probe machines, they could not generalize the skills. They had learned to look for a knob as the S+ for item selection. When this S+ feature differed (e.g., when a button was the S+ for item selection instead of the knob they had learned to use) from the one they had been trained to use, generalization did not occur.

The same type of problem befell Penny. She had learned to pay the person taking her order—when this stimuli did not lead to the consequences she expected, her behavior deteriorated. In both of these situations, the instructed S+s which controlled behavior differed significantly from the generalized S+s, and the student discriminated the difference and responded to the untrained S+s as if they were S-s or S*is*.

Second, generalization problems may occur when critical stimuli are omitted from the training situation. For example, Cheryl's vocational training instructor failed to teach a very significant S-for floor washing—wall-to-wall carpeting. In this case, although Cheryl successfully discriminated all of the steps involved in floor-washing, the teacher did not teach Cheryl that certain floors are to be washed while others are not.

Paul's responding came under the control of irrelevant stimuli. All of the objects used in training shared the characteristic of red coloring. In this situation, the irrelevant stimulus—a red color—has come to control responding. Paul picks up objects that are red and doesn't pick up objects that are not red. Although irrelevant, the red color is acting as a S+ while "not-red" is acting as an S-.

Strategy: Vary Stimuli

To remediate discriminative function problems, reinstitute training in which you systematically introduce and vary stimuli which occur in the generalization situation.

Analyze all of the instructional events/stimuli (i.e., what you taught) against all of the generalization stimuli in order to identify, for each class of stimuli, those that are necessary for proper generalization. If you can guess which stimuli are causing the problem, you will reduce the training time, although stimulus control problems often involve more than one stimulus. Then, you must reinstitute training in which behaviors that follow specific "poor" discriminations are not reinforced and behaviors that follow stimuli which should control responding are reinforced. Strategies which are effective in discrimination training may be useful here (see Haring, Liberty, & White, 1981; Liberty, 1985; Snell, 1987).

Whatever strategy is selected, all of the S+s are introduced and followed by reinforcement, and all of the S-s are introduced and any target behaviors which follow are ignored (i.e., not reinforced). All of the S*is* are also introduced, paired with the S+s in some cases and with the S-s in other cases. Irrelevant stimuli should be varied across S+s and S-s. The variation of stimuli must be systematic and thorough.

There are four basic methods for determining how to select stimuli for this intervention.

1. **All stimuli.** It would be ideal if all possible stimulus events could be included in training. For example, if you are teaching a student to pick up coins, and if the S+ of coin size is a problem, it would be possible and practical to teach all coins. But it will usually not be possible to train all stimulus events. For example, there would be no way to include all possible S+s in a "pick up objects" program—there are just too many objects.

2. **Frequent stimuli.** Survey the generalization situations and identify all of the stimuli for each class, or for the class you think is causing the problem. Then, pick those stimuli that occur most often or most usually across generalization situations.

3. **Multiple exemplars.** Survey the generalization situations and identify stimuli which are examples of stimuli (i.e., exemplars) and which represent the range of events the student might encounter. This method is suitable when it is not possible to identify all possible events, as in the suitable S+s for the pick up program. You will know that you have included "sufficient" exemplars when your reprobe for generalization meets with success.

4. **General case exemplars.** Identify the group of stimuli or situations across which generalization is desired; that group is known as the instructional universe (Sprague & Horner, 1984). Then, identify the range of stimulus and response variation that exists within that universe, and teach the minimum number of examples that sample the complete range of stimulus and response variation.

> The objective is to select a logistically feasible set of examples that sample the relevant stimulus variation in situations that the student will encounter after training. When selecting examples, begin by looking at each response that the student is to learn. For each response, define the stimulus that should exert control. Then examine how that controlling stimulus changes across the different stimulus conditions within the predefined instructional universe. (Horner, McDonnell, & Bellamy, 1986)

Criteria for selecting examples are shown in Table 8-7. This approach is based on the premise that generalization will be most successfully achieved when individuals are exposed, during training, to exemplars of the stimuli and responses which are associated with task performance across all targeted situations and materials.

Solution, Example 14. Each of these strategies could be applied to identify stimuli to teach vending machine use. To teach all of the possible variations in stimuli, Mr. Ferd would have to teach his students how to operate all of the vending machines around—he decided that this would be impossible.

The "frequent stimuli" strategy, as well as the other strategies, should be applied first to the S+, S-, or S*i* that you suspect may be causing the problem. Mr. Ferd thinks the location of the item cost (an S+) might be the problem area. In order to determine what "cost location" stimuli to train, he could first survey all of the machines that he thinks his students might use (i.e., frequent stimuli) and identify the kinds that occur most often. If, for example, costs are usually displayed right above the item or right below the item, he would choose machines for training which display the costs that way.

To use the multiple exemplars strategy, Mr. Ferd would include one machine that displayed cost above the item, one which displayed cost below item, cost displayed next to item, cost listed on panel below coin slot, and so on.

To apply a general case approach, Mr. Ferd would survey all of the vending machines he could, and identify stimulus groups with common characteristics for each stimulus event. He would then teach at least one example from each group so that the entire range of variation is sampled in the training. For example, at least one of each of the following would be included: cost displayed above item, cost displayed below item, cost displayed next to item, cost listed on panel below coin slot. This stimulus (i.e., cost location) would be systematically varied in a constellation with other S+ events (e.g., item viewing location, item choice activator, location of coin slot, amount/cost of item, etc.) (see Table 8-8).

In this example, the site of training (i.e., setting event) would be determined by several considerations. If Mr. Ferd can arrange to borrow the vending machines he needs, he can conduct his training in the school. Companies which distribute and operate vending machines may be

Table 8-7

Selecting and Teaching Examples for General Case Instruction[8]

Selecting Examples

1. The set of positive examples should be similar only with respect to relevant stimuli [S+]. Irrelevant stimuli [Si] should be as different as possible across examples.
2. The set of positive examples should sample the range of stimulus variation across which the learner is expected to respond (i.e., across the instructional universe).
3. A range of negative examples [S-] should be included (where appropriate) that are maximally similar to positive examples (e.g., when teaching the generalized skill of busing cafeteria and restaurant tables, the set of teaching examples should include tables that should not be bused).
4. Select a set of positive examples that included significant exceptions (e.g., for generalized street crossing, cars that pull away from curbs or out of driveways are "exceptions" that need to be taught).

Teaching Examples

1. Teach multiple components of an activity or skill within each training session. With simple skills (e.g., toothbrushing), teach all the behaviors within each session; with more complex skills, such as assembling circuit boards, teach portions of the skill that include multiple components rather than teaching a single component.
2. When the whole skill or activity is taught, use multiple examples within individual training sessions. Do not train one example at a time in an easy-to-hard sequence. While the learner experiences more success with an easy-to-hard sequence, she or he also learns generalization errors that decrease the efficiency of instruction and limit the utility of the acquired behavior. When presenting multiple examples of varying difficulty, however, it is reasonable to present a mix of 60% easy examples, 20% intermediate examples, and 20% hard examples within a session. This allows the student the opportunity to succeed with easy examples yet experience the full range of variation needed to prevent generalization errors.
3. Present maximally similar positive and negative examples one right after the other. This is especially important for behaviors in which learning when (or where) not to perform the behavior [S-] is as important as learning when (or where) to perform the behavior [S+]. This sequencing technique teaches the learner the specific stimuli that define the limits within which the target behavior is appropriate.
4. Review examples learned during previous sessions . . . When many examples are being taught, instructional sequences should include some new and some "old" examples during each training session.
5. Teach the general case before teaching exceptions.

---

[8] Adapted from "Teaching generalized skills: General case instruction in simulation and community settings" by R. H. Horner, J. J. McDonnell, & G. T. Bellamy, 1986, in *Education of learners with severe handicaps: Exemplary service strategies*, pp. 289-314, R. H. Horner, L. H. Meyer, & H. D. Fredericks (Eds.). Baltimore: Paul H. Brookes. Used with permission.

Table 8-8

General Case Analysis Form[9]

Student _____

Teacher _____

Activity: __Vending machine use__   Instructional universe: __All food and beverage vending machines in Eugene, OR__

Generic Responses	Generic Stimuli and Relevant Characteristics	Relevant Stimulus Variation	Relevant Response Variation	Exceptions/ Potential Errors
1. Select coins	1.1. Displayed cost 　　a. Location	By coin slot; 18 inches to left of item; above item; beside item; below item	Pull coins from pocket or purse	Other symbols of similar type, size, and location on machine
	b. Amount	20¢–75¢ in units of 5¢	Select one, two, or three quarters	"Out of order" sign
2. Insert coins	2.1. Coins in hand	One, two, or three quarters	Insert one, two, or three quarters	Other people using the machine
	2.2. Coin slot in machine 　　a. Location 　　b. Orientation	Right or left side 4 to 4½ feet high; horizontal or vertical	—	The Exact Change and All Out indicators look similar and are located similarly to the coin slot
3. Activate machine	3.1. Coins in machine	All coins in machine	—	—
	3.2. Item activator	Button; slide door; panel; lever	Push button; slide door; push panel; pull lever	Variation in number of buttons Variation in array of activators
	3.3. Item discriminator	Words; actual item; logo code; letters	—	Red light on selector
4. Obtain item	4.1. Item visible	Liquid in cup; actual item; item in chute; item drops	Grasp item; lift door with one hand and grasp item with other; push door with one hand and grasp item with other; lift cup of liquid	
	4.2. Noise from dispenser	Item drops; noise stops		
5. Check for change	5.1. Product in hand	Cup; can; packaged item	—	Bottle cap remover looks like coin return on soda machines
	5.2. Coin return slot	Right or left side; with or without door; 1½ to 2 feet high	Place finger in slot, push small door back	

[9] From "General case programming for community activities" by R. Horner, J. Sprague, and B. Wilcox, 1982, in *Design of high school programs for severely handicapped students*, pp. 84-85, B. Wilcox and G.T. Bellamy (Eds). Baltimore: Paul H. Brookes. Used with permission.

willing to loan them to the school. However, if he cannot arrange for the vending machines to be available, he could conduct training where the vending machines are located. If training "on-site" can't be arranged, he may have to either use vending machines that are available in the school or construct simulated vending machines. In any case, probes to untrained machines in other settings would need to be conducted.

Solution, Example 15. Lorraine's teacher identified the following groups of stimulus events:

S+: Greetings (words, phrases, gestures);
Recognition of person who has not been recently greeted;
Activity that can be interrupted to greet someone.

S−: Not a greeting statement ("See you later," any command, etc.);
Unknown person;
Person previously and recently greeted;
Activity which should not be interrupted to greet someone (e.g., work)

Si : Time of day;
Clothing worn by the greeter;
Setting where greeted (except as noted).

For our example, let us look at the types of specific stimuli identified for the S+, "Greetings."

For a frequent stimuli approach, the teacher would first write down all of the greetings that she observes in sample observations in the school and the community. She would then select the greetings that occur most often—for example, "Hi," "Hello there," "Good morning," "Hi, (name)," and "Say, (name)"—and train Lorraine to respond to them. Generalization probes (see Chapter 7) would include untrained greetings.

To use the multiple exemplar approach, Lorraine's teacher would select several different greetings and teach them. If Lorraine did generalize to untrained greetings, the number of exemplars selected would have been "sufficient" to produce generalization. Unfortunately, there are no empirically derived methods for determining how many are "sufficient."

The general case requires steps in addition to observing and recording greetings. Next, greetings are classified according to different characteristics or components, such as the number of words in the greeting, whether the person's name is included, interrogative case or not, time of day delivered, and resemblance to S− characteristics (e.g., "Good morning," an S+, is similar to "Good bye," which is an S− for greeting and an S+ for farewell). The teacher would include representatives of each combination of characteristics in this approach.

Solution, Example 16. Paul's teacher decides to vary the irrelevant stimulus. The color (Si) of both the S+ and the S− objects will have to be varied so that a particular color or color combination does not come to act as either an S+ or as an S−.

But what S+ and S− stimuli should she choose to represent the Si in training? Obviously, she can't possibly include all of the colors and color combinations that Paul will encounter. In order to include *frequent stimuli*, the teacher would survey all of the toys and other objects in Paul's current environment and note their colors and color combinations. Colors/combinations that occur most frequently would be trained.

The multiple exemplar approach would not necessarily include all "common stimuli," but should encompass a wide variety of colors/combinations.

In addition to a survey of all of the toys and other S− objects in Paul's current and subsequent environments, the Si colors would be classified (e.g., bright colors, subtle colors, monocolored, multicolored, patterned, changeable colors [e.g., doll clothing], transparent, etc.), and training would include at least one example of each.

Solution, Example 17. Ms. Olson surveys the fast food restaurants in Penny's community and identifies the different "order-pay-get served" options. These include:

(a) order, pay, receive food from one clerk at counter (McDonald's, Burger King, Wendy's);

(b) order and pay one clerk, get beverage from second clerk, wait to be called for food, pick up food at third location on counter (Flakey Jake's, Shakey's Pizza);

(c) order and pay one clerk, wait until number is called, get beverage and food from second clerk (Kidd Valley Hamburger, Hoagy's Deli);

(d) order food from one clerk, order beverage from second clerk, pay second clerk, wait, get food from second clerk (Ivar's Fish Bar);

(e) order, pay, wait, get food from same clerk (Dick's Drive-in where you can walk-in);
(f) take number, wait until number called, order, get served, pay (Baskin & Robbins, Schumacher's);
(g) order from one clerk, move down counter while second clerk fills order, pay and receive food from third clerk (Hank's).

For the frequent stimuli method, she would teach the chains that occur most often in the community or the ones that Penny currently favors; for the multiple exemplar method, she would teach several different sequences, and for the general case method, she would teach one example of each of the different classifications identified.

Solution, Example 18. One of the sets of stimuli that Cheryl must learn is the set of all S-s for floor-washing. These include:
(a) hardwood floors or any bare wood floor;
(b) floors with wall-to-wall carpeting;
(c) floors with area rugs (ask whether rugs should be moved, be washed around, or not be washed);
(d) stone/slate/brick floors that require special treatment.

For each of these classifications, there are many different stimuli that could serve as examples. Under the frequent stimuli method, the teacher would include stimuli that occur most frequently in the floors Cheryl would be most likely to clean. With the multiple exemplar method, the teacher would include several different stimuli from each classification. And, with the general case method, the teacher would include at least one from each class of the S- stimuli, in combinations of characteristics.

Generalization Format Problem

If you have followed the rules correctly, and you have eliminated the other problems, we suspect that there may be a combination of factors inhibiting generalization. To help you identify potential change strategies, first check that your instruction has included these basic format considerations introduced in the previous sections of this chapter:

1. **Proficient aim.** The aim set for the target response should ensure that the target response is the most efficient means of acquiring the reinforcer (p. 150).
2. **Natural reinforcers.** The reinforcers which control responding in training are identical to those which are available to control responding in the generalization situation (p. 153).
3. **Natural schedules.** The schedule of reinforcement used in training matches the naturally occurring schedule in the generalization situations (p. 154).
4. **Appropriate natural stimuli.** The S+, S-, Si, and setting events have been carefully selected and all have been systematically included in instruction (p. 160).

If you feel that your format meets these basic considerations, the following intervention may also be useful.

Strategy: Eliminate Training Stimuli

Eliminate all of the stimuli used in instruction which are not available in the generalization situation. Most often, these are events which are functionally irrelevant to the response (Si), but are used to facilitate acquisition and/or fluency-building. A discussion of the function of stimulus events begins on p. 160.

For example, while there might be a huge variety in the types of stimuli associated with eating, they generally include: a place where food is available (setting event), a desire to eat the food that is available, and specific food items (S+). These are the natural stimuli that are associated with eating.

During acquisition of eating behavior, however, the instructor may cut food in bite-sized pieces, verbally direct each bite (e.g., "Take a bite"), and schedule instruction to occur at a time when the student may not be hungry. Each of these stimuli (i.e., bite-sized pieces, verbal cue, and absence of hunger) is not usually associated with the response, but, since it is associated with reinforcement during training, it may come to control responding. For example, the cue "Take a bite" may come to control responding—when that cue is not given, the student may not eat.

Table 8-9

Examples of Training Stimuli

Example I: Desired Behavior = Head Up

Stimuli	**Type**
Activity in classroom	Natural S+
Teacher verbally cues"Head up"	Synthetic S+ (used for training)

Example II: Desired Behavior = Dresses Self

Stimuli	**Type**
Shortly after waking; before and after PE; before and after swimming; before and after special event	Natural S+
Dressing program occurs at 10 am daily, regardless of necessity of changing clothes	Synthetic S+ Natural S-
Puts shirt over bare chest or undershirt	Natural S+
Puts shirt over other shirt	Synthetic S+ Natural S-
Privacy	Natural S+
Lots of people around	Synthetic S+ Natural S-

Commonly used teaching events include verbal directions, demonstrations, prompts, massed trials, and so on. These events may be defined only through comparison with the events which precede the response in natural, nontraining situations. In addition, the classification of events may be related to the age of the behaver. For example, verbal directions to "Go to bed" may be natural with youngsters, but not natural with adults. Some examples are shown in Table 8-9.

Stimulus control exerted by teaching events can be avoided or eliminated by (a) varying the type of teaching event used during acquisition, (b) probing often to determine if performance can occur without the event, and, if it can, drop the use of that event immediately, and (c) gradually reducing the intensity, severity, or degree of event used (e.g., reduce verbal prompts from normal tone of voice to a whisper and then eliminate completely).

References

Bellamy, G. T., Horner, R. H., & Inman, D. P. (1979). *Vocational habilitation of severely retarded adults*. Baltimore: University Park Press.

Billingsley, F., & Neel, R. (1985). Competing behaviors and their effects on skill generalization and maintenance. *Analysis and Intervention in Developmental Disabilities*, 5(4), 357-372.

Falvey, M. (1986). *Community-based curriculum: Instructional strategies for students with severe handicaps*. Baltimore: Paul H. Brookes.

Haring, N. G., Liberty, K. A., & White, O. R. (1981). *An investigation of phases of learning and facilitating instructional events for the severely/profoundly handicapped (final project report).* (US Department of Education, Contract No. G007500593). Seattle: University of Washington, College of Education.

Horner, R. H., McDonnell, J. J., & Bellamy, G. T. (1986). Teaching generalized skills: General case instruction in simulation and community settings. In Horner, R., Meyer, L. H., & Fredericks, H. D. (Eds.), *Education of learners with severe handicaps: Exemplary service strategies,* (pp. 289-314). Baltimore: Paul H. Brookes.

Horner, R., Sprague, J., & Wilcox, B. (1982). General case programming for community activities. In B. Wilcox & G. T. Bellamy (Eds.), *Design of high school programs for severely handicapped students,* (pp. 61-98). Baltimore: Paul H. Brookes.

Liberty, K. A. (1985). Enhancing instruction for maintenance, generalization, and adaptation. In K. C. Lakin & R. H. Bruininks (Eds.), *Strategies for achieving community integration of developmentally disabled citizens.* Baltimore: Paul H. Brookes.

Snell, M. E. (Ed.) (1987). *Systematic instruction of persons with severe handicaps.* Columbus, OH: Charles E. Merrill.

Sprague, J. R., & Horner, R. H. (1984). The effects of single instance, multiple instance, and general case training on generalized vending machine use by moderately and severely handicapped students. *Journal of Applied Behavior Analysis, 17*(2), 273-278.

Stokes, T. F., & Baer, D. B. (1977). An implicit technology of generalization. *Journal of Applied Behavior Analysis, 10*(2), 349-367.

Walker, H. (1986). [Personal communication with Kathleen Liberty].

Bibliography

Further information and examples on *Train in Desired Situation*, *Reinforcing Function Strategies*, and *Discrimination Function Strategies* may be obtained by consulting the following resources.

Train in Desired Situation

Adkins, J., & Matson, J. L. (1980). Teaching institutionalized mentally retarded adults socially appropriate leisure skills. *Mental Retardation, 18*(5), 249-252.

Coon, M. E., Vogelsberg, R. T., & Williams, W. (1981). Effects of classroom public transportation instruction on generalization to the natural environment. *Journal of the Association for the Severely Handicapped, 6*(2), 46-53.

Correa, V. I., Poulson, C. L., & Salzberg, C. L. (1984). Training and generalization of reach-grasp behavior in blind, severely/profoundly mentally retarded young children. *Journal of Applied Behavior Analysis, 17*(1), 57-69

Cuvo, A. J., Leaf, R. B., & Borakove, L. S. (1978). Teaching janitorial skills to the mentally retarded: Acquisition, generalization, and maintenance. *Journal of Applied Behavior Analysis, 11*(3), 345-355.

Dineen, J. P., Clark, H. B., & Risely, T. R. (1977). Peer tutoring among elementary students: Educational benefits to the tutor. *Journal of Applied Behavior Analysis, 10*(2), 231-238.

Dowrick, P. W., & Dove, C. (1980). The use of self-modeling to improve the swimming performance of spina bifida children. *Journal of Applied Behavior Analysis, 13*(1), 51-56.

Hill, J. W., Wehman, P., & Horst, G. (1982). Toward generalization of appropriate leisure and social behavior in severely handicapped youth: Pinball machine use. *Journal of the Association for the Severely Handicapped, 6*(4), 38-44.

Koegel, R. L., Egel, A. L., & Williams, J. A. (1980). Behavioral contrast and generalization across settings in the treatment of autistic children. *Journal of Experimental Child Psychology, 30*(3), 422-437.

Kohl, F. L., Wilcox, B. L., & Karlan, G. R. (1978). Effects of training conditions on the generalization of manual signs with moderately handicapped students. *Education and Training of the Mentally Retarded, 13*(3), 327-335.

Neef, N. A., Iwata, B. A., & Page, T. J. (1978). Public transportation training: In vivo versus classroom instruction. *Journal of Applied Behavior Analysis, 11*(3), 331-344.

Sternberg, L., Pegnatore, L., & Hill, C. (1983). Establishing interactive communication behaviors with profoundly handicapped students. *Journal of the Association for the Severely Handicapped, 8*(2), 39-46.

Trap, J. J., Milner-Davis, P., Joseph, S., & Cooper, J. O. (1978). The effects of feedback and consequences on transitional cursive letter formation. *Journal of Applied Behavior Analysis, 11*(3), 381-394.

Tucker, D. J., & Berry, G. W. (1980). Teaching severely multihandicapped students to put on their own hearing aids. *Journal of Applied Behavior Analysis, 13*(1), 65-75.

Reinforcing Function Strategies

Combs, M. L., & Lahey, B. B. (1981). A cognitive social skills training program. *Behavior Modification, 5*(1), 39-59.

Cooke, T. P., & Apolloni, T. (1976). Developing positive social-emotional behaviors: A study of training and generalization effects. *Journal of Applied Behavior Analysis, 9*(1), 65-78.

Duker, P. C., & Michielsen, H. M. (1983). Cross-setting generalization of manual signs to verbal instructions with severely retarded children. *Journal of Applied Research in Mental Retardation, 4*(1), 29-40.

Fowler, S. A., & Baer, D. M. (1981). "Do I have to be good all day?" The timing of delayed reinforcement as a factor in generalization. *Journal of Applied Behavior Analysis, 14*(1), 13-24.

Garcia, E. E. (1976). The development and generalization of delayed imitation. *Journal of Applied Behavior Analysis, 9*(4), 499. (National Auxiliary Publications Service No. 02835.)

Hart, B., & Risley, T. R. (1980). In vivo language intervention. *Journal of Applied Behavior Analysis, 13*(3), 407-432.

Hendrickson, J. M., Strain, P. S., Tremblay, A., & Shores, R. E. (1982). Interactions of behaviorally handicapped children: Functional effects of peer social initiations. *Behavior Modification, 6*(3), 323-353.

Hurlbut, B. I., Iwata, B. A., & Green, J. D. (1982). Nonvocal language acquisition in adolescents with severe physical disabilities: Blissymbol versus iconic stimulus formats. *Journal of Applied Behavior Analysis, 15*(2), 241-258.

Jackson, G. M. (1979). The use of visual orientation feedback to facilitate attention and task performance. *Mental Retardation, 17*(6), 281-284.

Kirschenbaum, D. S., Dillman, J. S., & Karoly, P. (1982). Efficacy of behavioral contracting: Target behaviors, performance criteria, and settings. *Behavior Modification, 6*(4), 499-518.

Matson, J. L. (1981). Assessment and treatment of clinical fears in mentally retarded children. *Journal of Applied Behavior Analysis, 14*(3), 287-294.

Matson, J. L., & Adkins, J. (1980). A self-instructional social skills training program for mentally retarded persons. *Mental Retardation, 18*(5), 245-248.

Matson, J. L., & Andrasik, F. (1982). Training leisure time social-interaction skills to mentally retarded adults. *American Journal of Mental Deficiency, 86*(5), 533-542.

Mithaug, D. E., & Wolfe, M. S. (1976). Employing task arrangements and verbal contingencies to promote verbalizations between retarded children. *Journal of Applied Behavior Analysis, 9*(3), 301-314.

Oliver, C. B., & Halle, J. W. (1982). Language training in the everyday environment: Teaching functional sign use to a retarded child. *Journal of the Association for the Severely Handicapped, 7*(3), 50-62.

Paine, S. C., Hops, H., Walker, H. M., Greenwood, C. R., Fleischman, D. H., & Guild, J. J. (1982). Repeated treatment effects: A study of maintaining behavior change in socially withdrawn children. *Behavior Modification, 6*(2), 171-199.

Reese, S. C., & Filipczak, J. (1980). Assessment of skill generalization: Measurement across setting, behavior, and time in an educational setting. *Behavior Modification, 4*(2), 209-223.

Richman, J. S., Sonderby, T., & Kahn, J. V. (1980). Prerequisite vs. in vivo acquisition of self-feeding skill. *Behavior Research and Therapy, 18*, 327-332.

Risley, R., & Cuvo, A. J. (1980). Training mentally retarded adults to make emergency telephone calls. *Behavior Modification, 4*(4), 513-526.

Stokes, T., Fowler, S., & Baer, D. (1978). Training preschool children to recruit natural communities of reinforcement. *Journal of Applied Behavior Analysis, 11*(2), 285-303.

Tofte-Tipps, S., Mendonca, P., & Peach, R. V. (1982). Training and generalization of social skills: A study with two developmentally handicapped, socially isolated children. *Behavior Modification, 6*(1), 45-71.

VanBiervliet, A., Spangler, P. F., & Marshall, A. M. (1981). An ecobehavioral examination of a simple strategy for increasing mealtime language in residential facilities. *Journal of Applied Behavior Analysis, 14*(3), 295-305.

Wacker, D. P., & Berg, W. L. (1983). The effects of picture prompts on the acquisition of complex vocational tasks by mentally retarded adolescents. *Journal of Applied Behavior Analysis, 16*(4), 417-433.

Wacker, D. P., & Greenbaum, F. T. (1984). Efficacy of a verbal training sequence on the sorting performance of moderately and severely retarded adolescents. *American Journal of Mental Deficiency, 88*(6), 653-660.

Wehman, P., Renzaglia, A., Berry, G., Schultz, R., & Karan, O. (1978). Developing a leisure skill repertoire in severely and profoundly handicapped persons. *American Association for the Education of the Severely/Profoundly Handicapped Review, 3*(3), 162-172.

Discrimination Function Strategies

Anderson, S. R., & Spradlin, J. E. (1980). The generalized effects of productive labeling training involving common object classes. *Journal of the Association for the Severely Handicapped, 5*(2), 143-157.

Bourbeau, P. E., Sowers, J., & Close, D. W. (1986). An experimental analysis of generalization of banking skills from classroom to bank settings in the community. *Education and Training of the Mentally Retarded, 21*(2), 98-107.

Brady, M. P., Shores, R. E., Gunter, P., McEvoy, M. A., Fox, J. L., & White, C. (1984). Generalization of an adolescent's social interaction behavior via multiple peers in a classroom setting. *Journal of the Association for Persons with Severe Handicaps, 9*(4), 278-286.

Correa, V. I., Poulson, C. L., & Salzberg, C. L. (1984). Training and generalization of reach-grasp behavior in blind, severely/profoundly mentally retarded young children. Journal of Applied Behavior Analysis, 17(1), 57-69

Dunlap, G., Koegel, R. L., & Koegel, L. K. (1984). Continuity of treatment: Toilet training in multiple community settings. *Journal of the Association for Persons with Severe Handicaps, 9*(2), 134-141.

Frank, A. R., Wacker, D. P., Berg, W. K., & McMahon, C. M. (1985). Teaching selected microcomputer skills to retarded students via picture prompts. *Journal of Applied Behavior Analysis, 18*(2), 179-185.

Gaylord-Ross, R. J., Haring, T. G., Breen, C., & Pitts-Conway, V. (1984). The training and generalization of social interaction skills with autistic youth. *Journal of Applied Behavior Analysis, 17*(2), 229-247.

Hall, C., Sheldon-Wildgen, J., & Sherman, J. A. (1980). Teaching job interview skills to retarded clients. *Journal of Applied Behavior Analysis, 13*(3), 433-442.

Haring, T. (1985). Teaching between-class generalization of toy play behavior to handicapped children. *Journal of Applied Behavior Analysis, 18*(2), 127-139.

Hester, P., & Hendrickson, J. (1977). Training functionally expressive language. *Journal of Applied Behavior Analysis, 10*(2), 316. (National Auxiliary Publications Service No. 02915.)

Horner, R. H., & Budd, C. M. (1985). Acquisition of manual sign use: Collateral reduction of maladaptive behavior, and factors limiting generalization. *Education and Training of the Mentally Retarded, 20*(1), 39-47.

Horner, R. H., Jones, D. N., & Williams, J. A. (1985). A functional approach to teaching generalized street crossing. *Journal of the Association for Persons with Severe Handicaps, 10*(2), 71-78.

Horner, R. H., & McDonald, R. S. (1982). Comparison of single instance and general case instruction in teaching a generalized vocational skill. *Journal of the Association for Persons with Severe Handicaps, 7*(3), 7-20.

Jones, R. T., Sisson, L. A., & Van Hasselt, V. B. (1984). Emergency fire-safety skills for blind children and adolescents: Group training and generalization. *Behavior Modification, 8*(2), 267-286.

Kissel, R. C., & Whitman, T. L. (1977). An examination of the direct and generalized effects of a play-training and overcorrection procedure upon the self-stimulatory behavior of a profoundly retarded boy. *American Association for the Severely and Profoundly Handicapped Review, 2*(3), 131-146.

Koegel, R. L., Egel, A. L., & Williams, J. A. (1980). Behavioral contrast and generalization across settings in the treatment of autistic children. *Journal of Experimental Child Psychology, 30*(3), 422-437.

Kohl, F. L., Karlan, G. R., & Heal, L. W. (1979). Effects of pairing manual signs with verbal cues upon the acquisition of instruction following behaviors and the generalization to expressive language with severely handicapped students. *American Association for the Severely and Profoundly Handicapped Review, 4*(3), 291-300.

Lagomarcino, A., Reid, D. H., Ivancic, M. T., & Faw, G. D. (1984). Leisure-dance instruction for severely and profoundly retarded persons: Teaching an intermediate community living skill. *Journal of Applied Behavior Analysis, 17*(1), 71-84.

Lahey, B. B., Busmeyer, M. K., O'Hara, C., & Beggs, V. E. (1977). Treatment of severe perceptual-motor disorders in children diagnosed as learning disabled. *Behavior Modification, 1*(1), 123-140.

Lancioni, G. E., & Ceccarani, P. S. (1981). Teaching independent toileting within the normal daily program: Two studies with profoundly retarded children. *Behavior Research of Severe Developmental Disabilities, 2*, 79-96.

Lemanek, K. L., Williamson, D. A., Gresham, F. M., & Jensen, B. J. (1986). Social skills training with hearing-impaired children and adolescents. *Behavior Modification, 10*(1), 55-71.

Livi, J., & Ford, A. (1985). Skill transfer from a domestic training site to the actual homes of three moderately handicapped students. *Education and Training of the Mentally Retarded, 20*(1), 69-82.

MacKenzie, M. L., & Budd, K. S. (1981). A peer tutoring package to increase mathematics performance: Examination of generalized changes in classroom behavior. *Education and Treatment of Children, 4*(1), 1-15.

Marholin, D., O'Toole, K., Touchette, P. E., Berger, P. J., & Doyle, D. (1979). "I'll have a Big Mac, large fries, large coke, and apple pie . . . " or teaching adaptive community skills. *Behavior Therapy, 10*(2), 236-248.

Marholin, D., II, & Steinman, W. M. (1977). Stimulus control in the classroom as a function of the behavior reinforced. *Journal of Applied Behavior Analysis, 10*(3), 465-478.

McDonnell, J. J., Horner, R. H., & Williams, J. A. (1984). Comparison of three strategies for teaching generalized grocery purchasing to high school students with severe handicaps. *Journal of the Association for Persons with Severe Handicaps, 9*(2), 123-133.

McGee, G. G., Krantz, P. J., & McClannahan, L. E. (1985). The facilitative effects of incidental teaching on preposition use by autistic children. *Journal of Applied Behavior Analysis, 18*(1), 17-31.

Miller, S. M., & Sloane, H. N. (1976). The generalization effects of parent training across stimulus settings. *Journal of Applied Behavior Analysis, 9*(3), 355-370.

Mithaug, D. E. (1978). Case study in training generalized instruction-following responses to preposition-noun combinations in a severely retarded young adult. *American Association for the Severely and Profoundly Handicapped Review*, *4*(3), 230-245.

Murdock, G. Y., Garcia, E. E., & Hardman, M. L. (1977). Generalizing articulation training with trainable mentally retarded subjects. *Journal of Applied Behavior Analysis*, *10*(4), 717-733.

Neef, N. A., Iwata, B. A., & Page, T. J. (1978). Public transportation training: In vivo versus classroom instruction. *Journal of Applied Behavior Analysis*, *11*(3), 331-344.

Nietupski, J., Clancy, P., & Christiansen, C. (1984). Acquisition, maintenance, and generalization of vending machine purchasing skills by moderately handicapped students. *Education and Training of the Mentally Retarded*, *19*(2), 91-96.

Nietupski, J., Welch, J., & Wacker, D. (1983). Acquisition, maintenance, and transfer of grocery item purchasing skills by moderately and severely handicapped students. *Education and Training of the Mentally Retarded*, *18*(4), 279-286.

Nutter, D., & Reid, D. H. (1978). Teaching retarded women a clothing selection skill using community norms. *Journal of Applied Behavior Analysis*, *11*(4), 475-487.

Page, T. J., Iwata, B., & Neef, N. A. (1976). Teaching pedestrian skills to retarded persons: Generalization from the classroom to the natural environment. *Journal of Applied Behavior Analysis*, *9*(4), 433-444.

Pancsofar, E. L., & Bates, P. (1985). The impact of the acquisition of successive training exemplars on generalization. *Journal of the Association for Persons with Severe Handicaps*, *10*(2), 95-104.

Reichle, J., & Brown, L. (1986). Teaching the use of a multipage direct selection communication board to an adult with autism. *Journal of the Association for Persons with Severe Handicaps*, *11*(1), 68-73.

Reichle, J., Rogers, N., & Barrett, C. (1984). Establishing pragmatic discriminations among the communicative functions of requesting, rejecting, and commenting in an adolescent. *Journal of the Association for Persons with Severe Handicaps*, *9*(1), 31-36.

Richman, G. S., Reiss, M. L., Bauman, K. E., & Baily, J. S. (1984). Teaching menstrual care to mentally retarded women: Acquisition, generalization, and maintenance. *Journal of Applied Behavior Analysis*, *17*(4), 441-451.

Riordan, M. M., Iwata, B. A., Finney, J. W., Wohl, M. K., & Stanley, A. E. (1984). Behavioral assessment and treatment of chronic food refusal in handicapped children. *Journal of Applied Behavior Analysis*, *17*(3), 327-341.

Salmon, D. J., Pear, J. J., & Kuhn, B. A. (1986). Generalization of object naming after training with picture cards and with objects. *Journal of Applied Behavior Analysis*, *19*(1), 53-58.

Sarber, R. E., & Cuvo, A. J. (1983). Teaching nutritional meal planning to developmentally disabled clients. *Behavior Modification*, *7*(4), 503-530.

Schriebman, L., & Carr, E. G. (1978). Elimination of echolalic responding to questions through the training of a generalized verbal response. *Journal of Applied Behavior Analysis*, *11*(4), 453-463.

Sprague, J. R., & Horner, R. H. (1984). The effects of single instance, multiple instance, and general case training on generalized vending machine use by moderately and severely handicapped students. *Journal of Applied Behavior Analysis*, *17*(2), 273-278.

Stainback, S., Stainback, W., Wehman, P., & Spangiers, L. (1983). Acquisition and generalization of physical fitness exercises in three profoundly retarded adults. *Journal of the Association for the Severely Handicapped*, *8*(2), 47-55.

Sternberg, L., McNerney, C. D., & Pegnatore, L. (1985). Developing co-active imitative behaviors with profoundly mentally handicapped students. *Education and Training of the Mentally Retarded*, *20*(4), 260-267.

Storey, K., Bates, P., & Hanson, H. B. (1984). Acquisition and generalization of coffee purchase skills by adults with severe disabilities. *Journal of the Association for Persons with Severe Handicaps*, *9*(3), 178-185.

Thompson, T. J., Braam, S. J., & Fuqua, R. W. (1982). Training and generalization of laundry skills: A multiple probe evaluation with handicapped persons. *Journal of Applied Behavior Analysis, 15*(1), 177-182.

Trap, J. J., Milner-Davis, P., Joseph, S., & Cooper, J. O. (1978). The effects of feedback and consequences on transitional cursive letter formation. *Journal of Applied Behavior Analysis, 11*(3), 381-394.

Tucker, D. J., & Berry, G. W. (1980). Teaching severely multihandicapped students to put on their own hearing aids. *Journal of Applied Behavior Analysis, 13*(1), 65-75.

Warren, S. F., & Rogers-Warren, A. K. (1983). A longitudinal analysis of language generalization among adolescents with severe handicapping conditions. *Journal of the Association for Persons with Severe Handicaps, 8*(4), 18-31.

Welch, S. J., & Pear J. J. (1980). Generalization of naming responses to objects in the natural environment as a function of training stimulus modality with retarded children. *Journal of Applied Behavior Analysis, 13*(4), 629-643.

The steps in matching generalization strategies to learners are described in this chapter. Of course, we need more research to support the use of Decision Rules. But we believe that using these rules will increase our effectiveness in programming for generalization. The rules are not infallible. Use your data. Use your intelligence. And, if one strategy fails—TRY AGAIN! Generalization is the capstone of instruction. Without it, we fail as teachers. Achieve it, and increased independence and integration are the true results.

Chapter 9

DECISION RULES AND PROCEDURES FOR GENERALIZATION

Kathleen A. Liberty

The Decision Rules for Generalization consist of a series of questions regarding the current performance level of the target skill in probe and target situations and conditions in the generalization setting. It is assumed that, prior to the application of the Decision Rules, the target behavior and criterion levels of performance in the generalization setting have been identified.

When to Apply Decision Rules

Decision rules should be applied following a generalization probe.

1. **Before instruction occurs.** In one of five situations, we have found that initial assessment of students incorrectly identifies skills which need instruction for acquisition, when in fact the student is already performing that skill in another setting. In these cases, probes will help you recognize that the skill does not need instruction for acquisition, but procedures to make sure that the skill generalizes to the school situation. Once you have the information from the probe, you may use the Decision Rules to assist in selecting a particular strategy to facilitate the transfer to school.

2. **Following skill acquisition.** Generalization is not likely to occur until the skill has been acquired (see Chapters 4 and 5). Once the acquisition aim is met, a generalization probe should be conducted. The Decision Rules are then used to determine if the skill has generalized, and if not, to determine what type of strategy to use to facilitate generalization.

3. **Following use of generalization strategy.** Once you have implemented a generalization strategy and (a) the student has met aim under the new instructional procedures which incorporate generalization and/or (b) the target situation has been modified sufficiently, you should reprobe to determine the status of the skill and if an additional strategy should be used. These procedures continue until generalization is achieved.

How to Use the Decision Rules

1. **Probe for generalization.** To begin, you will need to conduct one or more generalization probes, as described in Chapter 7. The probe situations you select should match the conditions specified in the IEP objective for the skill (as described in Chapter 6). You may use the *Generalization Probe Report* (shown in Table 9–1) to record information about student performance, the probe situation, and events during the probe. Reading through the questions and procedures before

you probe will help you identify what to look for in your observations or what questions to ask in the probe interview.

2. **Follow step-by-step questions.** Once you have completed the probes, you will be ready to apply the Decision Rules for Generalization. These rules are presented as a sequence of questions (shown in Table 9–2). Information about student performance and probe events is used to answer each question, as described in the "Procedures" column of the Decision Rules (Table 9–2). The answer determines whether you continue in the sequence or stop, because you have identified the nature of the decision to be made. If you are unsure of whether the problem you identify is the real problem, you may wish to read the examples included in the previous chapter.

The *Generalization Decision Report* (see Table 9–3) may be used to record the decision process for a particular student's skill. A new report would be completed each time the process was initiated.

3. **Select a strategy** or combination of strategies. The list which accompanies the decision step will provide guidance. A description of each strategy and examples of how each can be applied is provided in the preceding chapter (see Table 9–4).

It will be necessary to develop an instructional plan incorporating the selected strategy or strategy combination. Depending on the strategy selected, it may also be necessary to train people in the new procedures; to arrange transportation; to adapt, construct, or purchase materials; to survey a number of settings; to identify natural reinforcers; and so forth.

4. **Implement the strategy**. Use the new strategy until the student has reached desired performance levels and/or the next generalization probe is conducted. You may wish to establish an aim date by which you expect the strategy to be effective, in keeping with the aim date established in the objective.

5. **Reprobe for generalization**. Conduct a new generalization probe while the strategy is in effect, at the aim date, and/or when the student has reached desired performance levels in training. Then repeat steps 1 through 5 as needed.

Examples

Examples of Probe and Generalization Decision Reports are provided in the tables at the end of the chapter.

Decision Rules Flow Chart

Once you have become familiar with the procedures involved in applying the Decision Rules, as described in Table 9–2, you may wish to use the flow chart at the back of the chapter (Figure 9–1) to guide your decision steps. To use this chart, you follow the lettered sequence of questions enclosed in the diamonds. In some cases, the questions have been slightly reworded so that the information will fit into the available space. The possible answers to each question are circled. If you find that you need more information to answer a particular question, you may need to review your probes, or reprobe to collect the needed information.

Table 9-1

Generalization Probe Report

Student: **Date:**

IEP Objective:[*]

Student Performance [*]

(1) Who provided the information on student performance?

(2) Was the skill directly observed for this probe?

(3) How many opportunities did the student have to perform the skill?

(4) When were the opportunities provided?

(5) Did the student perform the target skill?

(6) Did the student display inappropriate behavior or a previously learned skill instead of, or in addition to, the target skill?

(7) Did the student fail to respond?

(8) Describe the student's performance:

Probe Situation

Reinforcers Accessed by Student[*]

(9)   ( ) Were natural reinforcers for performance of the skill.
(10) ( ) Were not natural reinforcers for the skill.
(11) ( ) Included both natural and not natural reinforcers.
(12) ( ) Person reinforced inappropriate behavior, other behavior, or nonresponse, with reinforcer which should have been available for performance of skill.
(13) ( ) Student accessed natural reinforcer by doing something else.
(14) ( ) Person attended to other behavior.
(15) ( ) Person completed the skill task.
(16) ( ) Person physically assisted the student to complete the skill task.
(17) ( ) Person provided another reinforcer.
(18) ( ) Student did not access reinforcers.
         Describe what happened:

Stimuli Which Triggered the Opportunity to Perform the Skill[*]

(19) ( ) Were natural stimuli which occurred without need for intervention.
(20) ( ) Were naturally provided by persons in the generalization situation.
(21) ( ) Were not natural stimuli for the skill.
(22) ( ) Included both natural and not natural stimuli.
(23) ( ) Included training stimuli.
(24) ( ) Other:

Conditions Which Differed From Instruction (Check all that apply)[*]

(25) ( ) Materials or objects. Describe:

(26) ( ) Setting. Describe:

(27) ( ) Probe manager or persons who interacted with student.
(28) ( ) Person cued the student what to do.
(29) ( ) Person did not cue the student what to do.
(30) ( ) Person encouraged the student.
(31) ( ) Person did not encourage the student.
(32) ( ) Person physically assisted or physically prompted the student.
(33) ( ) Person did not physically assist or prompt the student.
(34) ( ) Person reinforced as often.
(35) ( ) Person reinforced less frequently.
(36) ( ) Student's performance criticized/corrected more frequently.
(37) ( ) Student's performance criticized/corrected less often.
         Person provided feedback on performance, especially errors or mistakes.
(38) ( ) Person did not provide feedback.
(39) ( ) Person praised the student during/after skill performance.
(40) ( ) Person did not praise the student.
(41) ( ) Other:

[*]Answers needed to apply Decision Rules.

Table 9-2

Decision Rules for Generalization

	QUESTION	PROCEDURES	ANSWER	NEXT STEP/DECISION
A.	Has skill generalized at the desired level in all target situations?	Probe for generalization in all desired situations, then compare performance with criteria (IEP objective).	yes	**1** SUCCESSFUL INSTRUCTION * Step ahead to a more difficult level of skill * Choose a new skill to teach EXIT sequence
			no	CONTINUE with question B.
B.	Has skill been acquired?	Compare performance in instructional situation with criteria for acquisition or performance levels specified in IEP objective. Answer yes if student has met performance levels in training situation but not in generalization.	yes	CONTINUE with question C.
			no	**2** SKILL MASTERY PROBLEM * Continue instruction EXIT sequence
C.	Is generalization desired to only a few situations?	Analyze function of skill in current and future environments available to student.	yes	CONTINUE with question D.
			no	CONTINUE with question E.
D.	Is it possible to train directly in those situations?	Are all situations frequently accessible for training so that training time is likely to be adequate to meet aim date in IEP objective?	yes	**3** LIMITED GENERALIZATION SITUATIONS * Train in desired situation * Train sequentially in all situations (i.e., sequential modification) EXIT sequence
			no	CONTINUE with question E.
E.	Is the student reinforced even though he/she does not do the target skill?	Observe student behavior during probes and note events which follow appropriate, inappropriate, target, and nontarget skills. Determine if those events which should follow the target skill, or have been shown to reinforce other skills, are presented to the student, or available even if he does not respond, or if he does the skill incorrectly, or if he misbehaves.	yes	CONTINUE with question F.
			no	CONTINUE with question H.

Continue to next page.

Table 9-2 (continued)

QUESTION	PROCEDURES	ANSWER	NEXT STEP/DECISION
F. Does the student fail to respond and is reinforced?	Answer yes only if the student is reinforced for doing nothing (i.e., accesses reinforcers for "no response").	yes	**4** NONCONTINGENT REINFORCER PROBLEM * Alter generalization contingencies
		no	CONTINUE with question G.
G. Is the behavior reinforced by the same reinforcers as the target skill?	If misbehavior or other behavior accesses same reinforcer available for target skill, answer yes.	yes	**5** COMPETING BEHAVIOR PROBLEM * Increase proficiency * Amplify instructed behavior * Alter generalization contingencies EXIT sequence
		no	**6** COMPETING REINFORCER PROBLEM * Alter generalization contingencies EXIT sequence
H. Did the student generalize once at or close to criterion performance levels and then not as well on other opportunities?	Consider performance in current and past probes. Compare student performance for each response opportunity with performance level specified in objective. If near criterion performance occurred on the first response opportunity, and performance was poor or nonexistent after that, answer yes.	yes	**7** REINFORCING FUNCTION PROBLEM * Program natural reinforcers * Eliminate training reinforcers * Use natural schedules * Use natural consequences * Teach self-reinforcement * Teach to solicit reinforcement * Reinforce generalized behavior * Alter generalization contingencies EXIT sequence
		no	CONTINUE with question I.
I. Did the student respond partially correctly during at least one response opportunity?	Analyze anecdotal data and observation notes from probe.	yes	**8** DISCRIMINATION FUNCTION PROBLEM Vary stimuli: * Use all stimuli * Use frequent stimuli * Use multiple exemplars * Use general case exemplars EXIT sequence
		no	CONTINUE with question J.
J. Did the student fail to perform any part of the target skill?	Analyze student performance during probe situation.	yes	**9** GENERALIZATION TRAINING FORMAT * Increase proficiency * Program natural reinforcers * Use natural schedules * Use appropriate natural stimuli * Eliminate training stimuli EXIT sequence
		no	*STOP.* You have made an error in the sequence. Begin again at Question A.

Table 9-3

Generalization Decision Report

Student _____   Skill _____

Decision-Maker _____   Date _____

QUESTION	*ANSWER*	*DECISION*	*COMMENTS*
A. Has skill generalized at the desired level in all target situations?	yes	**1** SUCCESSFUL INSTRUCTION ( ) Step ahead to a more difficult level of skill ( ) Choose a new skill to teach	
	no	CONTINUE with question B.	
B. Has skill been acquired?	yes	CONTINUE with question C.	
	no	**2** SKILL MASTERY PROBLEM ( ) Continue instruction	
C. Is generalization desired to only a few situations?	yes	CONTINUE with question D.	
	no	CONTINUE with question E.	
D. Is it possible to train directly in those situations?	yes	**3** LIMITED GENERALIZATION SITUATIONS ( ) Train in desired situation ( ) Train sequentially in all situations [i.e., sequential modification]	
	no	CONTINUE with question E.	
E. Is the student reinforced even though he/she does not do the target skill?	yes	CONTINUE with question F.	
	no	CONTINUE with question H.	
F. Does the student fail to respond and is reinforced?	yes	**4** NONCONTINGENT REINFORCER PROBLEM ( ) Alter generalization contingencies	
	no	CONTINUE with question G.	
G. Is the behavior reinforced by the same reinforcers as the target skill?	yes	**5** COMPETING BEHAVIOR PROBLEM ( ) Increase proficiency ( ) Amplify instructed behavior ( ) Alter generalization contingencies	
	no	**6** COMPETING REINFORCER PROBLEM ( ) Alter generalization contingencies	

Continue to next page.

Table 9-3 (continued)

QUESTION	ANSWER	DECISION	COMMENTS
H. Did the student generalize once at or close to criterion performance levels and then not as well on other opportunities?	yes	**7 REINFORCING FUNCTION PROBLEM** ( ) Program natural reinforcers ( ) Eliminate training reinforcers ( ) Use natural schedules ( ) Use natural consequences ( ) Teach self-reinforcement ( ) Teach to solicit reinforcement ( ) Reinforce generalized behavior ( ) Alter generalization contingencies	
	no	CONTINUE with question I.	
I. Did the student respond partially correctly during at least one response opportunity?	yes	**8 DISCRIMINATION FUNCTION PROBLEM** Vary stimuli: ( ) Use all stimuli ( ) Use frequent stimuli ( ) Use multiple exemplars ( ) Use general case exemplars	
	no	CONTINUE with question J.	
J. Did the student fail to perform any part of the target skill?	yes	**9 GENERALIZATION TRAINING FORMAT** ( ) Increase proficiency ( ) Program natural reinforcers ( ) Use natural schedules ( ) Use appropriate natural stimuli ( ) Eliminate training stimuli	
	no	*STOP.* You have made an error in the sequence. Begin again at Question A.	

Table 9-4

Index to Additional Information About Strategies

Table 9-5
Mark

Generalization Probe Report

Student: Mark   **Date:** Oct. 29

IEP Objective:* *Mark will demonstrate the ability to suck liquid through a straw without spilling liquid from his mouth. The straw will be placed through the plastic lid of a plastic glass. The glass will be held by a member of the classroom. Generalization to home & community settings, to other cup-straw combinations, & to other people holding cup will be determined when Mark sucks independently on 80% of opportunities before person signals that he/she has waited too long (e.g., by removing cup or leaving, etc.)*

Student Performance*

(1) Who provided the information on student performance?
staff not doing instruction; parent; volunteer

(2) Was the skill directly observed for this probe?
yes

(3) How many opportunities did the student have to perform the skill?
3 @ home; 3 @ school; 6 on field-trip

(4) When were the opportunities provided?
at natural meal times / school snack time

(5) Did the student perform the target skill?
yes

(6) Did the student display inappropriate behavior or a previously learned skill instead of, or in addition to, the target skill?
no

(7) Did the student fail to respond?
no

(8) Describe the student's performance:
field trip to zoo: 6 sips in 35 seconds, then drank 8 oz. of apple juice in about 5 minutes.
home: used a regular glass & regular plastic straw. "drank all of the juice right away at at a good rate"
school: 3 different people offered juice (4 oz. each). 3 different locations in room--standing table, in wheel-chair, w/out tray table; in wheelchair w/tray table. (Used regular cup used in classroom instruction). All finished w/in 2 minutes, no spilling. "very fast", "much faster than trying to get him to drink from a cup"

Probe Situation

Reinforcers Accessed by Student*

(9) (X) Were natural reinforcers for performance of the skill.
(10) (X) Were not natural reinforcers for the skill.
(11) ( ) Included both natural and not natural reinforcers.
(12) ( ) Person reinforced inappropriate behavior, other behavior, or nonresponse, with reinforcer which should have been available for performance of skill.
(13) ( ) Student accessed natural reinforcer by doing something else.
(14) ( ) Person attended to other behavior.
(15) ( ) Person completed the skill task.
(16) ( ) Person physically assisted the student to complete the skill task.
(17) ( ) Person provided another reinforcer.
(18) ( ) Student did not access reinforcers.
Describe what happened:

Stimuli Which Triggered the Opportunity to Perform the Skill*

(19) (X) Were natural stimuli which occurred without need for intervention.
(20) (X) Were naturally provided by persons in the generalizationsituation.
(21) ( ) Were not natural stimuli for the skill.
(22) ( ) Included both natural and not natural stimuli.
(23) ( ) Included training stimuli.
(24) ( ) Other:

Conditions Which Differed From Instruction (Check all that apply)*

(25) (X) Materials or objects. Describe: *paper glass & paper straw; glass tumbler & plastic straw + training glass*

(26) (X) Setting. Describe: *w/lid & straw* *classroom, picnic on field-trip, home*

(27) (X) Probe manager or persons who interacted with student.
(28) ( ) Person cued the student what to do.
(29) (X) Person did not cue the student what to do.
(30) ( ) Person encouraged the student.
(31) (X) Person did not encourage the student.
(32) ( ) Person physically assisted or physically prompted the student.
(33) (X) Person did not physically assist or prompt the student.
(34) ( ) Person reinforced as often.
(35) ( ) Person reinforced less frequently.
(36) ( ) Student's performance criticized/corrected more frequently.
(37) ( ) Student's performance criticized/corrected less often.
(38) (X) Person provided feedback on performance, especially errors or mistakes.
(39) (X) Person did not provide feedback.
(40) (X) Person praised the student during/after skill performance.
(41) ( ) Person did not praise the student.
Other:

*Answers needed to apply Decision Rules.

Table 9-5, **Mark** (continued)

Generalization Decision Report

Student ___Mark___   Skill ___Use a straw___

Decision-Maker _____   Date ___Nov. 1___

QUESTION	ANSWER	DECISION	COMMENTS
A. Has skill generalized at the desired level in all target situations?	(yes)	1 SUCCESSFUL INSTRUCTION (X) Step ahead to a more difficult level of skill ( ) Choose a new skill to teach	*Teach Mark to hold the glass by himself*
	no	CONTINUE with question B.	
B. Has skill been acquired?	yes	CONTINUE with question C.	
	no	2 SKILL MASTERY PROBLEM ( ) Continue instruction	
C. Is generalization desired to only a few situations?	yes	CONTINUE with question D.	
	no	CONTINUE with question E.	
D. Is it possible to train directly in those situations?	yes	3 LIMITED GENERALIZATION SITUATIONS ( ) Train in desired situation ( ) Train sequentially in all situations [i.e., sequential modification]	
	no	CONTINUE with question E.	
E. Is the student reinforced even though he/she does not do the target skill?	yes	CONTINUE with question F.	
	no	CONTINUE with question H.	
F. Does the student fail to respond and is reinforced?	yes	4 NONCONTINGENT REINFORCER PROBLEM ( ) Alter generalization contingenices	
	no	CONTINUE with question G.	
G. Is the behavior reinforced by the same reinforcers as the target skill?	yes	5 COMPETING BEHAVIOR PROBLEM ( ) Increase proficiency ( ) Amplify instructed behavior ( ) Alter generalization contingencies	
	no	6 COMPETING REINFORCER PROBLEM ( ) Alter generalization contingencies	

Continue to next page.

Table 9-5, **Mark** (continued)

QUESTION	ANSWER	DECISION	COMMENTS
H. Did the student generalize once at or close to criterion performance levels and then not as well on other opportunities?	yes	**7** REINFORCING FUNCTION PROBLEM ( ) Program natural reinforcers ( ) Eliminate training reinforcers ( ) Use natural schedules ( ) Use natural consequences ( ) Teach self-reinforcement ( ) Teach to solicit reinforcement ( ) Reinforce generalized behavior ( ) Alter generalization contingencies	
	no	CONTINUE with question I.	
I. Did the student respond partially correctly during at least one response opportunity?	yes	**8** DISCRIMINATION FUNCTION PROBLEM Vary stimuli: ( ) Use all stimuli ( ) Use frequent stimuli ( ) Use multiple exemplars ( ) Use general case exemplars	
	no	CONTINUE with question J.	
J. Did the student fail to perform any part of the target skill?	yes	**9** GENERALIZATION TRAINING FORMAT ( ) Increase proficiency ( ) Program natural reinforcers ( ) Use natural schedules ( ) Use appropriate natural stimuli ( ) Eliminate training stimuli	
	no	*STOP*. You have made an error in the sequence. Begin again at Question A.	

Table 9-6
Sally

Generalization Probe Report

Student: _Sally_   Date: _October 11_

IEP Objective:* _Sally will demonstrate the ability to turn on radios/tape recorder/t.v. with either turn-knob, roll-friction switch, push-button, or pull-button method of activation, when given untrained leisure appliance. She will be able to locate switch and turn on within 10 seconds without assistance or cues. (All appliances presented)_
Aim date: December 22

Student Performance*

(1) Who provided the information on student performance?
teacher

(2) Was the skill directly observed for this probe?
yes

(3) How many opportunities did the student have to perform the skill?
six

(4) When were the opportunities provided?
during "free" time in classroom

(5) Did the student perform the target skill?
yes, 3 of 6

(6) Did the student display inappropriate behavior or a previously learned skill instead of, or in addition to, the target skill?
_no_

(7) Did the student fail to respond?
no—always tried

(8) Describe the student's performance:
1. _radio w/turn-knob (Correct, 4 sec.)_
2. _radio w/friction switch (Error, 35 sec.), tried wrong switch, trying to turn knob_
3. _radio w/turn-knob (Correct, 9 sec.)_
4. _Walkman w/friction switch (Correct, 8 sec.)_
5. _portable tape recorer w/push button (Error, 35 sec.) kept trying to push, seemed not to push hard enough_
6. _t.v. w/pull button (Error, 25 sec.)—could not locate switch_

Probe Situation

Reinforcers Accessed by Student*

(9)	(X)	Were natural reinforcers for performance of the skill.
(10)	( )	Were not natural reinforcers for the skill.
(11)	( )	Included both natural and not natural reinforcers.
(12)	( )	Person reinforced inappropriate behavior, other behavior, or nonresponse, with reinforcer which should have been available for performance of skill.
(13)	( )	Student accessed natural reinforcer by doing something else.
(14)	( )	Person attended to other behavior.
(15)	( )	Person completed the skill task.
(16)	( )	Person physically assisted the student to complete the skill task.
(17)	( )	Person provided another reinforcer.
(18)	( )	Student did not access reinforcers.
		Describe what happened:

Stimuli Which Triggered the Opportunity to Perform the Skill*

(19)	(X)	Were natural stimuli which occurred without need for intervention.
(20)	( )	Were naturally provided by persons in the generalization situation.
(21)	( )	Were not natural stimuli for the skill.
(22)	( )	Included both natural and not natural stimuli.
(23)	( )	Included training stimuli.
(24)	( )	Other:

Conditions Which Differed From Instruction (Check all that apply)*

(25) ( ) Materials or objects. Describe:
see description in student performance

(26) ( ) Setting. Describe:
classroom & music room at school

(27)	( )	Probe manager or persons who interacted with student.
(28)	( )	Person cued the student what to do.
(29)	(X)	Person did not cue the student what to do.
(30)	( )	Person encouraged the student.
(31)	( )	Person did not encourage the student.
(32)	( )	Person physically assisted or physically prompted the student.
(33)	(X)	Person did not physically assist or prompt the student.
(34)	( )	Person reinforced as often.
(35)	( )	Person reinforced less frequently.
(36)	( )	Student's performance criticized/corrected more frequently.
(37)	(X)	Student's performance criticized/corrected less often.
(38)	(X)	Person provided feedback on performance, especially errors or mistakes.
(39)	(X)	Person did not provide feedback.
(40)	(X)	Person praised the student during/after skill performance.
(41)	( )	Person did not praise the student.
		Other:

*Answers needed to apply Decision Rules.

Table 9-6, **Sally** (continued)

Generalization Decision Report

Student _Sally_   Skill _activate switch on appliance_

Decision-Maker _____ Date _October 15_

	QUESTION	ANSWER	DECISION	COMMENTS
A.	Has skill generalized at the desired level in all target situations?	yes	**1 SUCCESSFUL INSTRUCTION** ( ) Step ahead to a more difficult level of skill ( ) Choose a new skill to teach	
		(no)	CONTINUE with question B.	
B.	Has skill been acquired?	(yes)	CONTINUE with question C.	
		no	**2 SKILL MASTERY PROBLEM** ( ) Continue instruction	
C.	Is generalization desired to only a few situations?	yes	CONTINUE with question D.	_lots of different types of radios, tvs, tape recorders, etc._
		(no)	CONTINUE with question E.	
D.	Is it possible to train directly in those situations?	yes	**3 LIMITED GENERALIZATION SITUATIONS** ( ) Train in desired situation ( ) Train sequentially in all situations [i.e., sequential modification]	
		no	CONTINUE with question E.	
E.	Is the student reinforced even though he/she does not do the target skill?	yes	CONTINUE with question F.	
		(no)	CONTINUE with question H.	
F.	Does the student fail to respond and is reinforced?	yes	**4 NONCONTINGENT REINFORCER PROBLEM** ( ) Alter generalization contingenices	
		no	CONTINUE with question G.	
G.	Is the behavior reinforced by the same reinforcers as the target skill?	yes	**5 COMPETING BEHAVIOR PROBLEM** ( ) Increase proficiency ( ) Amplify instructed behavior ( ) Alter generalization contingencies	
		no	**6 COMPETING REINFORCER PROBLEM** ( ) Alter generalization contingencies	

Continue to next page.

Table 9-6, **Sally** (continued)

QUESTION	ANSWER	DECISION	COMMENTS
H. Did the student generalize once at or close to criterion performance levels and then not as well on other opportunities?	yes	**7 REINFORCING FUNCTION PROBLEM** ( ) Program natural reinforcers ( ) Eliminate training reinforcers ( ) Use natural schedules ( ) Use natural consequences ( ) Teach self-reinforcement ( ) Teach to solicit reinforcement ( ) Reinforce generalized behavior ( ) Alter generalization contingencies	*Was not able to do "once well" for all switch types: once well for friction switch; did not do pull button or push button; twice well for turn knob.*
	(no)	CONTINUE with question I.	*From examples in Chapter 8, not a "reinforcing function" problem*
I. Did the student respond partially correctly during at least one response opportunity?	(yes)	**8 DISCRIMINATION FUNCTION PROBLEM** Vary stimuli: ( ) Use all stimuli ( ) Use frequent stimuli (X) Use multiple exemplars ( ) Use general case exemplars	*Sally tried to activate all of the switches. We'll try more training on a wider variety of switches, and vary the location of switches too.*
	no	CONTINUE with question J.	
J. Did the student fail to perform any part of the target skill?	yes	**9 GENERALIZATION TRAINING FORMAT** ( ) Increase proficiency ( ) Program natural reinforcers ( ) Use natural schedules ( ) Use appropriate natural stimuli ( ) Eliminate training stimuli	
	no	*STOP.* You have made an error in the sequence. Begin again at Question A.	

Table 9-7
George

Generalization Probe Report

Student: _George_   Date: _December 12_

IEP Objective: * _George will point to either a symbol
for 'yes' or a symbol for 'no' (green & red pieces of
cardboard, respectively) to answer "Do you want (object)?"
questions. He will answer 6 of 8 questions w/in 10
seconds. He will answer questions in at least 3 different
non-school settings, when asked by people other than the
classroom staff who instruct the skill. The aim date is
June 6._

Student Performance *

(1) Who provided the information on student performance?
People who asked questions

(2) Was the skill directly observed for this probe?
Yes

(3) How many opportunities did the student have to perform the skill?
_6_

(4) When were the opportunities provided?
Natural opportunities

(5) Did the student perform the target skill?
Yes--answered 3 questions

(6) Did the student display inappropriate behavior or a previously learned
skill instead of, or in addition to, the target skill? _Yes--reached for milk,
then pointed to yes when prompted to do so (trial 3 & 5)_

(7) Did the student fail to respond?
Yes--no response to 3 questions

(8) Describe the student's performance: _Questions and response:_

Do you want the napkin   (NR) (23 sec.)
cookies   (NR) (24 sec.)
milk   (yes) (23 sec.)
milk   (yes) (6 sec.)
milk   (yes) (19 sec.)
milk   (NR) (31 sec.)

Probe Situation

Reinforcers Accessed by Student *

(9) ⊗ Were natural reinforcers for performance of the skill.
(10) ⊗ Were not natural reinforcers for the skill.
(11) ◯ Included both natural and not natural reinforcers.
(12) ⊗ Person reinforced inappropriate behavior, other behavior, or nonresponse, with
reinforcer which should have been available for performance of skill.
(13) (X) Student accessed natural reinforcer by doing something else.
(14) ⊗ Person attended to other behavior.
(15) ◯ Person completed the skill task.
(16) ◯ Person physically assisted the student to complete the skill task.
(17) ◯ Person provided another reinforcer.
(18) ◯ Student did not access reinforcers.
Describe what happened:

Stimuli Which Triggered the Opportunity to Perform the Skill *

(19) ⊗ Were natural stimuli which occurred without need for intervention.
(20) ⊗ Were naturally provided by persons in the generalization situation.
(21) ⊗ Were not natural stimuli for the skill.
(22) ◯ Included both natural and not natural stimuli.
(23) ◯ Included training stimuli.
(24) ◯ Other:

Conditions Which Differed From Instruction (Check all that apply) *

(25) ( ) Materials or objects. Describe:

(26) ⊗ Setting. Describe:

(27) ⊗ Probe manager or persons who interacted with student.
(28) ⊗ Person cued the student what to do.
(29) ⊗ Person did not cue the student what to do.
(30) ◯ Person encouraged the student.
(31) ◯ Person did not encourage the student.
(32) ◯ Person physically assisted or physically prompted the student.
(33) ◯ Person did not physically assist or prompt the student.
(34) ◯ Person reinforced as often.
(35) ◯ Person reinforced less frequently.
(36) ⊗ Student's performance criticized/corrected more frequently.
(37) ⊗ Student's performance criticized/corrected less often.
(38) ◯ Person provided feedback on performance, especially errors or mistakes.
(39) ◯ Person did not provide feedback.
(40) ◯ Person praised the student during/after skill performance.
(41) ◯ Person did not praise the student.

* Answers needed to apply Decision Rules.

Table 9-7, **George** (continued)

Generalization Decision Report

Student _____George_____   Skill ___answers yes/no_____

Decision-Maker _____   Date ___January 8_____

QUESTION	ANSWER	DECISION	COMMENTS
A. Has skill generalized at the desired level in all target situations?	yes	**1 SUCCESSFUL INSTRUCTION** ( ) Step ahead to a more difficult level of skill ( ) Choose a new skill to teach	
	(no)	CONTINUE with question B.	
B. Has skill been acquired?	(yes)	CONTINUE with question C.	
	no	**2 SKILL MASTERY PROBLEM** ( ) Continue instruction	
C. Is generalization desired to only a few situations?	yes	CONTINUE with question D.	
	(no)	CONTINUE with question E.	
D. Is it possible to train directly in those situations?	yes	**3 LIMITED GENERALIZATION SITUATIONS** ( ) Train in desired situation ( ) Train sequentially in all situations [i.e., sequential modification]	
	no	CONTINUE with question E.	
E. Is the student reinforced even though he/she does not do the target skill?	(yes)	CONTINUE with question F.	*The 'no-response' functions like a "no" in this situation, since he doesn't get the item.*
	no	CONTINUE with question H.	
F. Does the student fail to respond and is reinforced?	(yes)	**4 NONCONTINGENT REINFORCER PROBLEM** (x) Alter generalization contingenices	*All questions asked seemed to be ones the questioner expected to be answered 'yes.' Also, gets asked another question even if didn't answer first*
	no	CONTINUE with question G.	
G. Is the behavior reinforced by the same reinforcers as the target skill?	yes	**5 COMPETING BEHAVIOR PROBLEM** ( ) Increase proficiency ( ) Amplify instructed behavior ( ) Alter generalization contingencies	*one. To change this situation, the questioner has the item &/or prevents George from taking it himself (maybe too artificial). Main problem is that he doesn't have to answer.*
	no	**6 COMPETING REINFORCER PROBLEM** ( ) Alter generalization contingencies	*Try changing the contingencies so that he does have to*

Continue to next page.

answer or else a long wait before the next question.

Table 9-7, **George** (continued)

QUESTION	ANSWER	DECISION	COMMENTS
H. Did the student generalize once at or close to criterion performance levels and then not as well on other opportunities?	yes	**7** REINFORCING FUNCTION PROBLEM ( ) Program natural reinforcers ( ) Eliminate training reinforcers ( ) Use natural schedules ( ) Use natural consequences ( ) Teach self-reinforcement ( ) Teach to solicit reinforcement ( ) Reinforce generalized behavior ( ) Alter generalization contingencies	
	no	CONTINUE with question I.	
I. Did the student respond partially correctly during at least one response opportunity?	yes	**8** DISCRIMINATION FUNCTION PROBLEM Vary stimuli: ( ) Use all stimuli ( ) Use frequent stimuli ( ) Use multiple exemplars ( ) Use general case exemplars	
	no	CONTINUE with question J.	
J. Did the student fail to perform any part of the target skill?	yes	**9** GENERALIZATION TRAINING FORMAT ( ) Increase proficiency ( ) Program natural reinforcers ( ) Use natural schedules ( ) Use appropriate natural stimuli ( ) Eliminate training stimuli	
	no	*STOP*. You have made an error in the sequence. Begin again at Question A.	

Table 9-8
Linda

Generalization Probe Report

Student: *Linda*   Date: *January 25*

IEP Objective:* *Linda will wipe her mouth to clear food/ drink from her face within 5 seconds of a request to do so—at home and at school. People requesting can be anyone seated at lunch table (exclude instructors for this program). Linda will follow this direction 2 out of 3 requests.*

Student Performance*

(1) Who provided the information on student performance?
person requesting skill & parent

(2) Was the skill directly observed for this probe?
yes

(3) How many opportunities did the student have to perform the skill?
9 at school/several at home

(4) When were the opportunities provided?
natural times @ meals (lunch @ school/dinner @ home)

(5) Did the student perform the target skill?
yes (2 of 9 trials @ school); none at home

(6) Did the student display inappropriate behavior or a previously learned skill instead of, or in addition to, the target skill? *yes: tear up napkin, play peek-a-boo (home); wipe hair, neck (school)*

(7) Did the student fail to respond?
no

(8) Describe the student's performance: *School probe conducted first: responded correctly w/in 2 sec. on trials 1 & 4 -- inappropriate behavior, which was ignored, on other trials. Got to continue eating w/out wiping mouth. Home probe: mother reported that she tore up paper napkins & laughed each time; played peek-a-boo w/cloth napkins. She has never seen her wipe her mouth. Reports that her dad taught her to tear up napkins.*

Probe Situation

Reinforcers Accessed by Student*

(9) ⊗ Were natural reinforcers for performance of the skill.
(10) ◯ Were not natural reinforcers for the skill.
(11) ◯ Included both natural and not natural reinforcers.
(12) ◯ Person reinforced inappropriate behavior, other behavior, or nonresponse, with reinforcer which should have been available for performance of skill.
(13) ⊗ Student accessed natural reinforcer by doing something else.
(14) ⊗ Person attended to other behavior.
(15) ◯ Person completed the skill task.
(16) ◯ Person physically assisted the student to complete the skill task.
(17) ◯ Person provided another reinforcer.
(18) ◯ Student did not access reinforcers.
     Describe what happened:

Stimuli Which Triggered the Opportunity to Perform the Skill*

(19) ◯ Were natural stimuli which occurred without need for intervention.
(20) ⊗ Were naturally provided by persons in the generalizationsituation.
(21) ◯ Were not natural stimuli for the skill.
(22) ◯ Included both natural and not natural stimuli.
(23) ⊗ Included training stimuli.
(24) ◯ Other:

Conditions Which Differed From Instruction (Check all that apply)*

(25) ( ) Materials or objects. Describe:

(26) ( ) Setting. Describe:

(27) ⊗ Probe manager or persons who interacted with student.
(28) ◯ Person cued the student what to do.
(29) ◯ Person did not cue the student what to do.
(30) ◯ Person encouraged the student.
(31) ◯ Person did not encourage the student.
(32) ◯ Person physically assisted or physically prompted the student. *1 trial at home*
(33) ⊗ Person did not physically assist or prompt the student.
(34) ◯ Person reinforced as often.
(35) ◯ Person reinforced less frequently.
(36) ◯ Student's performance criticized/corrected more frequently.
(37) ◯ Student's performance criticized/corrected less often.
(38) ◯ Person provided feedback on performance, especially errors or mistakes.
(39) ◯ Person did not provide feedback.
(40) ◯ Person praised the student during/after skill performance.
(41) ◯ Person did not praise the student.
     ◯ Other:

*Answers needed to apply Decision Rules.

Table 9-8, **Linda** (continued)

Generalization Decision Report

Student ___*Linda*___ Skill ___*wipes mouth with napkin*___

Decision-Maker _____ Date ___*February 2*___

QUESTION	ANSWER	DECISION	COMMENTS
A. Has skill generalized at the desired level in all target situations?	yes	**1 SUCCESSFUL INSTRUCTION** ( ) Step ahead to a more difficult level of skill ( ) Choose a new skill to teach	
	(no)	CONTINUE with question B.	
B. Has skill been acquired?	(yes)	CONTINUE with question C.	
	no	**2 SKILL MASTERY PROBLEM** ( ) Continue instruction	
C. Is generalization desired to only a few situations?	yes	CONTINUE with question D.	
	(no)	CONTINUE with question E.	
D. Is it possible to train directly in those situations?	yes	**3 LIMITED GENERALIZATION SITUATIONS** ( ) Train in desired situation ( ) Train sequentially in all situations [i.e., sequential modification]	
	no	CONTINUE with question E.	
E. Is the student reinforced even though he/she does not do the target skill?	(yes)	CONTINUE with question F.	*Three possible reinforcers: getting next bite whether she wipes or not; having*
	no	CONTINUE with question H.	
F. Does the student fail to respond and is reinforced?	yes	**4 NONCONTINGENT REINFORCER PROBLEM** ( ) Alter generalization contingenices	*clean face (when she wipes it or when someone wipes it for her), and attention for other behaviors like*
	(no)	CONTINUE with question G.	*tearing up the napkin or*
G. Is the behavior reinforced by the same reinforcers as the target skill?	yes	**5 COMPETING BEHAVIOR PROBLEM** ( ) Increase proficiency ( ) Amplify instructed behavior ( ) Alter generalization contingencies	*playing peek-a-boo.* *The only way I can see to figure this out is to start altering the consequences*
	(no)	**6 COMPETING REINFORCER PROBLEM** (X) Alter generalization contingencies	*(no attention for peek-a-boo; no going on w/meal) until she wipes.*

Continue to next page.

Table 9-8, **Linda** (continued)

QUESTION	ANSWER	DECISION	COMMENTS
H. Did the student generalize once at or close to criterion performance levels and then not as well on other opportunities?	yes	**7** REINFORCING FUNCTION PROBLEM ( ) Program natural reinforcers ( ) Eliminate training reinforcers ( ) Use natural schedules ( ) Use natural consequences ( ) Teach self-reinforcement ( ) Teach to solicit reinforcement ( ) Reinforce generalized behavior ( ) Alter generalization contingencies	
	no	CONTINUE with question I.	
I. Did the student respond partially correctly during at least one response opportunity?	yes	**8** DISCRIMINATION FUNCTION PROBLEM Vary stimuli: ( ) Use all stimuli ( ) Use frequent stimuli ( ) Use multiple exemplars ( ) Use general case exemplars	
	no	CONTINUE with question J.	
J. Did the student fail to perform any part of the target skill?	yes	**9** GENERALIZATION TRAINING FORMAT ( ) Increase proficiency ( ) Program natural reinforcers ( ) Use natural schedules ( ) Use appropriate natural stimuli ( ) Eliminate training stimuli	
	no	*STOP*. You have made an error in the sequence. Begin again at Question A.	

Table 9-9
Joe

Generalization Probe Report

Student: *Joe*   Date: *March 3*

IEP Objective:*
Joe will wash dishes at homes of senior citizens as part of work crew. Joe will finish all dishes satisfactorily (no soap, no grease, no food, etc.) as determined by supervisor, and will finish in time allotted to task by supervisor at start of work period. Generalization to different settings, types of dishes, work space, dish racks, etc.

Student Performance*

(1) Who provided the information on student performance?
independent observer

(2) Was the skill directly observed for this probe?
yes

(3) How many opportunities did the student have to perform the skill?
once to wash dishes in one home

(4) When were the opportunities provided?
as part of regular work crew training

(5) Did the student perform the target skill?
for first 2 or 3 dishes, only

(6) Did the student display inappropriate behavior or a previously learned skill instead of, or in addition to, the target skill?
yes

(7) Did the student fail to respond?
no

(8) Describe the student's performance: *Joe got set-up for washing under supervision, did very well (no errors); began washing dishes (good); supervisor left to see to other student, Joe merely rinsed dish under hot water and put it in the rack. He looked at me & I did nothing. He quickly "finished" all of the dishes by merely rinsing them. When the supervisor came back in the kitchen, he was surprised that Joe was done, but then looked at the dishes more closely and saw the food on them. The supervisor made Joe re-do the dishes, with some verbal prompts. The supervisor did not leave the kitchen while Joe was re-doing the dishes.*

Probe Situation

Reinforcers Accessed by Student*
(9) ( )	Were natural reinforcers for performance of the skill.
(10) ( )	Were not natural reinforcers for the skill.
(11) (X)	Included both natural and not natural reinforcers.
(12) ( )	Person reinforced inappropriate behavior, other behavior, or nonresponse, with reinforcer which should have been available for performance of skill.
(13) ( )	Student accessed natural reinforcer by doing something else.
(14) ( )	Person attended to other behavior.
(15) ( )	Person completed the skill task.
(16) ( )	Person physically assisted the student to complete the skill task.
(17) ( )	Person provided another reinforcer.
(18) ( )	Student did not access reinforcers.
	Describe what happened:

Stimuli Which Triggered the Opportunity to Perform the Skill*
(19) ( )	Were natural stimuli which occurred without need for intervention.
(20) (X)	Were naturally provided by persons in the generalizationsituation.
(21) ( )	Were not natural stimuli for the skill.
(22) ( )	Included both natural and not natural stimuli.
(23) ( )	Included training stimuli.
(24) ( )	Other:

Conditions Which Differed From Instruction (Check all that apply)*
(25) (X)	Materials or objects. Describe:
(26) (X)	Setting. Describe:
(27) ( )	Probe manager or persons who interacted with student.
(28) ( )	Person cued the student what to do.
(29) ( )	Person did not cue the student what to do.
(30) ( )	Person encouraged the student.
(31) ( )	Person did not encourage the student.
(32) ( )	Person physically assisted or physically prompted the student.
(33) ( )	Person did not physically assist or prompt the student.
(34) ( )	Person reinforced as often.
(35) ( )	Person reinforced less frequently.
(36) ( )	Student's performance criticized/corrected more frequently.
(37) ( )	Student's performance criticized/corrected less often.
(38) ( )	Person provided feedback on performance, especially errors or mistakes.
(39) ( )	Person did not provide feedback.
(40) ( )	Person praised the student during/after skill performance.
(41) ( )	Person did not praise the student.
	Other:

*Answers needed to apply Decision Rules.

Table 9-9, **Joe** (continued)

Generalization Decision Report

Student _____*Joe*_____   Skill _____*wash dishes*_____

Decision-Maker _____   Date _____*March 5*_____

	QUESTION	ANSWER	DECISION	COMMENTS
A.	Has skill generalized at the desired level in all target situations?	yes	**1** SUCCESSFUL INSTRUCTION ( ) Step ahead to a more difficult level of skill ( ) Choose a new skill to teach	
		(no)	CONTINUE with question B.	
B.	Has skill been acquired?	(yes)	CONTINUE with question C.	
		no	**2** SKILL MASTERY PROBLEM ( ) Continue instruction	
C.	Is generalization desired to only a few situations?	yes	CONTINUE with question D.	*too many different houses in work situation to use this alternative (see objective)*
		(no)	CONTINUE with question E.	
D.	Is it possible to train directly in those situations?	yes	**3** LIMITED GENERALIZATION SITUATIONS ( ) Train in desired situation ( ) Train sequentially in all situations [i.e., sequential modification]	
		no	CONTINUE with question E.	
E.	Is the student reinforced even though he/she does not do the target skill?	yes	CONTINUE with question F.	
		(no)	CONTINUE with question H.	
F.	Does the student fail to respond and is reinforced?	yes	**4** NONCONTINGENT REINFORCER PROBLEM ( ) Alter generalization contingenices	
		no	CONTINUE with question G.	
G.	Is the behavior reinforced by the same reinforcers as the target skill?	yes	**5** COMPETING BEHAVIOR PROBLEM ( ) Increase proficiency ( ) Amplify instructed behavior ( ) Alter generalization contingencies	
		no	**6** COMPETING REINFORCER PROBLEM ( ) Alter generalization contingencies	

Continue to next page.

Table 9-9, **Joe** (continued)

QUESTION	ANSWER	DECISION	COMMENTS
H. Did the student generalize once at or close to criterion performance levels and then not as well on other opportunities?	(yes)	**7** REINFORCING FUNCTION PROBLEM (X) Program natural reinforcers ( ) Eliminate training reinforcers ( ) Use natural schedules ( ) Use natural consequences ( ) Teach self-reinforcement ( ) Teach to solicit reinforcement ( ) Reinforce generalized behavior ( ) Alter generalization contingencies	*Did great on first few dishes until he figured out I wasn't going to do anything if he just rinsed them. A typical teenager. Maybe if he were getting money for this work, & then he didn't get it for poor performance, we might get him to do it right w/out needing constant supervision.*
	no	CONTINUE with question I.	
I. Did the student respond partially correctly during at least one response opportunity?	yes	**8** DISCRIMINATION FUNCTION PROBLEM Vary stimuli: ( ) Use all stimuli ( ) Use frequent stimuli ( ) Use multiple exemplars ( ) Use general case exemplars	
	no	CONTINUE with question J.	
J. Did the student fail to perform any part of the target skill?	yes	**9** GENERALIZATION TRAINING FORMAT ( ) Increase proficiency ( ) Program natural reinforcers ( ) Use natural schedules ( ) Use appropriate natural stimuli ( ) Eliminate training stimuli	
	no	*STOP.* You have made an error in the sequence. Begin again at Question A.	

Figure 9-1

Rules and Strategies for Generalization

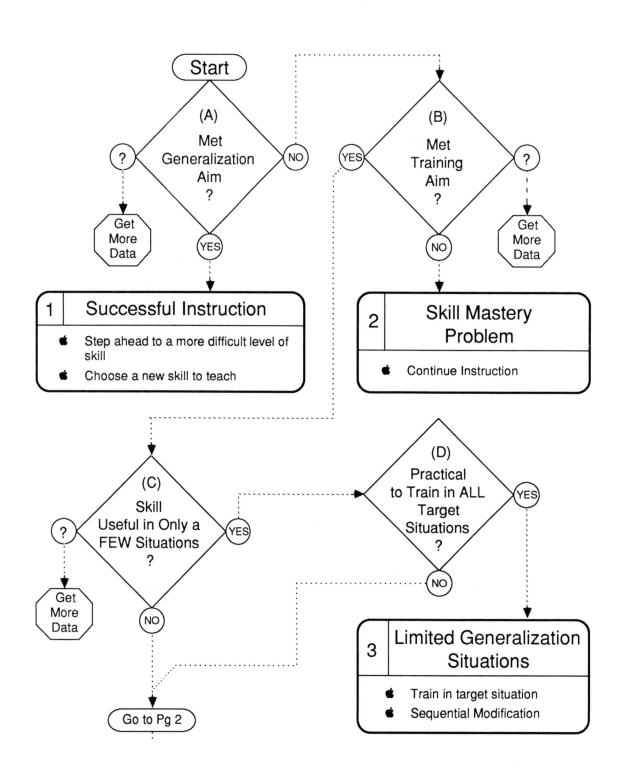

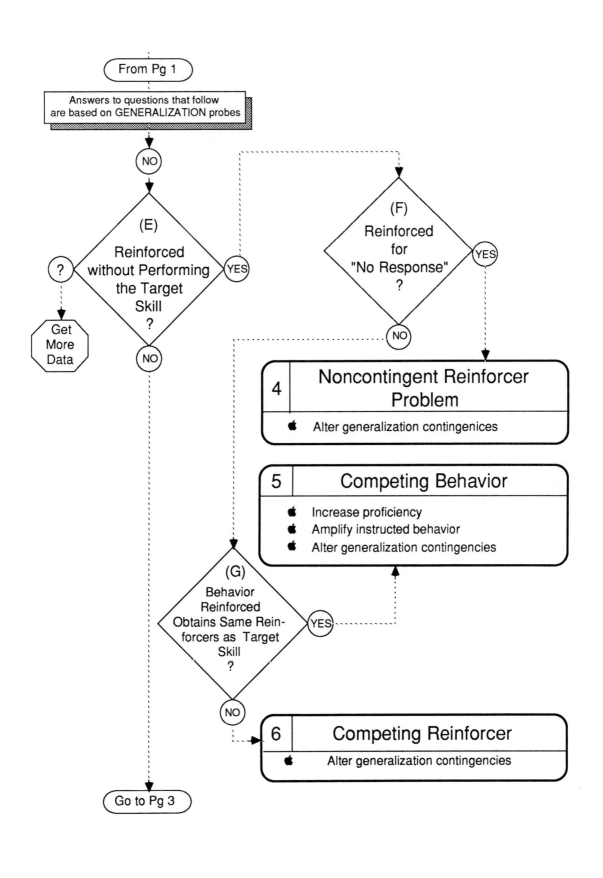

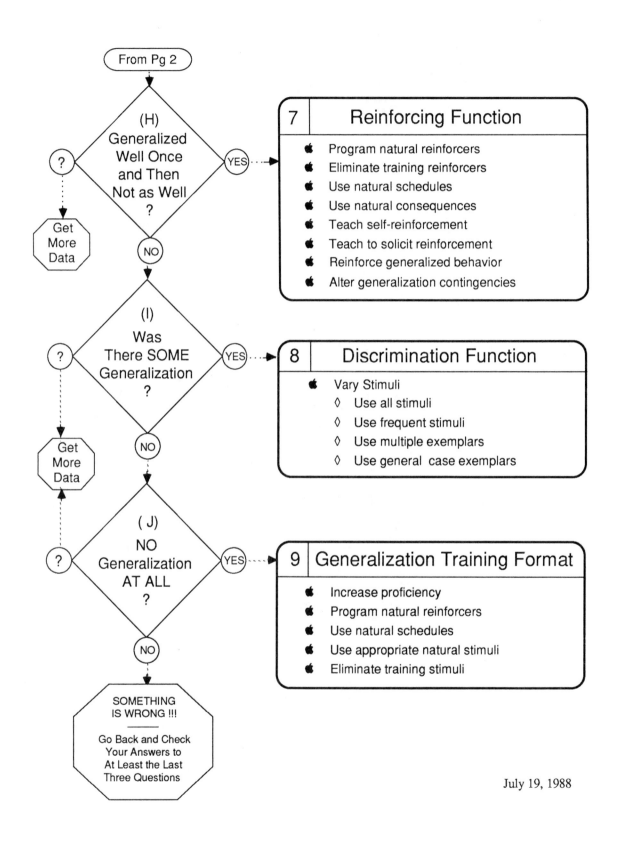

From Pg 2

(H)
Generalized
Well Once
and Then
Not as Well
?

?

Get
More
Data

YES

NO

7	Reinforcing Function

- Program natural reinforcers
- Eliminate training reinforcers
- Use natural schedules
- Use natural consequences
- Teach self-reinforcement
- Teach to solicit reinforcement
- Reinforce generalized behavior
- Alter generalization contingencies

(I)
Was
There SOME
Generalization
?

?

Get
More
Data

YES

NO

8	Discrimination Function

- Vary Stimuli
  - ◊ Use all stimuli
  - ◊ Use frequent stimuli
  - ◊ Use multiple exemplars
  - ◊ Use general case exemplars

(J)
NO
Generalization
AT ALL
?

?

YES

NO

9	Generalization Training Format

- Increase proficiency
- Program natural reinforcers
- Use natural schedules
- Use appropriate natural stimuli
- Eliminate training stimuli

SOMETHING
IS WRONG !!!
———
Go Back and Check
Your Answers to
At Least the Last
Three Questions

July 19, 1988